PAUL LITTLE'S WHAT & WHY BOOK

Paul E. Little's two paperback bestsellers *Know Why You Believe* and *Know What You Believe* are combined in this beautiful hardcover edition. Marie Little's biographical sketch of her husband portrays an intimate close-up of a man who wanted "all of God he could get."

Special Crusade Edition printed for
the Billy Graham Evangelistic Association

**world wide
publications**

1303 Hennepin Avenue
Minneapolis, Minnesota 55403

This special edition is published
with permission of the original publisher.
VICTOR BOOKS
A division of SP Publications, Inc.
P.O. Box 1825, Wheaton, Illinois 60187

Recommended Dewey Decimal Classification: 291.2
Suggested Subject heading: RELIGIOUS BELIEF; TRUST IN GOD
First paperback editions: *Know Why You Believe* © 1967; *Know What You Believe* © 1970

Library of Congress Catalog Card Number: 80-51159
ISBN: 0-88207-814-3

CONTENTS

Acknowledgments
Marie Little Talks about Paul

Know What You Believe
Testimonial   **36**
 1   The Bible   **37**
 2   God   **48**
 3   Jesus Christ   **59**
 4   Christ's Death   **70**
 5   Man and Sin   **80**
 6   The Holy Spirit   **91**
 7   The Church   **102**
 8   Angels, Satan, and Demons   **113**
 9   Salvation   **123**
10   Things to Come   **134**

Know Why You Believe
Dr. Dave Wright's Letter   **147**
 1   Is Christianity Rational?   **149**
 2   Is There a God?   **156**
 3   Is Christ God?   **164**
 4   Did Christ Rise from the Dead?   **171**
 5   Is the Bible God's Word?   **178**
 6   Are the Bible Documents Reliable?   **186**
 7   Does Archeology Help?   **194**
 8   Are Miracles Possible?   **202**
 9   Do Science and Scripture Conflict?   **210**
10   Why Does God Allow Suffering and Evil?   **221**
11   Does Christianity Differ from Other
     World Religions?   **230**
12   Is Christian Experience Valid?   **238**
     Notes   **249**

ACKNOWLEDGMENTS

Know Why You Believe

The publisher and the author gratefully acknowledge the permission granted by a number of publishers for the use of quotations from copyright material: The Macmillan Company, New York, for quotations from *God Our Contemporary*, by J. B. Phillips; the New American Library of World Literature, New York, for a quotation from *The Limitations of Science*, by J.W.N. Sullivan; E. P. Dutton & Co., Inc., New York, for a quotation from *Science Is a Sacred Cow,* by Anthony Standen; the Pergamon Press, New York, for a quotation from "Implications of Evolution," by G. A. Kerkut, in the *International Series of Monographs on Pure and Applied Biology,* Vol. 4; Farrar, Straus, & Giroux, Inc., New York, for a quotation from *Rivers in the Desert*, by Nelson Glueck; Encyclopedia Britannica, Chicago, for a quotation from *Great Books of the Western World*, Vol. II, edited by Mortimer Adler; InterVarsity Press, Downers Grove, Illinois, for a quotation from an article, "The Place of Reason," by John Montgomery in *His*, March 1966, and for quotations from *The Mystery of Suffering,* by Hugh Evan Hopkins, from *Conversions: Psychological and Spiritual*, by D. Martyn Lloyd-Jones, and from *Basic Christianity*, by John R. W. Stott; Baker Book House Grand Rapids, for quotations from *Revelation and the Bible*, edited by Carl F. H. Henry; Wm. B. Eerdmans Publishing Co., Grand Rapids, for quotations from *The Christian View of Science and Scripture*, by Bernard Ramm, from *An Introduction to Christian Apologetics*, by E. J. Carnell, and from *The New Testament Documents: Are They Reliable?* by F. F. Bruce; to Inter-Varsity Fellowship and Tyndale Press, London, for quotations from *Creation*, by R. E. D. Clark, from *Questions of Science and Faith*, by J. N. Hawthorne, and from *Christianity in a Mechanistic Universe*, edited by D. M. MacKay; and to Moody Press, Chicago, for quotations from *Protestant Christian Evidences*, by Bernard Ramm, *The Bible and Modern Science*, by Henry Morris, *An Introduction to Bible Archaeology* and *Genesis and Archaeology*, by Howard F. Vos, and *Can I Trust My Bible?* by Gordon Clark.

Know What You Believe

The publisher acknowledges with thanks permission to use materials from various sources, including such standard reference works as the *New Bible Dictionary* and the *International Standard Bible Encyclopedia* (published by Eerdmans Publishing Co., Grand Rapids) and the publications of Moody Press, Chicago. Material is also used from these publications of Inter-Varsity Fellowship, London: *Ministers of God*, © 1964; *The Death of Christ*, © 1951; *Evangelism and the Sovereignty of God*, © 1961; and *In Understanding Be Men*, © 1936. These four books are available from your Christian bookseller or InterVarsity Press, Box F, Downers Grove, Illinois 60515.

MARIE LITTLE
TALKS ABOUT PAUL

I first met my husband in March 1952 in the student lounge of Columbia University located in the heart of New York City. David Adeney, one of the senior Inter-Varsity Christian Fellowship staff, ushered me through the sprawling room to a form molded into one of the many sofas. As we approached, a young man unmolded himself and Paul Little shot forward to greet us.

That was my introduction to the man whose name I took a year and a half later. I had just returned from Red China, where I had been a missionary with the China Inland Mission, and had spent two years in "Free China" and two years in Red China. Now I was to join the Inter-Varsity staff in New York City, and my mission field was to be the multitude of Chinese students trapped in our country by the final thud of the "bamboo curtain."

The three of us sat there in the lounge for a long time. There was much to talk about. At first glance Paul was distinguished only by the ever-present rhythm of his crossed foot and the nervous opening and closing of his ball-point pen. A slightly rumpled suit jacket, draped casually over his "scholar's hump," tooted the message that he cared minimally about tailoring. There was something about his loose but graceful stance that identified him as "Ivy League," at home in a college lounge, and unthreatened by academic halls. His generous nose and stubborn, upright eyebrows were set against a clear, fair complexion which more than compensated for his scant brown hair. Behind "Coke bottle wire rim glasses" (as he called them before his days of contact lenses), his eyes burned brilliant blue. He spoke with a masculine intensity, gliding from jovial to spiritual without ambivalence. After a while we prayed, and I only remember thinking to myself, *He's a spiritual man*.

I couldn't foresee that the next year and a half I would spend virtually every day working with him in high-rise New York City campuses, dorm Bible studies, foreign student teas, prayer meetings, staff meetings, and summer camps. We visited International

House to make new friends, and we met incoming foreign ships to help international students adjust to their first hours in swirling New York City. We mixed coffee and conversation with Christian students, brainstorming ways to capture the interest of commuting students. We planned weekend conferences. We searched out lonely students. This was staff life. And "It was a subway romance," Paul used to say. "I had to show Marie the New York subway system."

What makes a man a leader? What seed of inspiration buds forth to raise a man above his peers? Such questions remind me of a summer at Cedar Campus, the Inter-Varsity camp in northern Michigan. During an afternoon break I was joined on a walk along the stony beach by a young staff man. He had been talking to my husband until 2 A.M. the night before and was literally exploding with enthusiasm about their conversation. Some of the questions he had wrestled with for months had been answered, and as an extra bonus, Paul had cranked out a few of his favorite rollicking jokes. I could feel the young man's searching eyes studying me. Finally he mustered enough courage to ask, "What's it like to live with Paul Little? Is life one long, exhilarating conversation? Is he always turned on? Is there no end to the bright stream of wisdom he puts out?"

He had seen Paul in fraternity houses and college auditoriums debating the skeptics, the relativists, and the materialists. He had heard Paul answering the challenges of Muslims, Hindus, and Mormons at international student house parties. He had listened to Paul's exhortations to affirm the will of God at the Urbana Missionary Conventions. He had seen him rap for hours with one student. On occasion he had heard Paul's expositions of a psalm, a parable, or a single verse.

"What's He Really Like?"
The question could not be answered easily then, nor can it now. At one of Paul's lectures on the well-traversed subject, "How to Give Away Your Faith," a student asked me, "Do you ever get tired of hearing the same sermon? I've heard your husband give this at least five times. You must have heard it 25." All I could think at the moment was, *It does make a difference if you love the person.* I knew almost each word and inflection Paul would give when he preached, and still found myself laughing instinctively at all the right places. There were times, as a part of Paul's audience, when the Lord spoke to me directly through a sermon I might have called "old hat." From this vantage point, I can only give bits and pieces from Paul's life to try to point out what made him tick. I hope it

will be understood that it will be less than a well-rounded, un-biased picture.

On the surface I saw Paul's gaiety and laughter—streams of never-ending mirth impatiently straining to break forth. He seemed to collect jokes without even trying. They weren't memorized, only absorbed, ready at any moment to lighten an occasion. His humor was always clean, side-splitting, and topical. Psychiatrists or elephants bore the brunt of his wit, and fast phrases, like commas, sprinkled his conversation.

Paul loved the music of Haydn. Its gaiety suited his temperament. Like Haydn, he too might have said about himself:

I cannot help it. I give forth what is in me. When I think of the Divine Being, my heart is so full of joy that the notes fly off as from a spindle, and as I have a cheerful heart, He will pardon me if I serve Him cheerfully.

From his joyful, zealous heart, Paul's words also flew off as from a spindle—with great abandon. Yet, his words had power, and some of them have become permanently grafted into our generation's evangelical patois. Many will never forget them.

On Witnessing

Put the cookies on the lower shelf.

Move out of the safety zone. We can't escape the traffic.

I'll lick stamps and stuff envelopes but someone else can witness.

Satan would like to isolate the Christian who is the carrier of the Christian disease.

I used to lunge at a non-Christian, spout my verses with a glassy stare, and then run!

The greatest favor we can do for any human being is introduce him to Jesus Christ.

Don't wait until you are good enough to pass for Gabriel's twin before you witness.

9

It's not a good idea to wear a sandwich board saying, "I am a Christian."

If we are clutched, the witnessee will be clutched.

Are we unloading unsolicited goods?

After 2,000 years no one is going to think of a question that will bring Christianity crashing.

On Understanding Belief

God doesn't grade on the curve.

We don't have to commit intellectual suicide to become Christians or kiss our brains good-bye.

Belief doesn't create truth but enables us to enter into what is already true.

Unbelief doesn't destroy truth.

Faith goes beyond reason, not against reason.

Man might believe the facts about Christ but shrink from the moral demands of belief.

It doesn't matter what you think of
  Playdoh,
    Napoleon, or
      President Nixon.
  It does matter what you think about Jesus Christ.

We can't ooze into faith in Christ.

Faith demands action.

On Jesus as Lord

The will of God is not a package on a string let down from heaven. It is like a scroll that unrolls one day at a time.

Faith, love, joy, peace are not little packages given in answer to prayer.

Fasten your spiritual seat belts or you'll get carried away.

God is not about to shortchange us in life.

Is our Bible knowledge stored like theological canned goods on the shelves of our minds?

When the Christian life has grown cold, it's like Pepsi that's lost its fizz. Or like cold mashed potatoes.

Separation from the world does not mean isolation.

Paul's grandfather was one of three brothers who migrated to Philadelphia from Germany. Family legend has it that one brother kept the German name of "Klein," the second translated it to "Small," and the third, Paul's progenitor, translated it into "Little." Paul's father, Robert J. Little, had such a dramatic conversion to Christ as a young man that studying the Bible for himself became his life's goal. This led to his wide itinerant preaching ministry, and eventually to the position of radio pastor at radio station WMBI of the Moody Bible Institute. Paul's Irish mother, Margaret Eagleson, was known for her bright blue eyes and irrepressible merry humor.

Paul Eagleson Little came into the world as a blue baby on December 30, 1928. He was Margaret and Robert's second child. Their first child Grace was already six years old. From his birth, Paul had trouble breathing and his parents despaired of his life. Doctors warned that he might not survive to a double digit age and that he might have a hole the size of a fountain pen in the septum of his heart.

Fortunately the blueness disappeared and Paul grew into an energetic boy. Physically, he still had limitations, but neither they nor parental prohibitions could restrain him. His parents told him not to play baseball, not to run in the playground, and not to sit on the cold steps. Although he couldn't run as well as his friends in school and his endurance gave out in baseball before he got to second base, his love for the game could not be bridled or benched. Sometimes he took his turn at bat and asked a friend to run the bases for him. Other times, he ran to first base and collapsed before another player took over. Always he carefully "dried off" his wet, sweaty clothes before returning home to avoid the searching questions of his parents. Baseball, as well as school and Boy Scouts, was his life.

Looking back, it is hard to believe that a small "storefront" church in Philadelphia was the humus in which his spiritual life took root. The Plymouth Brethren Assembly had no formal clergy, but the elders taught the Bible unceasingly. The Little family never missed a meeting. By osmosis Paul picked up a significant store of biblical knowledge.

Paul frequently told of his first spiritual awakening:

My friend Sam Kerr said to me, "Listen, don't you think it's time you and I became Christians?" (Everybody else but Sam thought I already was one! He knew better.)

"Yeah, a good idea," I told him. "Sometime."

Shortly after that we attended a children's conference. The speaker had an object lesson about bells. Most of the bells had clappers, but one did not. He told us, "From the outside we can't tell which one is deficient. Looking directly into my soul (I thought), he said, "Some of you are like the bell without a clapper. You look like a Christian, even do all the things Christians do. From the outside no one can tell the difference. But *you* know and *God* knows there is no clapper on the inside."

I thought to myself, *Who told him about me? Everybody used to pat me on the head and say, "My, what a fine boy you are." I'd groan inside and think that if they ever went through an entire week with me, they would get their adenoids cleared! They would see a different boy than I am on Sunday.*

That day, I made a commitment to Jesus Christ that began my growth into full-blown faith.

It soon became evident that Paul's clapper was not missing. He drove a bus around the neighborhood for the church's "Kids Club." In high school he was fully committed to the "Born Againers Club" and the local Youth for Christ Saturday night rallies.

When Paul turned 18, he entered the University of Pennsylvania Wharton School of Finance and backed into an accounting major because he "disliked it less than anything else." But student days proved to contain more than accounting. They were filled with spiritual beginnings for the man who years later started his first book by saying, "I stubbed my toe in the process of witnessing."

As a freshman at Penn, he admitted to cold fear as he silently followed an Inter-Varsity staff member going door to door in the Penn dormitories. Paul listened as the staff member invited students to dorm Bible studies. When Paul took his turn, his first attempt was a "flop" as he would say. He ground out a prepared speech, his eyes fixed beyond the student to a corner of the ceiling, and the

Future Inter-Varsity Christian Fellowship staff member, three years old

"Shall I be a ball player?"

Campus in the Woods, Canada, IVCF staff training

University of Pennsylvania graduate

13

student slammed the door in his face. The patient staff member commended Paul for his good memory but told him, "Next time, look the student in the eye, and speak directly to him." Eager, but still terrified, he tried again, and again! Gradually, it became easier. The Inter-Varsity group grew substantially and Paul threw his weight behind every activity: Bible studies, weekly meetings, monthly area meetings and summer camps.

Near the end of his senior year, Joe Bayly asked him, "Would you be interested in working with Inter-Varsity? Could your heart take it?" Paul told him, "I can't imagine a pace more strenuous than the last six months spent working in the dorms four nights a week." (He may not have mentioned keeping up his Ping-Pong championship at the Christian Association Building.)

In June 1950, Paul graduated from the Wharton School of Finance, but he did not attend the ceremonies. Rather, he spent the time enjoying the cool woods of northern Canada at Campus in the Woods training for the Inter-Varsity staff.

In Canada, Paul's acceptance on the Inter-Varsity staff could have been aborted by his penchant for clowning. Among the staff candidates, he stood out as a "clown and a jokester." Even after he was accepted as a full-fledged staff member, he heard that upon his arrival, a senior leader had strongly objected, saying, "Who sent this joker up here? Are you trying to wreck the place?" Nevertheless, his inner drive to serve the Lord was conspicuously fervent. He had made the team!

The state of Illinois was his first staff assignment. He also traveled through Kansas and Missouri. That year Leith Samuel from England held University Missions in the Midwest and Paul was a part of the backup team. The staff members penetrated the dorms and Greek houses with mini-sessions, and Leith Samuel preached daily in the main auditoriums.

One of their main objectives was to conduct question-and-answer periods in each of the mini-sessions. Paul said that the staff sometimes felt like Daniel in the lion's den. If the leader needed help in answering a question or wanted to close the meeting, he would signal the other staff to rescue him by pulling on his watchband.

During those meetings the staff started the practice of offering booklets to any student who wished further information. The booklets fell into at least two categories: basic information about Jesus Christ, or instruction in living the Christian life. Requests for either booklet gave the team some idea where the inquirer was spiritually. They mainly used the booklets entitled: "Have You Considered Him?" "Is Christianity Credible?" "Did Christ Die in Vain?" and "Becoming a Christian."

From that time on Paul rarely went anywhere without two booklets in his pocket to give to individuals or offer to an audience at the end of a speech. In later years he used "Becoming a Christian" and "How to Succeed in the Christian Life" almost exclusively.

After a year in Illinois, Paul was transferred to New York City, and in the middle of that year I arrived on the scene. We covered the dense concentration of students studying in Long Island, Queens, Brooklyn, and Manhattan. Their numbers alone were overwhelming, compounded by the fact that most of them commuted and worked part time. Weekly Bible studies had to be held in either classrooms or student center lounges. We divided our time between American and international students, and it was not unusual for us to travel from early morning until late at night.

By June 1953, after two years in New York, Paul felt the need for some concentrated biblical studies. He applied to the Wheaton Graduate School and was immediately accepted. However, as Paul prepared to leave, we both had mixed emotions. Drawn by some invisible magnet we had grown accustomed to being together.

I was delighted when, after a week at Wheaton, he called me on the phone and said, "It's bigger than both of us; let's get married." Not the usual proposal, I grant you, but by that time, I didn't need much persuading. As in the Peanuts cartoon, I felt just like Lucy who listened to Schroeder play Beethoven, and said, "You fascinate me!"

That December I left Inter-Varsity staff, and we were married in my home church, Tenth Presbyterian in Philadelphia, by Dr. Donald Grey Barnhouse. Paul was in the middle of his year at Wheaton, and I went back to nursing to help support us and pay for our $25-a-month basement room.

In August 1954 Paul had earned his M.A. degree cum laude and we returned to his folks' home in Philadelphia. His candid attitude toward his congenital heart condition always amazed me. We talked to every doctor friend we knew, read medical journals in the library, and prayed constantly about possible treatment.

Paul was rarely funnier than when he was telling stories about his hospital escapades. While he was still a student at Penn, he had his first heart catheterization, which resulted in a necrosis on his arm the size of an orange where the dye had leaked into the tissues. He always referred to the man who had done it as "Dr. Trembles." He could recall the doctors arguing if they were or were not in the vein while he lay there wondering what the problem was.

About a week passed before Paul saw a black surface developing under the bandage on his arm and wrote the doctor a letter to ask him what to do. Horrified, the doctor tracked him down by phone

Marie's home in WuWei, Kansu, Northwest China

Twins from the children's club in WuWei

Wedding—Tenth Presbyterian Church, Philadelphia—December 19, 1953

The engagement ring, August 1953

and told him to come immediately to the hospital to have a skin graft. Humor had a touch of cynicism this time.

In October 1954 after we had been married less than a year, Paul was admitted to Presbyterian Hospital in Philadelphia for closed heart surgery. The surgical team opened his funnel-shaped pulmonary valve with a scissors-like valvulotome and the valve became bicuspid. His inner heart blood pressure immediately returned to near normal. "A phenomenal result," the surgeon told us. We gave thanks that God's hand had touched him.

I can't imagine the energy Paul would have had without his heart problem. I couldn't keep up with him either before or after the surgery. In five months we were back in New York again looking for an apartment in Manhattan. As before, the number of ways we could spend our time staggered us. It wasn't often that we ate a meal alone or had an empty guest bed. Paul used to pray, "Lord, help me not be like an airplane and spin my propeller a thousand times a minute but never get off the ground."

We began to rub shoulders with students from virtually every country in the world. We met relatives of Chiang Kaishek; a son of an Indian maharaja; a son of a cabinet minister from Afghanistan; and a daughter of the majority leader in the Brazilian senate. One Indian student we met wore an ornate gold watch, so unusual that it immediately caught our eye. He took it off and showed it to Paul, casually mentioning that it was worth about $4,000. Paul told us later that he got weak and almost dropped it before quickly handing it back to him.

While in our country, the cloistered academic life isolated these students from contact with mainstream Americans. They were lonely, open for friendship, and anxious to meet American families to learn our customs. When they returned to their own countries, many would become top leaders in government and business. We prayed that God would give us a spiritual ministry among them. How could we get American students and families to meet them? We started giving teas or receptions early in the school year. These were usually "get acquainted" events between American Christians and foreign students. We played games and served refreshments. Then we announced monthly get-togethers and told the students that in addition to times of entertainment, each meeting would include lectures describing Christianity. The Americans were coached to get acquainted with one or two students and to establish an ongoing friendship. This strategy became a model for monthly "coffee hours" held across the country in university centers.

Two big events took place during this period in New York. The 16-week Billy Graham New York Crusade was the first one. Paul was responsible for counseling and follow-up for students who had made decisions. We attended the crusade six nights a week, and neither Billy nor the rest of us on the team will ever forget the grueling, yet singular experience of seeing Madison Square Garden turned into a harvest field. Billy preached night after night to 18,000 people, always seeking new ways to present the Christian message. We watched almost numbly as inquirers poured forward each night, seemingly regardless of the message preached. Some were idle inquisitors. Others were examples of genuine conversions happening right before our eyes.

The second big event came in June 1957 when we adopted a beautiful, three-day-old baby girl we named Deborah Ann. She was just four months old when Inter-Varsity needed someone to supervise the student work in the southwestern region, consisting of Oklahoma, Texas, New Mexico, and Arizona. We packed our trunks and journeyed south to Dallas.

The whole southwest area was new to us and relatively unplowed in student work. But in true Texan style, we were royally received and we loved every minute of our three years there. When Debi was 18 months old, we adopted our blonde son, Paul, Jr. As the four of us sat around our small table, Paul said in his inimitable style, "Now we are a group."

"Group" described our family well. While Paul traveled a great deal, he continually pressed us to go with him wherever and whenever possible. By the time Debi was only eight months old, she had traveled by car through more than eight states. Paul, Jr. was only two weeks old when we went to Bear Trap Ranch, the Inter-Varsity Camp in Colorado for the Christmas Foreign Student house party. Nestled in his yellow quilt at such a young age, he helped create a welcome, homelike atmosphere for the students away from home.

We spent every Christmas and Easter holiday at camps. Our summer routine consisted of traveling to one camp or another, anywhere between New Hampshire and California. I can still see Paul, Jr., knee-high among a forest of legs, running through a crowd of students and never failing to identify his father.

After three years in Texas, our family of four headed north again to Chicago in order to bring Paul closer to the headquarters office. Tom Stark, now senior pastor of the University Reformed Church in Lansing, Michigan, wrote me of his first exposure to the Inter-Varsity Staff:

Paul conducted a hilarious staff meeting but pulled us all back to serious praying and struggling with issues at the right time. The balance gave me a high model for staff relationships in the

With Afghan
student in
Central Park

Coffee hour
at home

Paul Jr.—
two months;
Deborah Ann—
twenty months

future. It was an election year, so for the month of new staff orientation, we ran a mock election with Paul and others as candidates for President. Someone did a charcoal sketch of "our founder," Stacey Woods, whose motto was, "I'd rather be right than wrong." Sounds silly but the fun brought us together.

Subsequently, I accompanied Paul as he spoke at the area campuses, staff conferences, and summer camps. There were many times of hilarity when we would double over with laughter. But more often in serious conversation, we struggled to understand problems in evangelical Christianity and in Inter-Varsity.

Paul and his good friend Jim McLeish could always be counted on to create waves of engulfing laughter. Both men had more than enough talents to become rousing successes in the business world. Their favorite phrase was "bottom-lining life." For them this involved the question: "What is the first and most important ingredient in life?" When they considered all the things they might do, they always came to the bottom line: the work of God came first for them. And God's work among students was *the* cause above all causes. There were times when things got tough and they felt the urge to quit. Failure, discouragement, and criticism were not unknown. But God's work was worth giving all they had. When it came right down to it, His work was not a duty or a chore, it was a flag to be raised high every morning and raised with no regrets.

Sometimes I feel Paul's life could be compared to the evolution of a butterfly, developing from the dormant chrysalis to full-blown maturity. There was genius there, but Paul's genius evolved with time and hard work. The hours spent with university students served to nurture his zeal for evangelism. His early diaries, which I call "event diaries," as opposed to "feeling diaries," remind me of his unremitting pattern of reaching out:

March 20th. Fair. Yesterday was a busy day, but very worthwhile. At noon I went back to the fraternity and talked with half a dozen guys. Social pressure on them is very strong, so I couldn't get a foothold for a Bible study, but a number of men sure heard the Gospel—I hope clearly.

March 22nd. Fair. In the afternoon I spoke to an English class. The instructor asked after I had finished, "How can students who want to know God do so since there is no Billy Graham on campus?" It was a modern version of "What must

I do to be saved?" I took that question as an opportunity to explain Revelation 3:20.

April 6th. Hot. I met a Vietnamese Army officer on the train. He is friendly—wants to learn English. A Roman Catholic, he accepted my New Testament tonight.

Paul's first fraternity meeting was assigned to him by the University of Kansas Inter-Varsity Student Committee. It took place at a scholarship hall that housed top students enrolled in individualized study programs. He was to speak 15 minutes while the fraternity brothers were eating and then open the floor for questions. Paul's growing pains surfaced in his dialogue with the Lord: "Lord, why does it have to be an honors frat reserved for brainy students for my first tryout? Why can't it be an ordinary unskeptical group?" But he made it. He put himself in a hard place and learned from it. Moreover, a young man became a Christian that night.

Through the years he faced hundreds of groups—some cold and skeptical, some indifferent and preoccupied. During each encounter he honed his skill in answering questions, and began to have a clearer understanding of the logic (or lack thereof) of unbelievers. His own faith deepened as he saw students transformed when they met Jesus Christ.

At one of the later missionary conventions, a young man brought Paul greetings from his father. Twenty years earlier the young man's father had trusted Jesus Christ at one of Paul's university bull sessions. His wife had become a Christian and then their whole family. Now, a generation later, the man's son was preparing to serve the Lord on the mission field.

Wherever college students congregated, Paul wanted to launch an evangelistic program. The Newport News Jazz Festival in Rhode Island brought an opportunity for our staff to cooperate with a local church. Homemade refreshments were offered along with discussions. Some students came in and said, "Forget the cake, I want to talk about purpose in life." The Inter-Varsity staff made similar outreaches at Estes Park, Colorado; Catalina Island, California; and other centers.

The concern for aggressive outreach and evangelism weighed heavily on Inter-Varsity's senior cabinet. They prayed for the wisdom to develop all the gifts and ministries of the Holy Spirit. "Paul became the real leader in challenging Inter-Varsity to move out more boldly in evangelism," Tom Stark wrote again:

In some staff discussions, I gave Paul a hard time on the whole

Stop off in Cairo on
trip to South Africa

Paul's room in the Illini Union,
University of Illinois

Student conference on trip to South America

Urbana '70

matter of a strong evangelistic thrust. I see now that I threw him all kinds of qualifications and cautions for moving out. Paul was persistent in turning our thoughts from an introverted, unexpectant approach to a much more biblical attitude about the practice of evangelism. Since leaving staff, I have changed in that regard myself, and many objections I once raised I now see as insecure defenses without substance.

During the summer of 1962, Debi, age five; Paul, age three; and I stumbled our way through the carpet of bodies lying on the beach at Fort Lauderdale, Florida. We were looking for "Dad" and the four-by-six yellow sign under the yellow umbrella declaring "Inter-Varsity Forum—Every Hour."

We were there for the Easter migration of students to the warm Florida beaches. Riots and disorder had been the annual ritual. The city of Fort Lauderdale had been beset by injuries, property damage in the millions, and even deaths. One motel found its bedroom furniture floating in the swimming pool. Police control proved impotent and the desperate city fathers invited Billy Graham to come to speak to the crowd in the heat of the riots. He definitely had a calming effect. This success encouraged a young pastor to ask the city for permission to invite Inter-Varsity students and a Christian music group to hold discussions and concerts. The city council opened their arms to us and our Christian beach invasion began.

Inter-Varsity selected Paul to lead the operation. He and his coterie of staff and students met each morning in prayer and evangelism classes, planning for the siege. They prepared religious surveys as conversation openers. And here, the battle began. Hourly beach talks near the sign under the yellow umbrella encouraged stimulating open discussion. As part of the crowd, the Christian students stood around ready to pick up on personal conversations. The city provided a band shell near the most crowded section of the beach for the Christian musical group, "The Excursions." The band was very well received and produced a climate for "rapping." The Christian students roamed the beach, having one conversation and then another. The children and I sat wherever we could find space, building sand castles, and making friends whenever we could. Our greatest joy was to see students becoming Christians and thus becoming a part of our group instead of peering at us from a distance. After a few years Paul relinquished the leadership of the "Christian beach invasion" to other staff for them to continue and expand.

Evangelism, Paul felt, must include every cultural and ethnic group. At the end of the turbulent '60s, when the activist period was at its height, Paul made a major breakthrough with the inclusion of black plenary speakers for the Urbana Missionary Convention. We had many close black friends ourselves. At times we went to inner-city churches and invited many of our friends to our own home or we went to theirs. It shattered us to learn of the hardships and dangers that were inconceivable to us but commonplace to them. A doctor's child told us he was afraid to go to school without a knife. He would be the only one in school without one! The many black colleges, without a witness for Christ, troubled Paul. Black students were socially cut off from contact with the white world and were likewise cut off from some of the natural avenues of learning about Christ. The entire Inter-Varsity staff felt this burden. As director of the 1970 Urbana Convention, Paul invited his friend Tom Skinner to be the first black man to give a major address. Tom was excellent. His message focused on the power of Christ as the liberating influence for all races, and abated some of the anger brooding among those students who were being pulled by the radical groups.

It could be said that the books Paul wrote were his autobiography. His experiences with his family, his church, the university, and with Inter-Varsity Christian Fellowship came together in a lecture series he gave at Wheaton College in 1963. "I was there for a week speaking three times a day," he explained. "It was the first time I'd ever spoken that long anywhere in my life. I wasn't sure I'd have enough material to last." But the student response was exceptional; the lectures were taped and transcribed, and they became the foundation for the book, *How to Give Away Your Faith*. The natural offspring of that first book was *Know Why You Believe* and then *Know What You Believe*.

As he spoke at Wheaton, it was obvious he knew how Wheaton students felt about witnessing. He himself had tried to witness and had failed. He knew the guilt feelings of a Christian who had been challenged to witness and still couldn't bring himself to do it. He knew what it was like to fear confrontation with a lifestyle different from his own. He constantly asked himself, "Why do non-Christians turn away from witnessing Christians?" He insisted on giving instruction that would give positive help.

When it came to the Christian faith, Paul told them that service in God's kingdom transcended any other attainment. To introduce someone to the Lord Jesus Christ was the greatest favor Paul or anyone could do for that person. He believed this passionately and he stated it passionately.

The exultant timbre of his voice caught the students' attention. Sometimes he spoke with rapid-fire fastness, leaving the audience breathless. Sometimes he held back, perfectly timing an aside or a pungent phrase. There was an electric quality about Paul's speaking that riveted their attention. The students loved him. And when the books were published, these same truths proved to be the ones the Christian church needed as well.

Paul's bank of stored knowledge was such that when the time came for him to write *Know What You Believe*, this knowledge was like a burden on his soul which had to be unloaded. He had scribbled the chapter subjects on yellow 8½ x 11 inch pads. The book finally came to full birth on a work vacation in Florida. "I'll finish it the first week and have two weeks to rest and enjoy the beach," he told us. The children and I spent each day at the beach to give him solitude. When he finished the yellow sheets, I deciphered and typed them while he played with the children. Well into the third week we finished the project, and that vacation will always be remembered as the vacation "Dad wrote a book."

Certain memorable characteristics come to my mind when I think of Paul. He was a people person. People endlessly fascinated him. He would rather interact with people in lively conversation than do almost anything else. In most ways, our household revolved around Paul and his gregarious nature. I shared that love for people too, I guess, but he had the instinct to attract them with warm, bright conversation. He had the ability to perceive their impalpable needs. He would sometimes downgrade himself and say that in social situations he was like an elephant on ice. Or when it came to matching ties with his suit, all his taste was in his mouth. But when it came to interacting with people, he knew how to make them feel comfortable. He could get them talking about themselves and then he would tell a few lively stories about himself. "There must be a permissive atmosphere," he would say, "permissive in the sense of kind, uncondemning, and accepting love that is not shocked when honest doubts are exposed."

One morning he planned to stay home to help move his office from one end of the house to the other. With the colossal stack of books and files, this was no small job. At the beginning of operation "book-move," a student came to the door bringing a package from InterVarsity Press. After putting the box down, his real mission surfaced. "May I talk to you for a few minutes?"

"Of course." The few minutes turned into four hours. Lunch was served amid the stack of unmoved books, while deep communication ensued. That was what satisfied. For us, contact with that student was far more important than any other project. The office got moved by midnight that night.

In counseling, Paul had the knack of "zeroing in" on the root of a problem. His nephew told me he had been working for a year on a pilot study for the teaching of earth science. Toward the end of the study, he'd had lunch with his Uncle Paul. "In one brief question, Uncle Paul pulled out of me the imperative conclusion that I'd been struggling all year to see. He asked me, 'Has your research produced anything that would be useful in the classroom?' I saw in an instant that the program should be shelved, but I needed him to ask me that $64,000 question."

Somewhere (could it have been from the Holy Spirit?), Paul gained the ability to make profound truths graphically clear. His explanations were uncluttered. One night he came home from a discussion at Northern Illinois University and expressed amazement and gratitude as he told me about a student who'd had a Christian background. After Paul had finished his talk, the student had signed a card for further information and, as was the custom, he'd put the card in a wastebasket placed at the door for that purpose. Paul had "grabbed" him and taken him out for coffee. The young man then explained, "I've heard about receiving Jesus Christ all of my life, but I've never really understood it before."

It was the same clarity that reached a surgeon from Portland. His wife had become a Christian, but he had a scientist's hang-up with the supernatural. While his wife was on vacation, he bought *Know Why You Believe* for his week's reading. Afterward he wrote me, "I was one third through the book when I knew for the first time that Jesus Christ was God's Son." His wife wrote me also: "When I came home from vacation, I knew by the way my husband hugged me that something good had happened to him while I was gone."

Paul was an unabashed hero worshiper. We attended the funeral of Samuel Zwemer, the veteran missionary to Muslims whom neither of us had ever met. The funeral was at the First Presbyterian Church in New York City. In the foyer Paul pointed out a well-known judge of the U.S. Supreme Court who had been trying a widely publicized case. I mused at Paul's ability to recognize him. "I saw his picture in *Time* magazine," he told me easily.

Martyn Lloyd-Jones, Leith Samuel, John Stott, Stacey Woods, Northcote Deck, Billy Graham, Leighton Ford, and Dr. Birch Rambo were among his heroes. He deeply revered his own father and admitted freely how much he was indebted to him for his example of a godly life. When they were together, he would take the opportunity to comb his father's brain for expositions of biblical passages or theological explanations. He often said sadly, but admiringly, "I'll never have the mastery of the Scriptures that my father has."

He felt secure enough of his abilities to freely compliment others,

With
Leighton Ford

Paul and his father,
Robert J. Little

The day we left
for Switzerland

In Switzerland

The whole family took
up skiing.

but he may have judged himself and his own biblical knowledge too harshly. His use of the Bible was different from his father's. His father had mastered its fine detail; Paul thought in terms of its broad truths—"the big picture," he called it. He lived by those truths and automatically peppered his answers to questions with phrases like, "The Scripture teaches such and such," or "There is no indication in the Scripture of such and such," or he might have said, "I don't know of any Scripture that would support such and such." His dependence on Scripture was like a firm inner core in the center of his being. He pored over the Bible alone, and together we read something each day. The last book we read together was the Book of Jeremiah with its strong promises of God's faithfulness, and I have literally clung to those truths as God's direction for my life since Paul has left.

Paul was a hero worshiper, but books were his interest too. Going over some of Paul's messages and files with a friend of his, and reading outlines and quotations Paul had used, I was surprised at his friend's explosion: "It always got to me that Paul had already read any book I referred to." Sometimes Paul and I spent more on books than our slim budget could afford. Books by Bruce Catton, Barbara Tuckman, Winston Churchill, Theodore White, and Harrison Salisbury decorate our shelves. World War II leaders were his heroes. With Christian books he seemed able to swiftly grasp their general thrusts and unique messages. Tournier, Thielicke, Schaeffer, C. S. Lewis—he had read them all. J. I. Packer's *Knowing God* was at Paul's bedside the day he left for heaven.

Joe Bayly reminded me of Paul's strong conviction concerning the sovereignty of God. He and Paul had both spoken at a Christian writer's conference in Minneapolis. Joe said that Paul's message had not been on writing, but on the sovereign will of God in the life of a writer. Paul had told them to write what God led them to write and trust God to get it published. It could be said that the word "intense" fit Paul in so many aspects of his life, but most clearly when it came to his belief in God's will for his life. From the family into which he was born, to our family that God gave us, and to the work that God led him into, he saw it all as the working of God's sovereign hand. If God brought blessing to something Paul did and people complimented him, he would shake his head and say without phoniness, "God has done it." And if at any time he became aware of self-aggrandizement, he would check himself with the words from Jeremiah 45:5; "Seekest thou great things for thyself? Seek them not" (KJV).

When the invitation came to teach at Trinity Evangelical Divinity School, Paul could see that God had laid the ground work for it years before. Paul had never intended to teach. Nor had he even projected it as a possibility. When he enrolled in Wheaton Graduate School, he'd merely wanted to pick and choose courses that he felt would fill in the gaps of his biblical knowledge. But the dean had advised him to take courses culminating in a master's degree that later qualified him to teach on the seminary level.

In some ways, Paul resisted teaching. For both of us, Inter-Varsity had been our life. A fellow student and I had founded the Inter-Varsity chapter at the University of Pennsylvania while I had been an undergraduate, and Paul had been president of the group in his junior year. So leaving student work was unthinkable to us even after the dean of Trinity had asked Paul on three different occasions to teach evangelism. Paul felt intensely loyal to university student work, but God's sovereign will was prodding him. He prayed a very simple prayer: "Lord, if You want me teaching at Trinity in addition to doing student work, cause Dean Kantzer to ask me the fourth time. I don't feel I should call him myself, so You move Kantzer to call me again." Very shortly thereafter, the dean called. "Let me ask you one more time. Would you come and teach evangelism at the seminary? We need realism in the curriculum and you are the man to put it here." Paul told him, "Yes, I will come and teach part time, and stay in student work, in the smoke of the battle, part time."

Paul found those first years of teaching to be very taxing. He complained about how different it was to face the same group week after week and remain charged up. "I run out of jokes," he would say. During the first few quarters of teaching, he felt the deadline pressure for each day's class, so he holed up in his study, his desk smothered with books, until near midnight every weeknight.

Eventually, he hit his stride and reveled in the high quality of students and in their eagerness to learn. His own involvement in the truths he taught and in the practical applications of those truths came through to his students. A young woman recalled how much it had meant to her own faith in Christ when "Dr. Little stretched his hands upward toward the ceiling and said, 'I don't know about you, but I want to get all of God that I can.' We all felt that his desire to know the Saviour in all His fullness was so great that at times it seemed he could hardly contain himself."

This desire spilled over unpredictably outside of the classroom as well. A fellow professor told me he and Paul had been having a very serious discussion while driving to a meeting. He was astonished when Paul, unannounced and unabashed, began to pray fervently, with his eyes open, of course, as they drove down the highway.

About the time when the Billy Graham Association began planning for the International Congress on World Evangelization, Paul made a chance remark to Leighton Ford. Paul said, "A congress should have substance, study papers, and practical know-how, not just inspiration." Not long afterward, Billy Graham invited Paul to join the team as program director for the world congress.

Imagine how I felt when Paul came home and asked me how I would like to live in Switzerland for a year! After the first shock waves receded, I realized he wasn't joking. So in 1973 our family flew to Lausanne, Switzerland, where we lived during the year prior to the start of the International Congress in August 1974. That year was the highlight of our entire lives! The beauty of the country wove a spell around us. Our apartment was perched on a palisade overlooking Lake Geneva. The entire length of the apartment boasted glass doors to ensure our enjoyment of every sunrise and sunset. The Swiss Christians took us in as their warmest friends. Our whole family took up skiing. As an added bonus we were able to take trips to Italy, Yugoslavia, and France.

The congress itself was unforgettable and unrepeatable. We met many of the 4,000 Christian leaders (the crème de la crème of God's worldwide family) from 156 countries. All of them were seeking to extend God's kingdom among their own people. Paul was responsible for the entire program, daily plenary sessions, and 60 study groups, considering both theological issues and mission strategies. His committee appointed the speakers for each session, had their work papers translated into seven languages, and had those papers duplicated for each delegate. During the congress, last minute crises and details kept three men outside Paul's office fielding small problems, saving the major ones for Paul's attention.

In the middle of this whirlwind, Paul's antennae brought in the personal touch. He noticed a young Ugandan delegate standing alone in the hallway. Some radar of Paul's made him stop in the rush to speak to Edward Bakaitwako, son of a tribal chieftain. Edward had just graduated from a European university. Paul immediately recognized this man's potential for helping to build God's kingdom. Where was he living now? What was he planning to do? Paul uncovered a roadblock. Edward was enrolling in a liberal seminary because it was the only school that had offered him adequate scholarship money. It was not a place where his faith would grow and be nurtured.

At a time like this, a divine restlessness would overtake Paul. I recall that evening he said he had to see Billy Graham and/or others who could obtain funds to finance Edward through an evangelical seminary and "bail Edward out." By the end of the week, a

Press conference for International Congress on World Evangelization, Lausanne, Switzerland

Driving our Volkswagen

Handsome professor

At home
Pre

solution had been found by a few Christians at the congress who made the commitment to provide scholarship funds. Edward graduated from Trinity Evangelical Divinity School four years later.

Any picture of Paul would have to contain whirling motion, and unremitting nervous energy. During the preparations for the congress in Switzerland, the work increased as the opening day drew near. We were all tense, working in the office from 7 A.M. to 11 P.M. On a rotating basis, the staff worked the Xerox machine 24 hours a day. Volunteer help was recruited. Physically, we were pushed to the limit. One evening Paul came out of his office and said, half seriously, half jokingly, "I'm going to put a sign on my door: Mark 14:8, 'He hath done what he could.' Let's go home."

When Paul was dressed in his best Harris tweed, his fine gray hair plastered neatly, and his bright blue eyes snapping, he looked every inch a handsome professor. A few minutes later, he could be seen flying across campus, books in hand, coattails flapping. He had many occupations: husband, father, professor, Inter-Varsity staff, Urbana Director, conference speaker, Bible class teacher, author, and convention director. His schedule was always too full, but he thrived on it. A section of his files marked "Invitations Refused" was about two inches deep, proving he was trying to slow down. Happily, he had the habit of instant relaxation and could fall asleep with airy abandon beside a mountain of demanding work. "It will be there when I wake up." He was not perfect, but he relied heavily on the grace of God which gave him an extra zest for life. He frequently requested the chorus, "Jesus Christ Is Made to Me, All I Need, All I Need." It became known in some circles as "Paul Little's Chorus."

Looking back on our almost 23 years together, I again remember Haydn's words:

When I think of the Divine Being . . . notes fly off as from a spindle. . . . He will pardon me if I serve Him cheerfully.

Paul spent his last day on earth vacationing in the beautiful lake ⌐ north of Toronto. We had gotten up early and sat on the ⌐atch Paul, Jr. take water-skiing lessons. The air had been ⌐ and the sun had given us that warm glow that both ⌐nervating. The two instructors had given us an ⌐ of trick skiing: barefoot, rolling on their ⌐ works. Then we had gone back to our ⌐rested.

⌐g ready to go speak to a summer ⌐ who lived next door stopped by to ask if Paul could come to an evening gathering a few days later. We all had a cup of tea. We talked of the Lord's power and grace. I remember the close feeling we had as I looked into Paul's kind blue eyes and said, "The Lord has given us peace, hasn't He?" He looked warm and thoughtful and nodded. "Yes, He has given us peace."

An hour and a half later, on the highway leading south to Toronto, the afternoon sun glared strongly through the car windshield. It seems clear that his penchant for dozing overtook him. Our tiny Volkswagen careened recklessly into the opposite lane and the high-speed northbound traffic. With the impact of a thundering LTD, Paul was mercifully ushered in an instant into Heaven.

The Lord has given us peace. In the midst of our engulfing loss, the mighty God hasn't changed. Paul is up there with Him. We are down here with Him.

KNOW WHAT YOU BELIEVE

"My husband and I were having problems getting along. I thought it would do him good to read *Know What You Believe*. When I began reading it myself I realized I was not a Christian. I knelt down and prayed to the Lord.

Now we are both trusting the Lord and our relationship has been completely healed."

Mrs. B.E.
Chicago, Illinois

ONE

THE BIBLE

What is the Bible—this Book that has far and away been the best seller of all history and has been translated into more languages than any other book?

Bible means "book." But what kind of book is the Bible? Some suggest it is a record of man's religious striving toward and encounters with God—an essentially human book. Until the latter half of the last century, however, the historic Christian church had always seen the Bible as far more than this—namely, as the written Word of God. There was no doctrine on which there was greater unity among Christians. Not until recently have widespread doubts been raised.

The question of the Bible is a crucial one because it involves the whole issue of revelation. How can we know God exists? How can we know about Him, even if He *does* exist? It is clear that our finite minds cannot penetrate His infinity. Job asked, "Canst thou by searching find out God?" (Job 11:7) The answer is: only as God takes the initiative in revealing Himself.

God has revealed Himself in several ways. Nature and creation are proof that God exists and that He is powerful (Rom. 1:19-20). God has revealed Himself through history, particularly in His dealings with Israel and the nations surrounding her. Such Old Testament expressions as, "Then Manasseh knew that the Lord He was God" (2 Chron. 33:13), reflect recognition of God because of His activity in the affairs of men and nations.

God's revelation came to man not only through events themselves, but through the words of the prophets who *interpreted* the events. "The Word of the Lord came to me" and, "thus saith the Lord," are recurring phrases throughout the Old Testament (Ezek. 7:1; 12:1; Zech. 8:1; Ex. 4:22; 1 Sam. 2:27) of what is called propositional revelation.

God's fullest revelation came in the person of His Son Jesus

Christ. The writer to the Hebrews summarizes it this way: "God, who at sundry times and in divers manners spake in time past unto the fathers by the prophets, hath in these last days spoken to us by His Son" (Heb. 1:1-2).

Written Record Needed

But what about people who were not present and so did not see God's involvement in history or the events surrounding Christ's incarnation, life, death, and resurrection? To reach *all* men, obviously, a written record was needed. God has given this to us in the Bible, through which He has revealed Himself.

The Bible consists of two sections: the Old Testament (or Covenant), consisting of 39 books, and the New Testament (or Covenant), consisting of 27 books. In the Hebrew Bible, the books of the Old Testament are arranged in three divisions—the Law, the Prophets, and the Writings.

In the Septuagint (often denoted LXX, the Roman numeral for the number of its translators), a translation of the Hebrew Old Testament into Greek made during the Third Century, B.C., the books are arranged according to similarity of subject matter. The Pentateuch (the Law, or five books of Moses) is followed by the historical books. Then come the books of poetry and wisdom and, finally, the prophets. This is the order of the books in most Christian editions of the Bible today. The writing of the Old Testament covered a span of a thousand years.

The 27 New Testament books are in four groups: the four Gospels, the Acts of the Apostles, 21 letters (epistles), and The Revelation. These books were written within the span of a century. The earliest documents were the first letters of Paul, which, along with perhaps the letter of James, were written between A.D. 48 and 60, and the Gospels and other books between A.D. 60 and 100.

How did the Bible come to be written? Two clear statements from the New Testament answer this question: "Knowing this first, that no prophecy of the Scirpture is of any private interpretation. For the prophecy came not in old time by the will of man; but holy men of God spake as they were moved by the Holy Spirit" (2 Peter 1:20-21); "All Scripture is given by inspiration of God, and is profitable for doctrine, for reproof, for correction, for instruction in righteousness" (2 Tim. 3:16).

Given by Inspiration

The Bible originated in the mind of God, not in the mind of man. It was given man by *inspiration*. It is important to understand this term, because its biblical meaning is different from that which we often give it in everyday language. The Bible is not inspired as the writings of a great novelist are inspired, or as Bach's music was inspired. Inspiration, in the biblical sense, means that God so superintended the writers of Scripture that they wrote what He wanted them to write and were kept from error in so doing. The word "inspired" (2 Tim. 3:16) actually means "outbreathed" (by God). Inspiration applies to the end result—the Scripture itself—as well as to the men whom God used to write the Scripture.

This does not mean that the human writers of Scripture were practically machines through whom God dictated. Nor does it means that they were human typewriters whom God punched. On the contrary, their full personalities entered into their writing. Their individual writing styles are evident, for instance. Their backgrounds also are often apparent in what they wrote. But though their human capacities came into play, they were superintended and borne along in a unique way by the Holy Spirit. Because of this, the Bible is called "The Word of God" (Mark 7:13; Heb. 4:12; etc.).

It is clear that some material in the Bible came directly from God; it could not otherwise have been known by the human mind. Genesis 1 and 2 are an example of this sort of material, which must have been made known to Moses supernaturally. In other cases, men recorded events which they themselves witnessed; e.g., John wrote about his approach, with Peter, to the empty tomb on the first Easter morning (John 20:3-10). Some writers used records that were already in existence, as Luke did in writing his Gospel (Luke 1:1-4). In other instances, God put into men's mouths the very words they should speak, or told them what to write: "The word that came to Jeremiah from the Lord, saying, 'Thus speaketh the Lord God of Israel, saying, "Write thee all the words that I have spoken unto thee in a book" ' " (Jer. 30:1-2).

To say that the Scripture is inspired is not to say that all of the attitudes and ideas mentioned in the Bible are directly from God. Some of the record includes the words of evil and foolish men and even of Satan himself. Such parts are not revelation as such, nor are they the words of God, yet they are recorded in Scripture by God's intention and inspiration.

In the Book of Job, for instance, the words of Jehovah, the words of Satan, the speeches of Job's three friends, and the words of Job himself are given. All are not equally authoritative, but inspiration guarantees that what each one said was accurately recorded.

It is a striking fact that however the words came to be recorded, all Scripture is viewed by the writers as from God. Paul speaks of

Scripture as "the oracles of God" (Rom. 3:2). Most significant of all, the apostles and our Lord Himself quoted the Old Testament—not merely as the counsel of a particular patriarch or prophet, but as the counsel of *God,* given through the writers: "Lord, Thou . . . by the mouth of Thy servant David hast said . . ." (Acts 4:24-25).

Other passages speak of God as if *He* were the Scriptures. For example: "For the Scripture says to Pharaoh, 'I have raised you up for the very purpose of showing My power in you, so that My name may be proclaimed in all the earth' " (Rom. 9:17, NASB; cf. Ex. 9:16). Benjamin Warfield pointed out that these instances of the Scriptures being spoken of as if they were God, and of God being spoken of as if He were the Scriptures, could only result from a habitual identification of the text of Scripture with God speaking. It became natural to use the terms "Scripture says," and "God says," synonymously. In other words, "Scripture" and the speaking of God were seen as identical.[1]

Extent of Inspiration

The question of the extent of inspiration is frequently raised and is an important issue today. The terms *plenary* and *verbal* inspiration are used. *Plenary* means full. When used in connection with inspiration, it means that *all* of Scripture is inspired—not merely some parts. Some take the position that the only inspired (and therefore inerrant) parts of the Bible are those having to do with spiritual issues and salvation. These people maintain that to apply the claim of inspiration (and consequently inerrancy or trustworthiness) to matters involving human history or the physical world (science) is to encounter insuperable barriers.

Some scholars hold that the Bible "contains" the Word of God rather than *is* the Word of God. This view, however, confronts us with a serious problem. How can we know what parts of the Bible are trustworthy and what parts are not? How do we know which aspects have to do entirely with salvation and which are "only" matters of history? Often the two—salvation and history—are inextricably intertwined. For instance, if the Cross and the Resurrection were not historical events, of what value are they in salvation?

Moreover, if the Bible's references to the physical world and to history are not trustworthy, on what basis can we be sure that those portions dealing with salvation are trustworthy? If we are going to pick and choose the parts of the Bible we can believe, we must depend on personal subjective judgment. On matters involving eternal destiny, this is a shaky basis on which to proceed.

There have been three bases of religious authority. The first is tradition, or the authority of the church, to which Roman Catholics have adhered. The second is human reason, which liberal thinkers have adopted. The third is the Bible itself, which evangelicals have always recognized as authoritative. To take this third position is not to deny the value of tradition and of human reason, but to submit them, in case of conflict, to the authority of Scripture.

Evangelicals do not deny that there are problems in reconciling some statements of Scripture with what historical data we possess. But the evidence of modern archeology has, with few exceptions, confirmed the Bible record, so it would not seem unreasonable to postpone judgment on the questions still in doubt.

The term *verbal inspiration* indicates that inspiration extends to the *words* of the Bible themselves, not only to the ideas. We have already seen that God did not "dictate" the Scripture mechanically, but guided and superintended the writers within the framework of their own personalities and backgrounds. This guidance would of necessity include their choice of words, since thoughts are composed of words, much as a bar of music consists of individual notes. To alter the notes alters the music. Verbal inspiration holds that God, by His Spirit, has guaranteed the authenticity and reliability of the very words that were written, without depriving the writers of their individuality. A Christian who has a high view of inspiration is, of all people, sincerely interested in using modern tools in textual study to determine the original text.

The inspiration of which the Scripture speaks applies only to the text *as originally produced by the writers*. There have been some errors in copying, though they are fewer and less significant than one would think.

We have observed that the Bible *is* the Word of God; it does not merely *contain* the Word of God, as many believe. Others say the Bible *becomes* the Word of God to an individual when the person has an "existential encounter" with God in his reading of Scripture—when the truth of a passage makes a powerful and indelible impression on him. Those who hold this position are often in strong reaction to *dead* orthodoxy—to the profession of evangelical beliefs unaccompanied by evidence of the believer's having been changed by God's power.

Holy Spirit Illuminates

Scripture must be illuminated in the heart of an individual by the Holy Spirit before it becomes meaningful to him. Before the coming of the Spirit, at Pentecost, the Father and the Son had revealed divine truth. When Peter answered our Lord's climactic question, "Who do you say I am?" with, "Thou art the Christ, the Son of the living God," Jesus said, "Blessed art thou, Simon Bar-Jona, for flesh and blood hath not revealed it unto thee, but *My Father* which is in heaven" (Matt. 16:15-17). When Jesus was talking to the two disciples on the road to Emmaus after His resurrection, *He* "expounded unto them in all the Scriptures the things concerning Himself." As He sat with them, "their eyes were opened, and they knew Him" (Luke 24:27, 31). "Then opened *He* their understanding, that they might understand the Scriptures" (24:45). In telling the disciples about His going away, He said, "Howbeit when He, the Spirit of truth [the Holy Spirit], is come, He will guide you into all truth" (John 16:13).

Paul speaks of God's revealing by the Spirit what He has prepared for those who love Him (1 Cor. 2:9-10). The illuminating work of the Spirit of God is necessary if we are to know *anything* about God. What the Holy Spirit illumines is "the Sword of the Spirit, which is the Word of God" (Eph. 6:17). It does not *become* the Word of God; it *is* the Word of God.

A television set, sitting in the corner but not turned on, is still a television set. I won't get any images or sound until I turn it on, but it *is* a television set, whether turned on or not. It doesn't *become* a television set when turned on.

So, too, the Scripture *is* the Word of God, whether anybody ever responds to it or not. The Holy Spirit must illumine Scripture in a person's heart before it becomes *meaningful,* but what He illumines *is* the Word of God, not something less. It doesn't *become* something it wasn't before.

Having seen that the Bible *is* the Word of God, we must now consider the principles of interpreting and understanding it. Considerable confusion has resulted because people have oversimplified the kinds of biblical interpretation as either *literal* or *figurative*. Those who take the Bible literally are made to look foolish by their apparent denial of any use of figures of speech in the Bible. Those, on the other hand, who take it figuratively often appear to be capricious in evading the clear meaning of statements they do not want to accept.

The fact is that some parts of the Bible are to be taken literally and other parts figuratively.

The key question is, What did the writer intend his readers to understand? We must ask to whom the passage was written. Is the promise or command, for instance, one that has universal application or one that has limited reference? Often there are primary and secondary applications. A primary application has to do with the person or people directly addressed. A secondary application relates a scriptural principle to those to whom the passage is not applied directly.

It is important to consider the context in which a Bible statement is made. What is the primary teaching of the passage? Statements must not be lifted out of context in such a way as to cause misunderstanding. A skeptic once triumphantly asserted, "The Bible says, 'There is no God.' " He was considerably deflated when reminded of the context: "The fool hath said in his heart, 'There is no God' " (Ps. 14:1).

Literal or Figurative?

It is important to decide whether a statement is literal or figurative. The Bible uses such literary forms as poetry, allegory, and parable. Though there are passages on which there is strong difference of opinion, it is usually no more difficult to distinguish between figurative and literal statements in the Bible than in a daily newspaper. The statement, "Two people were killed in an accident on Main Street," is obviously literal. "He shot home from third in the last half of the ninth with the winning run under his arm, and the crowd went mad," is readily recognized as figurative language. A player does not "shoot" home or carry runs under his arm. And the folks in the bleachers, though they may get excited, do not become insane.

A final word about Bible study. Simply using a dictionary to investigate the full meaning of the words of Scripture will reveal surprising riches. Try it! And consult several translations.

It has been said that the Scripture is its own best commentary. Often a verse or a passage becomes clear when studied in the light of other Bible statements on the same subject. Though humanly the Bible has many writers, in the final analysis there was only one Author—God Himself. As we compare Scripture with Scripture, we are guarded against becoming unbalanced in our views. We need to study individual books and we also need to trace themes through the whole Bible. This is the difference between biblical theology and systematic theology. One scholar compares biblical theology to "the profusion of nature in which the various plants and flowers are scattered with a bountiful hand in 'ordered disorder.' " He compared systematic theology to a botanical garden "where plants and flowers are gathered and arranged according to species." [2] Both kinds of arrangements are useful; both have their place in a study of botany. Both kinds of Bible study are useful, too.

The Canon of Scripture

A separate question from that of inspiration is that of the canon, i.e., *which* writings, or books, are recognized as *inspired?* It is important to realize that a book did not become inspired by being included in the canon. Inclusion in the canon was merely recognition of the authority the book already possessed.

We do not know exactly when the Old Testament canon was completed. The Old Testament itself says that collections of "authorized" books were put in the sacred buildings—the tabernacle and then the temple. Hilkiah rediscovered the Book of the Law there (2 Kings 22). The Jews recognized as their Scriptures certain books that recorded Jehovah's dealings with Israel.

In our Lord's time, the Old Testament was viewed as a completed collection. He and the apostles referred to this collection as "the Scripture." Most of the books of the Old Testament are quoted in the New Testament, always as authoritative.

In tracing the canonicity of a particular book—that is, its recognition as one of the inspired writings—we must keep three questions in mind: (1) Is it mentioned by the Early Church Fathers in the Christian literature of the first centuries of our era? (2) What attitude do these early writers take toward the inspiration of the book? (3) Do they regard it as part of a canon, or list of books recognized as inspired?

The definition of the canon was important in the early church, because claims were being advanced for many writings which were patently spurious, and because heretics were attacking the validity of the genuine Scriptures. The canon, as we know it today, became fixed in the fourth century. Athanasius (A.D. 297-373), known as the father of orthodoxy, became patriarch of Alexandria. In his 39th Paschal Letter (A.D. 367), he listed the books of the New Testament as we know them.

The canon of the New Testament was also confirmed at a church council held in Carthage in A.D. 397. The council used three criteria in recognizing canonicity. First, was a book apostolic in origin? Mark and Luke were accepted, for example, because they were recognized as the work of close associates of the apostles. Second, was the book used and recognized by the churches? Third, did the book teach sound doctrine? [3]

It is on these bases that the orthodox protestant church today does not receive as canonical the books of the Apocrypha (1 and 2 Maccabees, 1 and 2 Esdras, Tobit, Judith, Wisdom of Solomon, Ecclesiasticus, Baruch, Song of the Three Holy Children, Susanna, Bel and the Dragon, and the Prayer of Manasses), which the Roman Catholic Church accepts. The Jews never recognized these books as part of their Old Testament.

To accept the Bible as the Word of God today is not fashionable. Some, even within the professing church, deny its reliability. Generally, attacks on Scripture follow certain lines. Perhaps the foremost is that of contending that the Bible is incompatible with 20th century science. Many conflicts are said to exist between scientific facts and statements in the Bible. There are, admittedly, some problems. But the following considerations usually bridge what on first sight may seem a yawning chasm.

Understanding the Bible

First, the Bible speaks in *phenomenological* language—that is, it describes things *as they appear to be* rather than in precise scientific terms. To say the sun rises in the east is a phenomenological statement. Technically, we know the sun does not really *rise*, but even the *Naval Almanac* uses the term *sunrise,* and we would not charge the *Almanac* with error. The Bible has been understandable in all cultures and throughout history because of the phenomenological way it describes things. It does not claim to be a textbook on science, but where it touches scientific matters, it does not give misinformation.

Second, when Bible information is incomplete, it is not necessarily incorrect. Science is always building on previous knowledge. Advancement on incomplete theories does not mean the theories were incorrect.

Third, we must always guard against making the Bible say things which, on closer examination, it really doesn't say. And it is most important to determine whether, in a given instance, the Bible is speaking figuratively or literally.

Fourth, we must carefully investigate to see whether the supposed conflict is between biblical teaching and scientific facts or simply between an *interpretation* of Scripture and an *interpretation* of the facts. Often an interpretation at variance with biblical truth is more philosophic than scientific.

Fifth, it would be foolish to *freeze* the points of conflict and assume the Bible wrong. The Bible has not changed in 2,000 years, but science admittedly is a moving train. To have reconciled the Bible to scientific views current a century ago would have been to make Scripture obsolete today! Far better to *admit* an apparent conflict and await the development of additional evidence.

That there is no basic conflict between science and Scripture is suggested by the fact that modern science was born and developed largely by earnest Christians. Believing in a personal God as Creator, they were convinced that the universe was orderly and therefore capable of meaningful investigation. In scientific research they felt they were thinking God's thoughts after Him. There can be no ultimate conflict between truth of biblical revelation and that discovered by science, for all truth is from God and is therefore consistent. In our day, when some 90 percent of all scientists who have ever lived are alive, many outstanding scientists are also earnest Christians.

Dating Problems Explained

In another line of attack it is contended that the Bible is not reliable historically and that there are "internal" contradictions in parallel accounts of the same event. Some apparent numerical errors may be due to mistakes in transmission of the text over many years. Recent archeological discoveries, however, show that the ancients' system of dating explains many numerical problems. If one king, for example, ended his rule and another began ruling in a given calendar year, *both* were given credit for ruling the entire year. Also, it is important to remember that the biblical writers often used round figures which, though not precise, are at the same time not incorrect.

Admittedly we do not presently have complete explanations for all seeming Bible discrepancies. But it would be unscientific, in the light of modern archeological discoveries, to adopt the prevalent assumption that the Bible is wrong until proven right, rather than the reverse. Dr. W. F. Albright, one of the world's leading archeologists, has said, "There can be no doubt that archeology has confirmed the substantial historicity of the Old Testament tradition." [4]

Nelson Glueck, famed Jewish archeologist, writes, "It may be stated categorically that no archeological discovery has ever controverted a biblical reference." [5]

We do not *prove* the Bible by archeology. The Holy Spirit confirms in our hearts the conviction that the Bible is the Word of God. But it is gratifying to know that scientific evidence is consistent with Scripture.

We can with confidence affirm, with the hymn writer:

> The Bible stands like a rock undaunted
>   'Mid the raging storms of time;
> Its pages burn with the truth eternal,
>   And they glow with a light sublime.
> The Bible stands though the hills may tumble;
>   It will firmly stand when the earth shall crumble;
> I will plant my feet on its firm foundation,
>   For the Bible stands!
>   Haldor Lillenas

"Forever, O Lord, Thy Word is settled in heaven" (Ps. 119:89).

For Further Reading

Bruce, F. F. *The New Testament Documents: Are They Reliable?* Downers Grove, Ill.: InterVarsity Press, 1960.

Henry, C. F. H., ed. *Revelation and the Bible*. Grand Rapids: Baker Book House, 1958.

Mickelsen, A. B. *Interpreting the Bible*. Grand Rapids: Wm. B. Eerdmans Co., 1963.

Packer, J. I. *Fundamentalism and the Word of God*. Grand Rapids: Wm. B. Eerdmans Co., 1958.

Ramm, Bernard. *The Christian View of Science and Scripture*. Grand Rapids: Wm. B. Eerdmans Co., 1955.

TWO
GOD

"**W**hat we believe about God," said the late A. W. Tozer, "is the most important thing about us." Our belief or lack of it inevitably translates itself into our actions and attitudes.

It is interesting, on the basis of how Joseph reacted to his traitorous brothers and to his unjust imprisonment for refusing the seduction of Potiphar's wife, to reconstruct the God Joseph believed in. Moses, because of the God he trusted, "endured as seeing Him who is invisible" (Heb. 11:27). He gave up the king's palace for the desert and God's people. Significantly, faith, in Hebrews 11, is illustrated by what people *did* rather than what they *said* or professed.

The word "God" is one of the most widely used—but vague and undefined—terms in our language. Some people, such as Einstein, think of God as "a pure mathematical mind." Others see Him as a shadowy superhuman person or force. Still others see God as a ball of fire to which we, as sparks of life, will ultimately be reunited. A few think of Him as a sentimental grandfather of the sky or as a celestial policeman.

Increasing godlessness causes some people to urge us to agree simply to use the word "God" without even trying to define it lest we breed division. It is obvious, however, that if God *is*, His existence and His nature do not depend on what anyone thinks about Him. To conceive of God as a stone idol or as a mystical idea does not *make* Him either. If I am interested in *reality*, I must know what God is *really* like. This I cannot know apart from His revealing Himself to me. How God has done this is summed up by the writer to the Hebrews: "God . . . at sundry times in divers manners spake in time past unto the fathers by the prophets . . . [and] hath in these last days spoken unto us by His Son" (Heb. 1:1-2).

Because God has spoken and has revealed Himself, we no longer have the need or the option of conjuring up ideas and images of

God by our own imaginations. Our personal concept of God—when we pray, for instance—is *worthless* unless it coincides with His revelation of Himself.

God's "Natural" Attributes

The terms that describe the nature of God—love, holiness, sovereignty, etc.—are known as His attributes. They are classified as "natural" attributes and "moral" attributes. Let's think first about God's "natural" attributes, as revealed by His self-disclosure in Scripture.

First, God is separate from His creation. He is *transcendent*—above and beyond His creation, the heavens and the earth. He is not a slave to natural law He authored, but is independent of it and above it. He can override it at will—though normally He does not interfere with it. He is exalted and eternal, the world's Creator, Sovereign, and Judge.

But God is *immanent* as well as transcendent. By this we mean that His presence and power pervade His entire creation. He does not stand apart from the world, a mere spectator of the things He has made.

The prophet spoke of God's *transcendence* when he wrote of "the high and lofty One that inhabiteth eternity, whose name is Holy [set apart]," and of His *immanence* when he spoke of Him as the One who dwells "with him also that is of a contrite and humble spirit" (Isa. 57:15).

God is not so totally transcendent that He set the universe in motion and then left it, as Deists would have us believe. Nor is He so immanent that He is indistinguishable from the universe. Pantheism holds that God is all and that all is God. But that means you and I would be part of God, which ultimately means that God sins when we sin. If all is God, and everything else is illusion, as some hold, then what could exist to *have* the illusion? Does God have illusions?

One who sees God in nature is not necessarily a pantheist. The Bible itself tells us that the universe which God has made speaks to us of His eternal power (*omnipotence*) and Deity (Rom. 1:19-20). The Rocky Mountains, Niagara Falls, the starry hosts of heaven, the ocean's vastness—all remind us that God made them and is sovereign over them.

The prophet observed, "Oh, Lord God . . . there is nothing too hard for Thee" (Jer. 32:17), and the Angel Gabriel assured Mary, after informing her of her privilege of bearing the Son of God as a virgin, "For with God nothing shall be impossible" (Luke 1:37).

The omnipotence of God is limited by His moral character. For

example, though "nothing [is] impossible" with God, He cannot lie
(Heb. 6:18). His omnipotence applies to inherent possibilities, not
inherent impossibilities. Someone has asked, "Is it possible for God
to make anything too heavy for Himself to lift? If not, can we say
He is omnipotent?" Nonsense is still nonsense, as C. S. Lewis says,
whether we are talking about something else or about God.

God's Eternity

God is *eternal*—that is, He never had a beginning and will never
have an end. He is the "One who inhabiteth eternity" (Isa. 57:15).
"The eternal God is our refuge" (Deut. 33:27). From everlasting
to everlasting, He is God (cf. Ps. 90:2). He is not a prisoner of
time, because time—as we know it—began with Creation. The
answer to the question, "Who created God?" is, "No one and
nothing," because God is completely self-existent. There was never
a time when He did not exist.

God is *infinite*. By this we mean that He is not limited by or
confined to the universe. He is entirely independent of finite (measurable) things and beings. There have been times when God has
put limitations on Himself, as when He appeared to Old Testament
believers in the form of an angel or a man (e.g., Gen. 18:1) and
when He became incarnate in the person of Jesus Christ. He im-
posed such limitation on Himself in order to bless His creatures,
not because He *had* to.[1]

It has been pointed out that our minds cannot adequately conceive of an *infinite* quantity of anything—space, power, potatoes.
Such a concept baffles and frustrates us. We *can,* however, imagine
a being—God—who is infinite in the sense that He has no limitations. God's infinite holiness does not mean that He has a boundless *amount* of holiness—for holiness cannot be measured in this
way. Rather, it means that His holiness has no limitations and no
defects. The same may be said for each of His other attributes.

God's infinity is also a matter of "boundless activity"—that is,
His power (omnipotence) is at work in and in control of everything, anywhere, that exists.[2]

God is *unchangeable*. With Him "no variation occurs, nor shadow
cast by turning" (James 1:17, BERK). It is important that we not
think of God in terms of human personality, which is ordinarily
volatile and unsteady. God's love is steadfast and constant, and is
not subject to the ebbs and flows of human love. His wrath is a
fixed attitude toward sin and is not like our fits of temper when
something displeases us.

A man who walks east into a strong east wind, and then turns
around and walks west, would say, "The wind *was* on my face, but

now it is on my back." But there would have been no change in the wind. His *direction* was what changed, and this change brought him into a new relationship with the wind. God never changes, and when He *seems* to be different it is because *we* have changed and in so doing have come into a different relationship toward Him.

When God "Repents"

The Bible speaks of God as *repenting* (changing His mind). The term describes what *seems* to us to have happened. As an instance, God threatened to destroy the ancient city of Nineveh, but after Jonah had preached there the people turned to God for forgiveness and He is said to have repented (Jonah 3:10) of His plan to destroy them. Actually, the people of Nineveh had turned from rebellion to repentance, and so they came under God's mercy and forgiveness instead of His wrath. God Himself had not changed.

God is *omnipresent,* which means He is fully present everywhere. He is not like a substance spread out in a thin layer all over the earth—*all* of Him is in Chicago, in Calcutta, in Cairo, and in Caracas, at one and the same time.

God is *omniscient*—that is, He knows everything, including our own thoughts. "Thou understandest my thought afar off" (Ps. 139:2), David wrote about God, and the Apostle John wrote of our Lord that He needed no testimony from anyone about [men], for He well knew what was in human nature (John 2:25, WMS). Moreover, He declares the end from the beginning (Isa. 46:10), and nothing takes Him by surprise.

Jesus declared that God is *a Spirit* and that those who worship Him must do so in [the] Spirit and in truth (John 4:24). God does not have a physical body. When we speak of the "hand of God" or the "nostrils of God" we are using *anthropomorphisms*—human expressions—to describe God; we know they are not *literally* true.

We have saved for last the fact about God which, among His "natural" attributes, is of the greatest importance. God is all-powerful, all-wise, infinite and eternal, and changeless, and we are not to think of Him as an impersonal force behind the universe. God is *personal*—that is, He is a Person. He has the elements of personality—intellect, feelings, and will. He is self-determining—as, within our limitations, we also are. He does according to His own purpose and will.

We know this of God because He created man in His own image and after His own likeness (Gen. 1:26). Since *we* are persons, God cannot possibly be something less than a person. What is created cannot be of a higher order than its Creator.

Because God is personal, we know that His sovereign will is not akin to the blind fate ("Kismet") of Islam's Allah. It is, rather, the loving purpose of a heavenly Father to whom His children are precious. And because God is a Person and we are persons, communication between Him and us is possible.

God's Moral Attributes

God's other qualities are called His "moral" attributes. It is not enough to know merely that God exists; it is desperately important to know about His moral nature. Suppose we knew God existed, but thought He was like Adolf Hitler. What a horrible truth to contemplate, and what a heinous existence we would have!

Holiness is perhaps the most comprehensive of all of God's attributes. "It is a term for the moral excellence of God and His freedom from all limitation in His moral perfection. 'Thou art of purer eyes than to behold evil' (Hab. 1:13)." [3] In this exalted sense, only God is holy. He is therefore the standard of ethical purity by which His creatures must measure themselves.

"Since holiness embraces every distinctive attribute of the Godhead, it may be defined as the outshining of all that God is. As the sun's rays, combining all the colors of the spectrum, come together in the sun's shining and blend into light, so in His self-manifestation all the attributes of God come together and blend into holiness. Holiness has, for that reason, been called 'an attribute of attributes' —that which lends unity to all the attributes of God. To conceive of God's being and character as merely a [collection] of abstract perfectness is to deprive God of all reality." [4] Holiness is the sum total of the perfections of the God of the Bible.

All the attributes of God are in perfect harmony and are in no way antagonistic to each other. God's love and mercy are not opposed to, or exercised at the expense of, His righteousness and holiness. Sometimes it is wrongly suggested that the God of the Old Testament is a God of wrath and anger, but that in the New Testament we have God in Christ portrayed as love and gentleness. The implication is sometimes drawn that these are two different Gods. This, of course, is completely false. The God of the Old Testament, who repeatedly had mercy on the Israelites after they repented, is the same God who wept over Jerusalem because her people killed the prophets and would not turn to the Lord. The Jesus who spoke frequently of hell and eternal judgment is the same God who moved in judgment on Jerusalem in 586 B.C., and on the pagan Belshazzar some years later.

Our Triune God

At the heart of the Christian view of God is the concept of the

Trinity. Rather than being "excess baggage," as former Episcopal Bishop James A. Pike called it, this truth is central to an understanding of biblical revelation and the Christian Gospel. Departure from the doctrine of the Trinity has been and is one of the major sources of heresy in the Christian Church.

The term *Trinity* does not occur in the Bible, but this does not mean that the idea is a later development or one that is a product of philosophic speculation rather than divine revelation.

The Trinity is a difficult concept, not fully susceptible to human explanation, because it involves categories which our finite mental powers cannot grasp. Anyone who has ever tried to explain the Trinity to an unbeliever will agree that it could hardly be a human invention. It is a teaching which God Himself has revealed to us.

The doctrine is that "God is one in His essential being, but that the 'divine essence' exists in three modes or forms, each constituting a Person, yet in such a way that the divine essence is wholly in each Person." [5] God is one Being, but He exists in three Persons.

The first Old Testament clue concerning the Trinity comes in the story of creation. God (Elohim) created by means of the Word and the Spirit (Gen. 1:1-3). These immortal words were read by Commander Frank Borman in Apollo 8 as the spacecraft circled the moon: "In the beginning God created the heaven and the earth. And the earth was without form, and void, and darkness was upon the face of the deep. And the Spirit of God moved upon the face of the waters. And God said, Let there be light, and there was light."

"Here we are introduced . . . to the Word as a personal creative power, and to the Spirit as the bringer of life and order to the creation. There is revealed thus early a threefold center of activity. God, as Creator, thought out the universe, expressed His thought in a Word, and made His Spirit its animating principle." [6]

Some believe that when God (Elohim) said, "Let Us make man in Our image" (Gen. 1:26), the plural forms used (Elohim, us, our) are to be understood as a revelation of the Trinity by God to man, and that man's awareness of this truth was later lost through the Fall.

Other indications of the Trinity are to be found in Genesis 48:15-16; Exodus 31:3; Numbers 11:25; Judges 3:10; Proverbs 8:22-31 (the Word is here personified as Wisdom); and Isaiah 11:2; 42:1; 61:1. In these passages the Spirit is clearly the source of blessing, power, and strength.

The Bible's emphasis throughout, however, is on the fact that God is *one.* "Hear, O Israel: the Lord our God is one Lord" (Deut.

6:4). This truth was in sharp contrast to the rampant polytheism that surrounded the nation of Israel. We must not allow the scriptural truth of the Trinity to deprive us of the equally important teaching that there is only *one* God.

It is both interesting and significant that in the New Testament, where the distinctness of the persons of the Godhead is more clear, the disciples were taught by our Lord to baptize in *the name,* singular, of the Father and of the Son and of the Holy Spirit (Matt. 28:19).

John the Baptist spoke of the coming baptism of the (Holy) Spirit, of which his own water baptism was a symbol. When John baptized Him, Jesus saw "the heavens opened and the Spirit like a dove descending upon Him. And there came a voice from heaven saying, 'Thou art My beloved Son, in whom I am well pleased' " (Mark 1:10-11). This was a clear manifestation of the Trinity, all of the three Persons of the Godhead being referred to.

Earlier, at the birth of Jesus, all three Persons of the Godhead are also mentioned. The angel told Mary that her child would be the *Son of God* conceived by the *Holy Spirit* (Luke 1:35).

Jesus explicitly spoke of the Father and the Spirit as being distinct Persons from Himself (John 14:16).

Salvation itself portrays the work of the triune God. The Father sent the Son to accomplish the work of redemption. The Son sent the Spirit to bring conviction and to apply to men what Christ had accomplished.

The apostolic benediction, "The grace of the Lord Jesus Christ, and the love of God, and the communion of the Holy Spirit, be with you all" (2 Cor. 13:14), is another instance of apostolic teaching on the Trinity.

Each person of the Trinity is fully God. Paul wrote of "God our Father" (Rom. 1:7), and spoke of Christ as the "dear Son . . . who is the image of the invisible God" (Col. 1:13, 15) and as "God our Saviour" (Tit. 3:4).

The deity of the Holy Spirit is also clear. Peter told Ananias that in lying to the Holy Spirit, he had "not lied unto men, but unto God" (Acts 5:3-4).

A Semantic Problem

Part of the problem of understanding the Trinity is the inadequacy of human words to express divine reality. For instance, we speak of the *Persons* in the Godhead. We use this term because it describes a being who has intellect, emotion, and will. We can understand this. But we must be careful in applying such terms to God. "In most [cases] the doctrine is stated by saying that God is one in His essential being, but that in this being there are three Persons, yet so as not to form separate and distinct individuals. They are three modes or forms in which the divine essence exists. 'Person' is, however, an imperfect expression of the truth, inasmuch as the term denotes to us a *separate* rational and moral individual. But in the being of God there are not three *individuals,* but only three *personal self distinctions* within the one divine essence.

"Then again, personality in man implies independence of will, actions, and feelings, leading to behavior peculiar to the [individual]. This cannot be thought of in connection with the Trinity: each Person is self-conscious and self-directing, yet never acts independently or in opposition [to the others]. When we say that God is a Unity, we mean that though [He] is in Himself a threefold center of life, His life is not split into three. He is one in essence, in personality, and in will. When we say that God is a Trinity in Unity, we mean that there is unity in diversity, and that diversity manifests itself in Persons, in characteristics, and in operations." [7]

Just as the word "person" is not exact when applied to the Godhead, but is the best approximation available, so it is with the word "substance." The Trinity was spoken of in the early church as "three Persons in one Substance." But here "substance is, of course, immaterial; it must not be thought of either as a common spiritual 'stuff' or 'material' out of which three Beings of the same divine nature are produced (as we talk of silver as the *substance* from which coins may be made). The divine essence is not *divided* into three: it is fully present in each of the Persons. 'Substance' thus relates to the one Being who is God, rather than to the nature or being of that God." [8]

It is also important to understand the relationships of the Persons of the Trinity. The Son and the Spirit are said to be *subordinate* to the Father, but this does not mean they are inferior. Their subordination has been called a matter of relationship, but not of nature.

"The Father, as the fount of Deity, is first. He is said to *originate.* The Son, eternally begotten of the Father, is second. He is said to *reveal.* The Spirit, eternally proceeding from the Father and the Son, is third. He is said to *execute.* . . . Thus we can say that creation is from the Father, through the Son, by the Holy Spirit." [9]

The Spirit of God is said to proceed from the Son as well as from the Father. The Father is the one by whom the Son is begotten and from whom the Spirit proceeds.

Two Major Heresies

There have been two major heretical distortions of the Trinity, and they exist at present. One is an attempt to get away from any implication that there are three separate and distinct Persons in the Godhead. Originating with a man named Sabellius in the third century, this error claims that Father, Son and Holy Spirit are merely different manifestations of the one God which He assumes temporarily to achieve His purposes. At times God appears as Father, at times as Son, and at times as the Holy Spirit, say the Sabellians.

The other emphasis was originated by Arius (about A.D. 325). Though Arius emphasized the unity of God, he so stressed the Persons of the Trinity that he ended up by dividing the substance of the Godhead. "This resulted chiefly from his definition of the Son and the Holy Spirit as being lesser, subordinate Beings whom the Father willed into existence for the purpose of acting as His agents in His dealings with the world and men. In effect, Arius reduced our Lord (and the Spirit) below the level of strict Deity." [10] He would admit (Christ's) Deity in a secondary sense, but denied His *eternal* Sonship. He admitted that Christ existed before the foundation of the world, but denied that He was coeternal with the Father. The disciples of Arius, by teaching that the Spirit was brought into existence by the Son, reduced Him to a lesser form of Deity.

In more recent times, some movements, such as Unitarianism, Russellism (Jehovah's Witnesses), and Mormonism assign our Lord and the Holy Spirit a nature and position below that of true Deity. "This is one of the most important battlegrounds in the history of the church, and no true Christian should for one moment tolerate any description of our Master other than that which assigns to Him the fullest Deity, co-equal and co-eternal with the Father." [11]

It is also important that we know about God's providence and will if our knowledge of God is to be accurate. He is not only the Creator of the universe—He is also its Sustainer in the physical sense, and is the moral Governor of the intelligent beings He has created. The sweep of God's providence and sovereignty are complete and comprehensive. "Whatsoever the Lord pleased, that did He in heaven, and in earth, in the seas, and all deep places" (Ps. 135:6). This truth is echoed in the New Testament: "For to do whatsoever Thy hand and Thy counsel determined before to be done" (Acts 4:28). God is the One in whom "all things hold together" (cf. Col. 1:17, NASB). He is the One "who worketh all things after the counsel of His own will" (Eph. 1:11).

God's Decrees
God's control of the universe is often spoken of in terms of His

decrees. Someone has defined the decrees of God as that eternal plan by which God makes sure that all the events of the universe—past, present, and future—take place. To our finite, limited minds there appear to be a great many events, but with God there is no time and everything happens in one eternal moment. This is why we say God knows the end from the beginning.

A distinction is sometimes made between the absolute *decrees* of God, which determine what happens, and His *purposes* for His creatures—that is, His revelation to them of their duties. God's decrees are always accomplished, but men frequently ignore and disobey His purposes for them.

Another distinction is made between the *directive* will and the *permissive* will of God. His directive will is what He brings to pass; His permissive will is what he allows to take place. God *permitted,* but did not *direct,* the entrance of sin into the world. But whether actively (by decree) or passively (by permission), God is sovereign over all that happens. He is *free* in that He is under no other influence or power of anything or anyone but Himself. "Who hath directed the Spirit of the Lord, or being His counselor hath taught Him?" (Isa. 40:13) He is *sovereign*—He has power to bring His purposes to pass.

What about Free Will?

The question of God's sovereignty and its relation to human freedom troubles many people. If God directs everything, how can man be a free agent and therefore morally responsible? If God knows in advance what man is going to do, what choice has he in the matter? Admittedly there are profound aspects to this question which are not altogether clear, but it is helpful to keep several other things in mind:

First, man's will is always a relatively small part of any given circumstances. Man has no control over where he is born, into what family, or with what abilities or disabilities, advantages or disadvantages. He is subject to many influences beyond his control. He is rather like a baby in a playpen. He has real freedom, but only within certain prescribed bounds. Francis Schaeffer points out that when someone throws a man a ball, he can either catch it or let it fall. Barring some physical defect, he is not so limited that he has no power of decision or choice.

Second, God's foreknowledge (which is not to be confused with His election or with predestination) is not in itself the *cause* of what happens. For example, God foreknew that Demas would forsake the Apostle Paul for love of this world, but God's foreknowledge did not *predispose* Demas to turn back, much less *compel* him to do so. Demas acted in freedom; he made his own personal choice, under no compulsion.

Again, God foreknew that Saul would receive Christ and become Paul the Apostle, but on the Damascus Road Saul exercised his own will in answering the Lord's summons. God foreknows your decisions before you make them—He knows what you will do and where you will go—but this foreknowledge does not interfere in the slightest with your complete freedom to act.

Packer calls this difficulty—reconciling divine sovereignty and human freedom—an *antinomy*—an apparent contradiction between conclusions that seem equally logical, reasonable, or necessary. He says:

> An antinomy exists when a pair of principles stand side by side, seemingly irreconcilable, yet both undeniable. There are cogent reasons for believing each of them: each rests on clear, solid evidence; but it is a mystery to you how they can be squared with each other. You see that each must be true on its own, but you do not see how they can both be true together. . . .
>
> Modern physics faces an antinomy, in this sense, in its study of light. There is cogent evidence to show that light consists of waves, and equally cogent evidence to show that it consists of particles. It is not apparent how light can be both waves and particles, but the evidence is there, and so neither view can be ruled out in favor of the other. Neither, however, can be reduced to the other or explained in terms of the other; the two seemingly incompatible positions must be held together, and both must be treated as true. Such a necessity scandalizes our tidy minds, no doubt, but there is no help for it if we are to be loyal to the facts.[12]

We may take comfort that divine sovereignty is exercised by a personal, all-loving, all-knowing God. But His sovereignty in no way lessens our freedom—or our privilege and responsibility to know and do His good will.

For Further Reading

Orr, James. *A Christian View of God and the World*. New York: Charles Scribner's Sons, 1908.

Schaeffer, Francis. *The God Who Is There*. Downers Grove, Ill.: InterVarsity Press, 1968.

THREE
JESUS CHRIST

D r. W. H. Griffith Thomas wrote a book entitled *Christianity Is Christ*. This title sums up the heart and uniqueness of Christianity.

Buddha is not essential to the teaching of Buddhism, or Mohammed to Islam, but everything about Christianity is determined by the person and work of Jesus Christ. Christianity owes its life and character in every detail to Christ. Its teachings are teachings about Him. He was the origin and will be the fulfillment of its hopes. He is the source of its ideas, which were born of what He said and did. The strength of Christ's church is the strength of His own Spirit, who is omnipotent.

But who is this Man, Jesus Christ? He Himself made His identity the central question of His ministry: "But whom say ye that I am?" (Matt. 16:15). To be wrong at this point is fatal, as the history of the church has shown.

We must be clear, first, that Jesus Christ was fully God. He is expressly called God in various passages of Scripture, of which the following are a few examples: "The Word was God" (John 1:1; that the Word is Christ is confirmed in v. 14); "the great God and our Saviour Jesus Christ" (Titus 2:13); "His Son Jesus Christ. This is the true God" (1 John 5:20).

Christ Claimed Deity
Jesus claimed Deity for Himself in a way quite clear to His listeners. He said, on one occasion, "I and the Father are one" (John 10:30). His claim to Deity was considered by the religious leaders to be blasphemy, and led to His crucifixion: "We have a law, and by our law He ought to die, because He made Himself the Son of God" (John 19:7). The high priest expressly asked Christ, "Tell us whether Thou be the Christ, the Son of God," and Jesus answered, "Thou hast said" (Matt. 26:63-64). This was a clear affirmative answer, and the high priest said there was no further need of

witnesses because they had heard His "blasphemy" with their own ears. He had said "that God was His Father, making Himself equal with God" (John 5:18).

Jesus Christ claimed the prerogatives and authority of God. He said He had authority to forgive sins (Mark 2:10) and that He would come in the clouds of heaven, sitting at the right hand of power (Mark 14:62), implying authority to judge men: "For the Father judgeth no man, but hath committed all judgment unto the Son" (John 5:22). Several times Jesus asserted that He Himself had the authority and power to raise the dead (John 6:39-40, 54; 10:17-18).

Jesus possessed attributes which belong to God alone. He claimed omnipotence, or all power (Matt. 28:18), and during His life He demonstrated this power over nature by stilling the stormy waves (Mark 4:39) and by turning water into wine (John 2:7-11); over physical disease (Mark 3:10); over the spirit world of demons (Luke 4:35); and over death by raising Lazarus from the grave (John 11:43-44). He has also been designated as having power over all the heavenly hosts (Eph. 1:20-22).

He is omniscient, or all-knowing. He knew, as only God could know, what was in men's minds before they spoke (Mark 2:8; John 2:25). He was omnipresent, and promised to be with all His disciples to the end of the age (Matt. 28:20).

Christ the Creator
He is the Creator (John 1:3) and Sustainer (Heb. 1:3) of the universe. Perhaps the most comprehensive statement about the Deity of Christ is that "in Him dwelleth all the fullness of the Godhead bodily" (Col. 2:9).

Christ accepted the worship of men, which is due to God alone. He commended rather than rebuked doubting Thomas, who fell at His feet and declared in awe, "My Lord and my God!" (John 20:28, BERK) This was the same Jesus who scorned Satan's invitation to worship him by replying, "Thou shalt worship the Lord thy God, and Him only shalt thou serve" (Matt. 4:10).

Another dimension of Christ's Deity to be kept in mind is His preexistence. He did not *become* the Son of God, either at His birth or sometime during His earthly life. He *was* and *is* the eternal Son, coexistent and coeternal with the Father. John declared, "In the beginning was the Word," and, "without Him was not anything made that was made" (John 1:1, 3). Jesus made clear reference to His own preexistence when the Jews challenged Him concerning His age. "You're not 50 years old yet," they said; and He replied, "Before Abraham was, I am" (John 8:57-58).

The Deity of Christ is woven into the warp and woof of everything He said and taught. It is confirmed by what others clearly understood Him to say. The things that He did were conclusive evidence that His words were not clever deceit or the babblings of a demented person.

Christ Also Fully Man

But Jesus was not only fully God—He was also fully man, fully human. This is a vital aspect of the person of Christ. If He were not fully human, He could not have represented us on the cross and He could not be the High Priest who comforts and strengthens us. But He *has* gone through our human experience (Heb. 2:16-18) and is fully able to understand us and sympathize with us.

Though His conception was supernatural, Jesus' birth was that of a normal child born of a human mother (Matt. 1:18). He is spoken of as being born of the seed of the woman (Gen. 3:15) and of the seed of Abraham (Heb. 2:16). In this way, in the virgin birth, "The Word became flesh" (John 1:14, NASB).

Jesus, as a normal child, grew physically and mentally. "And the Child grew, and waxed strong in spirit, filled with wisdom . . . and Jesus increased in wisdom and stature, and in favor with God and man" (Luke 2:40, 52).

Jesus referred to Himself as a man: "Ye seek to kill Me, a man that hath told you the truth" (John 8:40). He was recognized by others as a man (Acts 2:22). He had a body, soul, and spirit, and shared our physical and emotional experiences.

Jesus got hungry (Matt. 4:2) and thirsty (John 19:28). His feet ached and He got weary from traveling (John 4:6). He needed sleep and refreshment (Matt. 8:24). He experienced and expressed love and compassion (Matt. 9:36). He was angry at those who defiled His Father's house (Matt. 21:13) and who deliberately refused the truth of God (Mark 3:5). He wept at the tomb of a dear friend (John 11:35), and as He faced the agony of the cross, He was troubled within (John 12:27).

The Son of Man

Jesus calls Himself the Son of man 80 times in the Gospels. Though He claimed attributes of Deity as Son of man, He at the same time asserted His identification with *us* as sons of men. His humanity, in fact, was unique in that it was *complete*. Our Lord, as a man, was "free from both hereditary depravity and from actual sin, as is shown by His never offering sacrifice, never praying for [His own] forgiveness, teaching that all but He needed the new birth, challenging all to convict Him of a single sin." [1]

Christ's humanity was as real and genuine as His deity. Both must be maintained and neither may be emphasized at the expense of the other.

Mostly Man or Mostly God?

A brief review of church history will illustrate how easy it is to emphasize one aspect of Christ's nature over the other. Some of these tendencies are with us to this day and we must guard against them. Heresies forced the early church to define clearly her belief in the deity and humanity of Christ. These definitions were not innovations, but merely crystallized what was already held to be biblical truth.

The Ebionites, early in the second century, denied the Deity of Christ. They maintained He was merely a man, though perhaps supernaturally conceived. They conceded that, though a man, He held a peculiar relationship to God, especially from the time of His baptism—when, they held, the fullness of the Holy Spirit rested on Him.

On the other hand, the Docetists, later in the same century, denied the true humanity of Jesus. They rejected the reality of His human body and suggested that it was merely a phantom and only appeared to be human. This view was the logical conclusion of their assumption that matter is inherently evil. They implied that the divine Christ was not hungry and thirsty, nor did He suffer and die. Jesus' life on earth, they maintained, was largely an illusion.

The Arians, forerunners of today's Unitarians, mistook the biblical statements about Christ's subordination to the Father as teaching His inferiority. They taught that Christ was somehow created by the Father as the first and highest of created beings, but that He Himself was not eternally self-existent. This belief is current today in several major cults.

Another deviation was that of the Apollinarians, who were condemned at the Council of Constantinople in A.D. 381. Heavily influenced by Greek philosophy, Apollinarius taught that Christ had a true body and soul and that in Him the place of the human mind or spirit was taken by His divine being. If this were true, however, it would mean that Jesus was not fully human and therefore was not tried or tempted in every respect as we are.

In the fifth century, Nestorius so emphasized the distinctness of Christ's two natures that he denied the real union between the divine and human in our Lord. He made this union a moral one rather than an organic one. Nestorians virtually believed in two natures and two persons instead of two natures in one person.

The Eutychians, on the other hand, were on the opposite extreme, denying the distinction and coexistence of the two natures. They said that the divine and the human natures in Christ mingled into a third sort of nature, peculiar to Christ. They seemed to believe that Christ's human nature was really absorbed into His divine nature, though the divine nature was, by this *merger,* somewhat changed from what it had been before the union. This group was condemned as heretical at the Council of Chalcedon in A.D. 451.

The question of the two natures of Christ is obviously complex, with numerous subtleties. The orthodox doctrine, promulgated at Chalcedon in 451, says that "in the one person, Jesus Christ, there are two natures, a human nature and a divine nature, each in its completeness and integrity, and that these two natures are organically and indissolubly united, yet so that no third nature is formed thereby. In brief, to use the antiquated dictum, orthodox doctrine forbids us either to divide the person or confound the natures." [2]

The deity and humanity of Christ's one Person is admittedly a profound subject, and it raises many questions. This concept is similar to that of the Trinity—we know by relevation that it is true, but have no satisfactory explanation.

In an attempt to explain Christ's two natures, some have suggested various "kenosis" theories. The term *kenosis* comes from the Greek word for "emptied" (Phil 2:7). Some have contended that Christ totally emptied Himself of deity and was limited to the natural knowledge and ability of an ordinary man. Others have held that though He renounced His divine attributes, He still somehow possessed them. Still others have suggested that our Lord suspended His divine consciousness at His conception and reassumed it in manhood. Hammond comments that, "our Lord's attributes of deity were at no time laid aside. Any 'explanation' of His divine-human nature which violates the integrity of His deity is obviously to be rejected, and there seems to be no explanation that is without grave difficulties. The nearest we can get is that our Lord's perfect divine nature (with the possession of all its attributes) was so united with a perfect human nature that a single divine-human Personality developed with the divine element (if such a distinction can be made here) controlling the normal development of the human. Beyond this we cannot safely go." [3]

The early church creeds did not try to explain the mystery of how Christ's two natures were united in one Person. They recognized His full manhood and His true deity, but they did not solve the problem of bringing the two modes of His self-manifestation— manhood and deity—into the unity of a single person. From the beginning, it must have been obvious that the truth lay between two unacceptable tendencies—to break the Person into two, or to mingle the natures so that the result was neither truly human nor truly divine. In a statement which the early church found acceptable, and which has been used ever since, Athanasius said, "He became what He was not; He continued to be what He was." This is really a terse affirmation rather than an explanation.

In an effort to eliminate the difficulties that arise from the problem of Christ's two natures, theologians—as we have seen—go to either of two extremes. Some exalt Christ's human nature to a level that would separate Him from the rest of humanity. For example, they say His nature was that of unfallen Adam. For this, there is no evidence in the Gospel records of His earthly life. Others, on the other hand, water down His deity, defining the Incarnation as involving a *kenosis* or self-emptying, for which the word used in Philippians 2:7 gives no support. This view makes our Lord, on earth, subject to all human limitation—with, of course, the exception of sin.

"The factor that is forgotten, and may well be the only key to the problem, is the ministry of the Holy Spirit in the Person and life of Christ. That Spirit, who had prepared His humanity and kept the unborn Child free from the taint of a mother's sin, never left Him, but throughout all the temptations and sufferings of His life and death brought to His human soul the light and comfort and strength which He needed to accomplish His task. In the light of that gracious ministry, we can understand, in some measure, how the divine nature was acting under human conditions, and how the human nature was acting in the fullet unity with the divine. The Spirit, who shared the eternal counsels of the Godhead, unified the consciousness of Christ so that there could be no possibility of division or dualism within Him. For this reason we can understand how there was nothing unnatural or unhuman about the self-consciousness of Jesus, even when He was in unbroken communion with the supernatural and eternal.

"However we explain it—and a full knowledge passes our comprehension—saving faith has always reached out to One who is perfect man, true God, and one Christ, and in the strength and fellowship of this faith we as Christians are called to abide." [4]

A proper knowledge of Christ's Person is crucial in understanding His work. If He were not the God-man, His work could not have eternal and personal significance for us.

What Christ Did

We have already considered the claims of our Lord to deity and the way He vindicated His claims by an authority over natural forces which could only have been supernatural. While fully appreciating who Jesus *is,* however, we must not overlook the equally important significance of what He has *done*—and is doing—for believers.

If Jesus were not fully God, He *could* not be our Saviour. But if He were God and yet did nothing on our behalf—that is, did not *do* something to bring us to God—He *would* not be our Saviour. Being God *qualified* Jesus Christ to be Saviour, but His atoning death for us *made* Him our Saviour. Jesus not only *could* save men; He *did*.

Christ was the perfect Man. As such, He was without sin in thought, word, or deed. He was able to challenge His enemies with the question, "Which of you convicts Me of sin?" (cf. John 8:46, NASB). His foes had no reply. He was totally obedient to the Father. "My meat," He told His disciples, "is to do the will of Him that sent Me, and to finish His work" (John 4:34).

There are three reasons why our Lord's perfect life was a necessity.

1. It qualified Him to become the sacrificial offering for sin. Old Testament types all insist on the purity of the victim for sacrifice.

2. It meant that perfect obedience was rendered to God, in contrast to Adam's disobedience. Scripture emphasizes this repeatedly (Rom. 5:19; Heb. 10:6-7).

3. By it He became a qualified Mediator and High Priest for His people (Heb. 2:11-18).[5]

Our Lord was, par excellence, "a Man with a mission." He frequently said, at a point of crisis, "Mine hour is *not yet* come" (John 2:4; cf. 7:6). Finally He said, "The hour *is come* that the Son of man should be glorified" (John 12:23). A little later, as He contemplated the awfulness of the cross, He said, "Now is My soul troubled; and what shall I say? Father, save Me from this hour. But for this cause came I unto this hour" (John 12:27). The reason He had come, as He had said, was to "seek and to save that which was lost" (Luke 19:10) and to "give His life a ransom for many" (Mark 10:45). So central is the death of Christ to an understanding of Christianity that we will discuss it more fully in a later chapter.

Christ Left the Grave

But not only did our Lord live and die. The triumphant dynamic of Christianity is that *He arose from the dead*. The common greeting of the early church was the dramatic reminder, "He is risen!" The thing that changed a handful of cowardly, frightened disciples, who denied that they even knew their Leader (Matt. 26:56, 70, 72, 74), into roaring lions proclaiming the faith, was the fact that they had seen Jesus, alive from the dead. Peter declared in Jerusalem, at the risk of his life, and just 50 days after the Resurrection, "This Jesus hath God raised up, whereof we all are witnesses" (Acts 2:32). Both the death and the resurrection of Christ show His supremacy and His uniqueness among all the religious leaders of the world.

A number of times Jesus predicted both His death and His resurrection (Mark 8:31; 10:32-34; cf. Matt. 16:21, etc.). But such a statement was so fantastic that the disciples didn't believe it until, after His entombment, they had the firsthand evidence of seeing Him themselves.

It is important to understand that the resurrection of Christ was a *bodily* resurrection, not one of "spirit" or "influence," as is sometimes suggested. The disciples, on first seeing Jesus after He rose, thought they were seeing a ghost and were terribly frightened. Our Lord had to say to them, "Behold My hands and My feet, that it is I Myself: handle Me, and see; for a spirit hath not flesh and bones as ye see Me have" (Luke 24.39). He proceeded to eat fish and honey with them to further demonstrate His physical reality. He invited doubting Thomas to put his finger in the nailprints and put his hand in the pierced side (John 20:27), so giving further testimony to the physical nature of His resurrection body and also indicating that this was the body that had been crucified and buried.

His risen body, however, differed from our bodies and from His own previous body. For instance, our risen Lord passed through closed doors when He met with the disciples for the first time in the Upper Room (John 20:19). Paul discusses at some length the subject of the Resurrection and the resurrection body (1 Cor. 15). This passage should be studied carefully.

Resurrection Implications

The implications of the Resurrection are enormous. We should understand them as fully as possible—and *enjoy* them.

First, as we have seen, the Resurrection fully confirms the truth and value of what Jesus taught and did. Paul says, "If Christ be not raised, your faith is vain; ye are yet in your sins" (1 Cor. 15:17). Because of the Resurrection, we know we are not trusting in a myth; we know that our sins are actually forgiven through the death of Christ. Certainty and forgiveness are based on the empty tomb! Christ is the only One who has ever come back from death to tell men about the beyond. In *His* words we know we have the authoritative Word of God Himself.

Second, Christ's resurrection is the guarantee of our own resurrection. Jesus said, "Because I live, ye shall live also" (John 14:19). We know with assurance that the grave is not our end, and that we shall be raised as He was.

Third, we know that the body is in itself good, not inherently evil, as some have mistakenly thought. The fact that our Lord became flesh and took a physical body in the Incarnation shows this. It is confirmed by the Resurrection, which tells us that in the eternal state, body and soul will be reunited, though the body will, of course, be a glorified body like our Lord's. Christ is the One "who shall change our vile [weak] body that it may be fashioned like unto His glorious body" (Phil. 3:21).

Fourth, we have assurance of the contemporary power of Christ in life today. We do not believe in a dead Christ hanging on a cross or lying in a grave, but in the risen Christ of the empty tomb. Christ gives us His life in salvation. This is the contemporary power, the dynamic, of Christian faith.

Many attempts have been made to explain away the Resurrection. A full discussion cannot be gone into here.

In summary, we can say that some false theories of the Resurrection (such as the swoon theory) revolve around denial of Christ's actual death. Other views hold that the disciples made an honest error which led them sincerely but wrongly to proclaim that Jesus had risen from the dead.

But all attempts to explain away the Resurrection founder on the rocks of the actual evidence. Christ would have been a deceiver had He only swooned and allowed the disciples to think He had actually risen from the dead. The disciples were not prepared for a hallucination. They didn't *expect* He *would* rise and they didn't *believe* He *had* risen from the dead. They had to be persuaded against their "better judgment" that it was so (Luke 24:36-45). Furthermore, Christ appeared ten different times, in different places, and in one case to more than 500 people at once. Such an event cannot be explained by "hallucination." The disciples would have been deceivers at best if they had stolen Christ's body. Nearly all of them died for their faith, however, in martyrdom. People will die for what they mistakenly *think* is true, but they don't die for what they *know* is false. The inability of the enemies of Christ to produce His body is further evidence that it had not been stolen.

The empty tomb, the revolutionized lives of the disciples, the Lord's Day (worship being shifted from Saturday to Sunday because of the Resurrection), the existence of the Christian church (which can be traced back to approximately A.D. 30)—all are conclusive evidence that the Resurrection is fact, not fiction. The final evidence is the transformation of those today who have met and been given new life by the risen Christ.

Ascension, Exaltation

Jesus not only predicted His death and resurrection, but also His ascension and exaltation (John 6:62; 17:1). In the ascension, He visibly left His disciples and the earth and returned to heaven, 40 days after His resurrection. His exit from this life was as miraculous as His entrance. The account of it is given in Acts 1:9-11.

Christ having ascended, God the Father has given Him a place of exaltation in heaven. God has "set Him at His own right hand in the heavenly places, far above all principality and power and might and dominion, and every name that is named" (Eph. 1:20-21). Christ has a position of power and glory. His ascension and exaltation were necessary for the completion of His work of redemption. As the ascended and exalted Christ, He has entered heaven as a forerunner for us (Heb. 6:20). We are to follow Him. He is able to enter into the heavenly counterpart of the holy of holies in the earthly tabernacle because of the merits of His atonement. Believers will be able to follow Him because the blood of His atonement has been applied to them.

Christ is now before God as our High Priest and Advocate. He appears "in the presence of God for us" (Heb. 9:24). "If any man sin, we have an Advocate with the Father, Jesus Christ the righteous" (1 John 2:1). As our Mediator, Christ is now active for us before the throne of God.

Christ has gone to prepare a place for us in heaven. He clearly told the disciples that He would do so and come again "and receive you unto Myself, that where I am, there ye may be also" (John 14:3-4). Every Christian should look forward with deep anticipation to the return of his Lord for him.

Because of the ascension and exaltation of Christ, we have free and confident access into the very presence of God. We can "come boldly unto the throne of grace" (Heb. 4:16). In Old Testament times, access to the presence of God was limited to one person—the high priest; to one place—the holy of holies in the tabernacle (or the temple); and to one time—the Day of Atonement. But because Christ is our High Priest and has passed into the heavens, *each* of us has access to the Creator at *any* time and at *any* place. How the angels must wonder that we make so little use of this privilege of audience with the King!

Christianity is Christ from beginning to end. To know who Christ is and what He has done is to increase our awe, wonder, and appreciation of the One who, though He was rich, for our sakes became poor, that we through His poverty might be rich (2 Cor. 8:9).

For Further Reading

Anderson, J. N. D. *Evidence for the Resurrection.* Downers Grove, Ill.: InterVarsity Press, 1966.

Berkouwer, G. C. *The Person of Christ.* Grand Rapids: Eerdmans, 1954.

Harrison, E. F. *A Short Life of Christ.* Grand Rapids: Eerdmans, 1968.

Little, Paul. *Know Why You Believe.* Wheaton, Ill.: Scripture Press, 1967.

Morris, Leon. *The Lord From Heaven.* London: InterVarsity Fellowship, 1958.

Warfield, B. B. *The Person and Work of Christ,* ed. S. G. Craig. Nutley, N.J.: Presbyterian and Reformed Publishing Co., 1950.

FOUR

CHRIST'S DEATH

Christianity is Christ, and unless we understand the death of Christ, we cannot possibly appreciate why our Lord came into human history. Without the death of Christ, there could be no forgiveness of sins and hence no salvation. Jesus Himself said, "The Son of man is come to seek and to save that which was lost" (Luke 19:10) and, "The Son of man came not to be ministered to, but to minister, and to give His life a ransom for many" (Mark 10:45), clearly pointing to the redemptive nature of His death.

In the death of Christ we have another *uniqueness* of Christianity. Here God has done for man what man cannot do for himself. God provided a way by which man, who is sinful and corrupt, can be forgiven, cleansed, and brought into vital and intimate relationship with his Maker—not on the basis of something *man* must do, but on the basis of what God Himself, in His Son, has *done*.

Every other religious system in the world is essentially a "do-it-yourself" proposition. Only in Christianity is salvation a free gift, offered not because man deserves it but because of the incomprehensible goodness of God's love. The cross of Christ is the central fact of human history. Jesus was the only Man born to die (Heb. 2:14). His death is the basis for His personal worthiness to receive the worship of the whole creation (Rev. 5:9, 12-13).

Christ's death is a central theme of the Scriptures, both Old Testament and New. As far back as the Garden of Eden, when God cursed the serpent, He promised the Deliverer (Gen. 3:15). The Prophet Isaiah gives us a clear promise of One who would die for our sins: "He was wounded for our transgressions; He was bruised for our iniquities; the chastisement of our peace was upon Him; and with His stripes we are healed. All we like sheep have gone astray; we have turned every one to his own way, and the Lord hath laid on Him the iniquity of us all" (Isa. 53:5-6).

In order to explain the recent puzzling events in Jerusalem to the two disciples walking to Emmaus, Jesus showed them *all* the Scriptures pointing to His death (Luke 24:25-27). His conversation must have been one of the most exciting Bible studies of all time. His death was a subject about which the prophets wrote much. They spoke of His sufferings without knowing exactly who He was or when He would come. They were told they were writing for the benefit of others than themselves (1 Peter 1:10-12).

Some question the necessity for *understanding* the meaning of the Cross and the Atonement. After all, they argue, we are not saved by any theory of the Atonement, but by the actual death of Christ. This, of course, is true. We must be careful not to try to reduce the Atonement into merely a neat formula. On the other hand, just as what we believe about Christ's person is crucial—even though we are saved by what He has *done*—so it is important for us to understand the meaning of His mission to die for man's sin. Otherwise we may find ourselves wittingly or unwittingly opposing the Gospel in one of its most vital and fundamental teachings.

Old Testament Background
A clear understanding of the significance of the death of Christ requires an understanding of the Old Testament background which led up to it.

Man is hopelessly separated from God because of his sin: "But your iniquities have separated between you and your God, and your sins have hid His face from you, that He will not hear" (Isa. 59:2). God takes the initiative and provides the way by which our estrangement may be ended.

Leon Morris comments: "In the Old Testament, [atonement] is usually said to be obtained by the sacrifices, but it must never be forgotten that God says of the atoning blood, '*I* have given it to you upon the altar to make an atonement for your souls' (Lev. 17:11). Atonement is secured not by any value inherent in the sacrificial victim, but because sacrifice is the divinely appointed way of securing atonement." [1]

The whole sacrificial system of the Old Testament was a symbolic portrayal of what would be completely fulfilled in Christ. The Passover, celebrated at the time of the Exodus of the Israelites from Egypt, is the fullest picture. Each believing family slew a perfect lamb and put its blood on the doorposts and lintels of the house. The angel of death, when he saw the blood, passed over that household, which in this way escaped the judgment of having its firstborn die. As with other sacrifices, the elements of perfection, the shedding of blood, and substitution were all present.

Christ was the fulfillment of all that the Passover lamb stood for. He was "the Lamb of God which taketh away the sin of the world" (John 1:29). Those who in faith offered animal sacrifices in Old Testament times looked forward to the coming Messiah, just as we by faith look back to the cross of Christ. The animal sacrifices did not save, but faith in what they symbolized *did*. We by faith lay hold on the fulfillment of the symbols.

> Not all the blood of beasts
> > On Jewish altars slain,
> Could give the guilty conscience peace,
> > Or wash away the stain.
> But Christ the heavenly Lamb,
> > Takes all our sins away;
> A sacrifice of nobler name
> > And richer blood than they.

Atonement for Sin

Christ's death is spoken of as the atonement for our sin. It has been suggested that "atonement" means, basically, "at-one-ment"—that is to say, a bringing together of those who are estranged. But the Old Testament word means, essentially, "to cover." The animal sacrifices provided a "covering" for sin until the death of Christ would put it forever away.

In the New Testament, various ideas are presented which explain and illustrate Atonement. It is spoken of as a reconciliation: "When we were enemies, we were reconciled to God by the death of His Son" (Rom. 5:10; cf. 2 Cor. 5:18-19; Eph. 2:16; and Col. 1:20). Reconciliation implies former hostility between the reconciled parties. As sinners, we were enemies of God. God, because of His holy character, is opposed to that which is sinful and unholy. The death of Christ did away with the cause of God's enmity by taking away our sin. We have been reconciled to God, the root cause of alienation having been removed and our attitude toward God having been changed. God has always loved us, and still loves us. But His wrath—the fixed, permanent attitude of God's holiness against evil—has been turned away from us. It has been carried totally by Christ.

The death of Christ is also spoken of as a propitiation: "God hath set [Him] forth to be a propitiation through faith in His blood, to declare His righteousness for the remission of sins that were past, through the forebearance of God" (Rom. 3:25). Propitiation has within it the concept of "the removing of wrath by the offering of a gift." [2] It has a personal quality to it. A young man might propitiate his girlfriend, for example, by sending her a bouquet of roses. God, in this case, is propitiated because the perfect sacrifice of Christ, in laying down His life for us, has fully met the holy and just requirements of God's law.

It is important to understand that God does not first reconcile us and then love us. Rather, *because* God has loved us, He reconciles us and opens the way for propitiation.

Ransom is another term used to define the death of Christ. It is closely linked with the idea of redemption. "[Christ] gave Himself a ransom for all, to be testified in due time" (1 Tim. 2:6; cf. 1 Peter 1:18). Though some church leaders seem to have thought this ransom was paid to Satan, the general conviction has been that it is the price paid to meet the holy requirements of God's law and redeem us from its curse. "Ye know that ye were not redeemed with corruptible things, as silver and gold . . . but with the precious blood of Christ, as a Lamb without blemish and without spot" (1 Peter 1:18-19).

Our Substitute
Among the terms that give the clearest explanations of the death of Christ is *substitute*. "Christ also hath once suffered for sins, the just for the unjust, that He might bring us to God" (1 Peter 3:18). Christ died *for* us—that is, in our place. "[God] hath made Him who knew no sin to be sin for us, that we might be made the righteousness of God in Him" (cf. 2 Cor. 5:21). The whole concept of sacrifice for sin carries with it the idea of substitution, which is fulfilled in Christ, "who His own self bore our sins in His own body on the tree, that we, being dead to sins, should live unto righteousness; by whose stripes we are healed" (1 Peter 2:24).

In the doctrinal statements of many Bible-believing churches and institutions, specific and particular mention is made of the "substitutionary" atonement of Christ. The reason for this is that other interpretations of the atonement have been advanced which, though some of them contain partial truth, have tended to eclipse, if not deny outright, the central truth of substitutionary atonement. Some theologians openly attack this doctrine, suggesting that the idea of substitution is a Pauline addition to the teaching of Christ. Even from the small portion of Scripture we have examined, however, it is clear that such claims are not the case. The teaching that Christ has taken our place and suffered and died in our behalf is as present in the Gospels as in the rest of the New Testament.

Often the viewpoint of a speaker, minister, or author on the substitutionary atonement is a reliable indicator of the orthodoxy of his other theological views.

Among the many perverted views of the atonement are the following:

1. The *moral influence* or *example* theory. The idea here is that man needs only to repent and reform to be reconciled to God. Advocates of this view believe the death of Christ is merely the powerful example of a man committed to truth and righteousness at all costs, and that we are redeemed as we allow His example to have a determining influence on our own efforts at moral improvement.

There is, of course, great moral influence in Christ's example. It is true that "Christ also suffered for us, leaving us an example that ye should follow in His steps" (1 Peter 2:21). But Scripture clearly teaches not only that sin has defiled us personally, but that because of it we are guilty before a holy God. Many passages of Scripture clearly teach that Christ died *for our sins,* and the moral influence theory ignores these passages entirely.

Other Erroneous Views

2. The *governmental* theory holds that the Atonement is a requirement of God's government of the universe, which "cannot be maintained, nor can the divine law preserve its authority over its subjects, unless the pardon of the offenders is accompanied by some exhibition of the high estimate which God sets upon His law and on the heinous guilt of violating it." [3] But why is *Christ* necessary, if this is all there is to the Atonement? And why should One who is *perfect* suffer, rather than one who is *guilty?*

It is true that the Cross shows man, with extreme vividness, the awfulness of sin, and that it is eloquent testimony that man may not ignore or toy with the law of God. But this surely is incidental to Christ's being made sin for us so that we may be made the righteousness of God in Him (2 Cor. 5:21). This view also fails to do justice to all the passages of Scripture already referred to.

3. Some have felt that the crucifixion of Christ was simply an untimely *accident of history,* unexpected and unforeseen. But Scripture clearly contradicts this view. Christ Himself assured His disciples that it was for this purpose that He had come into the world (John 12:27). In the Garden of Gethsemane He prayed to His heavenly Father, "Nevertheless, not as I will but as Thou wilt" (Matt. 26:39). He says further, "Therefore doth My Father love Me, because I lay down My life, that I may take it again. No man taketh it from Me, but I lay it down of Myself. I have power to lay it down, and I have power to take it again" (John 10:17-18). The prophets predicted the Messiah's sacrificial death and, in fact, all scriptural evidence opposes the idea that Christ's death was

accidental. That Christ did not *have* to die, but voluntarily endured the cross for us, is one of the central and most moving aspects of His sacrifice.

4. Others would suggest that though Christ's death might have been anticipated by sensitivity to the gathering storm, He died, essentially, as *another martyr* of history. But if this were the case, how could forgiveness come from His death, and how do we account for Jesus' statement, when He began the ceremony we celebrate as the Lord's Supper, "This is My blood of the New Testament, which is shed for many for the remission of sins" (Matt. 26:28)? The whole emphasis of the Scripture is opposed to any view of the Cross that is less than supernatural.

The idea of substitution is a basic theme throughout the Bible. There are other lessons to be learned from the Atonement, to be sure, but none is so prominent as to obscure this basic and wonderful truth.

Objections to Substitution

There have always been objections to the substitutionary atonement, and we should consider some of them.

Some insist that if God does not pardon sin without requiring atonement, He must either not be all-powerful or else not be a God of love. "Why can't He simply forgive sin out of His pure mercy?" skeptics want to know. "Could not an all-powerful God, in His omnipotence, have redeemed the world as easily as He created it? Since God commands man to forgive freely, why does He Himself not freely forgive?"

Finlayson summarizes the answer given such questions by Anselm in the Twelfth Century: "God cannot so forgive because He is not a private person, but God. God's will is not His own in the sense that anything is permissible to Him or becomes right because He wills it. What God determines is what God does. God cannot deal with sin except as in His holiness He sees it to be. If He did not punish it, or make adequate satisfaction for it, then He would be forgiving it unjustly." [4]

It is important to realize, as we have previously pointed out, that God exercises all His attributes in harmony with each other. His holiness demands atonement for sin. His love provides it. God's attributes never violate one another, nor are they antagonistic to each other. They are not in an uneasy equilibrium, but they work together in full and complete harmony. "Mercy is shown not by trampling upon the claims of justice, but by vicariously satisfying them." [5] In the cross of Christ, "Mercy and truth are met together: righteousness and peace have kissed each other" (Ps. 85:10).

Love and Holiness

The New Testament speaks of the *wedding*, or coming together, of the attributes of God's love and holiness in the cross of Christ so that "He might be just and the justifier of him which believeth in Jesus" (Rom. 3:26). In the very act of forgiving sin, or, to use Paul's "daring word . . . of 'justifying the ungodly,' God must act in harmony with His whole character. He must show what He is in relation to sin—that evil cannot dwell with Him because He refuses to tolerate sin in any form. In the very process of making forgiveness available to men, He must show His complete abhorrence of sin. In other words, God must not merely forgive men, but must forgive in a way which shows that He forever hates evil and can never treat it as other than completely hateful. Sin makes a real difference to God, and even in forgiving, He cannot ignore sin or regard it as other or less than it is. If He did so, He would not be more gracious than He is in the Atonement—He would cease to be God." [6]

Others have said that the very idea of God's permitting *Christ* to die for *our* sin, as an innocent victim for guilty sinners, was injustice rather than justice. Some go so far as actually to call it immoral. But such charges would be true only if Christ were an unwilling victim. As we have seen, the glory of the Cross is in the *voluntary* nature of Christ's coming to earth. "He did not consider equality with God a thing to be grasped, but humbled Himself and became obedient to death, even the death of the cross" (cf. Phil. 2:6-8). Hammond observes, "The Sufferer must have a double connection between God and Himself on the one hand, and the sinner and Himself on the other." [7] Only a solidly scriptural objection could fairly be raised against evangelical teaching on this subject.

Though we must consider alternative interpretations, we must note that critics approach the doctrine of substitution from their preconceived notions of what God *ought to have done* and their own superficial and humanistic ethical standards.

Other Questions

In addition to the objections we have already mentioned, certain other questions may come to your mind about the substitutionary death of Christ. How, for example, could the death of one Person atone for the innumerable sins of the whole world?

At the human level, such atonement would obviously be impossible. One person may die for one other, but for no more than one other. But when we consider the effectiveness of the death of Christ, we must remember who died. Christ was not merely a man;

He was the God-man: "God was in Christ" (2 Cor. 5:19). Christ's life was of infinite value, and His death likewise had infinite worth. The sum total of the value of all of those for whom He died does not approximate the infinite value of the divine life that was given at Calvary in sacrifice for our sakes.

In the *value* of the One who died is also the answer to the question, "Since Christ was only dead for three days, how can His experience be compared with the eternal death millions will experience if they do not trust Him?" The death Christ died was an infinite death, both in value and in the intensity of the spiritual suffering the Son of God went through. We simply cannot comprehend what it must have been for the sinless Son of God to become sin (2 Cor. 5:21) for us.

There is also the question as to whether, when Christ died, it is true to say that "*God* died." Robert J. Little points out, in answer to this question, that Christ "became a man in order to die, for without dying as a man He could not have delivered men from the penalty of sin. . . . Yet when He died, His *divine being* did not die. And when He died as a man, it was only His body which died. Scripture makes it clear that when *any* human being dies, it is the body which dies. The soul and spirit live on. Hence, when Christ died, we do not say that God died, though He who died on the cross was God. No finite mind can fully understand everything about the infinite God, but we can have some understanding of what is involved." [8]

A number of clear implications arise out of an understanding of the Atonement.

One is that in the Atonement we are dealing with an absolute issue of life and death. The Bible clearly tells us that "the wages of sin is death, but the gift of God is eternal life through Jesus Christ our Lord" (Rom. 6:23). Some tend to hedge on drawing lines between those who are saved and those who are lost. This hedging is perhaps due to their reluctance to judge individuals and perhaps also because of their incipient hope that all are saved.

It is true that only the Lord knows those who are His, and that our judgment, based on a man's profession in words and on the external nature of his life, may be faulty. But the Scripture knows no such vagueness. "He that believeth on the Son *hath everlasting life;* and he that believeth not the Son *shall not see life,* but the wrath of God *abideth* on him" (John 3:36). Men are in sin and Christ died for their sin. A man is *now* either in Christ by faith, or still in sin because of unbelief. There is no in-between ground. A person has either life or death, lives either in light or in darkness, is either saved or lost.

Other Implications

It is in the death of Christ that we can see clearly why some widespread ideas of the universal Fatherhood of God are erroneous. Often accompanying a reluctance to draw distinctions, people who hold these ideas suggest that all men are God's children and that therefore efforts to "convert" them are in bad taste. But though we all *are* God's offspring by creation (Acts 17:28), we are not God's children spiritually, else the Atonement would have been unnecessary. Jesus spoke sharply to those who refused to recognize Him as God, saying, "Ye are of your father the devil" (John 8:44). On the other hand, "to all who did accept Him, and trust in His name, He gave the right to *become* the children of God" (John 1:12, WMS). We cannot *become* what we already *are*.

The death of Christ is what makes the Gospel good *news* rather than good *advice*. Christ did not die for us because we recognized our need and cried out to God for help. "But God proves His own love for us by Christ's dying for us when we were still sinners" (Rom. 5:8, BERK). The Gospel is not a set of swimming instructions for a drowning man, but a pardon and reprieve from death for a man who does not deserve it. There is nothing we must or can *do* to benefit from it, except simply to receive it as a free gift and so experience eternal life.

Basis for Assurance

The Atonement is what gives a Christian his basis for assurance of forgiveness of sin and eternity in heaven. This assurance is not arrogant presumption that *we* are better than anyone else, but rather confidence, based on God's own Word, in what Christ has done for us by dying on the cross. From the cross, just before He died, Jesus said, "It is finished" (John 19:30). So we speak of the "*finished* work of Christ." By this we mean that our Lord has already done everything necessary for our salvation. We still need daily cleansing and forgiveness of sin, of course, and we receive it when we confess our sin (1 John 1:9). But we receive forgiveness on the basis of what has already been accomplished in us—as sons, not as alienated sinners. God intends us to have assurance of our salvation: "These things have I written to you that believe on the name of the Son of God, *that ye may know* that ye have eternal life" (1 John 5:13).

Assurance need not lead to indifference and smug contentment, as many contend it does. It can also result in deep joy and a loving response to Christ because of His love for us. We are continually reminded, "Ye are not your own . . . ye are bought with a price; therefore glorify God in your body and in your spirit, which are

God's" (1 Cor. 6:19-20). The new life we receive changes our attitudes, motives, values, and will. In ourselves we are incapable of such changes, but in Christ we become new creations (2 Cor. 5:17). It is for this reason that Paul was so daring and so adamant in maintaining that the church add nothing to simple trust as a requirement for salvation, and add nothing afterward by way of legal regulation to maintain salvation. The Gospel is not Christ "plus" something, however good the something may be, but Christ *alone* in His atoning death for us.

Demonstrates God's Love

The Atonement also demonstrates the nature and character of God's love. We live in a world which is acutely aware of man's pain, suffering, and misery. No one is interested in a God who is aloof and untouched by human need, or even in a God who might save sinners from a distance. In the cross of Christ the affirmation, "God is love," takes concrete expression. People will believe a demonstration of love in action before they will believe a person who declares it only in words. God's love for us is no exception. John says, "Hereby perceive we the love of God, because He laid down His life for us" (1 John 3:16).

God, in Christ, became involved in this life. He assumed its burdens and entered into its tragedies. Finally He took on full responsibility for this life by "becoming sin for us . . . that we might be made the righteousness of God in Him" (2 Cor. 5:21). Through the Atonement, we know dramatically that God is not indifferent to man's tragedy and suffering.

The death of Christ, in its objective accomplishment and in its subjective impact, is the central fact of history.

> Love so amazing, so divine
> Demands my soul, my life, my all.

For Further Reading

James Denney. *The Death of Christ*. Downers Grove, Ill.: Inter-Varsity Fellowship, 1964.

Guillebaud, H. E. *Why the Cross?* London: Inter-Varsity Fellowship, 1967.

Morris, Leon. *The Apostolic Preaching of the Cross*. London: Tyndale Press, 1965.

————. *The Cross in the New Testament*. Grand Rapids: Eerdmans, 1964.

FIVE

MAN AND SIN

"**W**hat is man?" asked the Psalmist David, centuries ago. It is striking that this is also the burning question of the 20th century and the Space Age. Is man merely a glorified animal? Is he merely the sum total of all his chemicals and their reactions? Or is he more than this?

As the genetic code is deciphered and the electronic aspects of the brain's functioning are understood, the problem becomes increasingly urgent.

"Who am I?" The piercing question of identity must be answered by every person. Our answer, whether we realize it or not, has enormous influence upon our thinking and acting, our outlook, and our living. Never was it more important for a Christian to understand what the Bible says about man in order to have an anchor on the sea of human speculation.

Where Did Man Come From?

The first question to be answered is that of man's origin. "In the beginning God created the heaven and the earth" (Gen. 1:1), says the Bible, and, "God said, 'Let Us make man in Our image, after Our likeness; and let them have dominion over the fish of the sea, and over the fowl of the air, and over the cattle, and over all the earth, and over every creeping thing that creepeth upon the earth.' So God created man in His own image, in the image of God created He him; male and female created He them" (vv. 26-27).

Scripture consistently teaches that neither the universe nor man himself is the product of blind chance. Man, especially, is the result of careful and purposeful deliberation on the part of the members of the triune Godhead.

Adam, the first man, was created in God's image. Adam is a proper name, but the Hebrew term also has the connotation of *mankind*. It is frequently so used in the Old Testament.

God said, "It is not good that the man should be alone," and to complement man He made a woman to be Adam's helper (Gen. 2:18, 22).

"Through faith we understand that the worlds [universe] were framed by the Word of God, so that things which are seen were not made of things which do appear" (Heb. 11:3). In other words, God created matter *ex nihilo* (out of nothing). He then formed matter into animate objects—plants, animals, and man.

The Bible does not claim to tell us *how* man and the universe were created. It does, however, assert emphatically and unambiguously *that God brought them into being*. Nowhere does the Bible attempt to *prove* God. It *assumes* Him. A Christian unashamedly begins with the assumption that God exists. He is convinced that the life, death, and resurrection of Christ clearly bear out this assumption. Such assumption is not naive or unintellectual, and we should keep in mind that unbelievers who reject the biblical view of Creation also begin with presuppositions and assumptions on which they base *their* claims. *Everyone* begins somewhere with an assumption that is not provable in the scientific sense. For a helpful, brief, contemporary discussion of the issues involved, see *The Creation of Matter, Life, and Man,* by Addison H. Leitch.

It is also important to realize that New Testament writers saw Adam as a person as historical as our Lord Himself. Paul clearly considered Adam to be a distinct individual as well as the prototype of fallen man (Rom. 5:12-21; 1 Cor. 15:22). Our Lord spoke about the creation of man, confirming the Genesis account (Matt. 19:4). There is no room for mythical or allegorical interpretations of the historicity of Adam's creation and subsequent fall.

Man was distinct and unique from the rest of creation. He was to subdue it and have dominion over it. He is at the top of all living beings. Man's self-consciousness, his capacity for intelligent reasoning, and, above all, his moral and spiritual sense, set him completely apart from all other creatures. No creature other than man has ever been observed building a chapel.

Body, Soul, and Spirit

Genesis 2 gives further information on the creation of man: "And the Lord God formed man of the dust of the ground and breathed into his nostrils the breath of life; and man became a living soul" (v. 7). It is clear that two elements were involved in man's creation. One is "the dust of the ground." The other is "the breath of life," which was given by God. The union of these two elements makes man a living being.

Man is clearly more than one substance. But are the components

of his being *three* (body, soul, and spirit) or *two* (body and soul)?
The Old Testament does not have a fixed term for the immaterial
part of man's nature. The terms *soul, heart,* and *spirit* are used as
counterparts of the material side. Along with the term *body,* they
include the whole man. The psalmist says, "My *soul* thirsteth for
Thee, my *flesh* longeth for Thee" (63:1). But not all such biblical
expressions indicate a twofold nature of man. Others just as plainly
speak of *three* aspects of man's being: "My *soul* longeth . . . for
the courts of the Lord: my *heart* and my *flesh* crieth out for the
living God" (Ps. 84:2).

Should the God-breathed part of man be viewed as *two* parts—
i.e., *soul* and *spirit* separately—or as *one?* Hammond observes,
" 'Soul' and 'spirit' are certainly not to be regarded as synonymous
in scriptural language. But, on the other hand, they are not kept
invariably distinct. Compare Psalm 74:19 with Ecclesiastes 3:21;
Matthew 10:28 with Luke 23:46; Acts 2:27 with 7:59. The references invoked in suggesting [threefold] division are those of
1 Thessalonians 5:23; Hebrews 4:12; cf. Luke 1:46-47. . . . But
those who suggest [such a division] admit that soul and spirit, in
the body, are separable only in thought. It would seem best to
regard them as differing aspects of the same essence, and to remember that whatever distinctions are made for the spiritual
purposes of scriptural teaching, there is a substratum which is
common to both soul and spirit." [1]

Man a Unity

In any case, the Bible always views man as a unity, both material
and immaterial. The Resurrection shows that man is as essentially
body as he is essentially soul or spirit. The notion that man is a
soul imprisoned in a body is a Greek concept, not a biblical one.

What does it mean that man was created in the image and
likeness of God? It certainly does not mean that he has any *physical*
likeness to God. Scripture clearly teaches that God is a Spirit and
does not have physical parts like a man (John 4:24). The Bible
uses anthropomorphic expressions, such as "the hand of God," only
to accommodate our human incapacity to think in any other terms.
The strong prohibition against man's representing God by graven
images was given because no one had ever seen God and therefore
could not know how He looked. Nothing on earth *could* represent
Him (Deut. 4:15-23; Ex. 20:4).

The image of God in man has to do, rather, with *personality.*
Man has "a free, self-conscious, rational and moral personality
like that of God—a nature capable of distinguishing right and
wrong, of choosing the right and rejecting the wrong, and of

ascending to the heights of spiritual attainment and communion with God." [2]

The original man was intelligent. He could give names to all the animals when they were presented to him (Gen. 2:19-20). He had the power of reasoning and thought. In speaking, he could connect words and ideas. He had moral and spiritual qualities. He could and did commune with God and had the power to resist moral evil or yield to it (Gen. 3).

Because man has been created in the image of God, human life is inviolate. God instituted capital punishment (Gen. 9:6) for this reason.

The new man is *renewed* in the image of God in righteousness (Eph. 4:23-24; Col. 3:10). The implication of "renewed" is that man once had a moral likeness to God, but that it was lost. Originally man was holy and the basic inclination of his nature was toward God. He was not *neutral* toward God, for the creation of the "new man" is after the pattern of the original. Nevertheless, from the beginning man had freedom to choose evil, and so to sin.

At the same time it is important to realize that man was also free *not* to sin. He had no original inward tendency to sin, as we have. Though he was capable of being tempted, he was not either *compelled* or *impelled* to sin. Adam *chose* to do so deliberately, as a free act. In the words of the famous phrase, man did not have inability to sin; he had ability *not* to sin.

Image versus Likeness

Roman Catholics and some others distinguish between "image" and "likeness" because both words are used in Genesis 1:26. They have suggested that the *image* of God in man is only in his personality, and that the *likeness* of God is a supernatural gift given man by God in creation—i.e., "an original righteousness and perfect self-determination before God which could be, and indeed was, lost in the Fall. The *image,* on the other hand, consists of what belongs to man by nature, i.e., his free will, rational nature, and dominion over the animal world, which could not be lost even in the Fall. This would mean that the Fall destroyed what was originally supernatural in man, but left his nature and the image of God in him wounded, and his will free." [3]

This distinction, however, is not borne out by Scripture. The word "image" is used alone in Genesis 1:27 to describe what is meant by the two terms together in verse 26. In a similar construction elsewhere (Gen. 5:1), the word "likeness" is used alone.

Had things remained as they were in the original creation, all would have been well. Sin and death, with all their disastrous consequences for the human race, would never have come into being if Adam and Eve had chosen to obey rather than disobey God. But they *did* assert their wills against God, and their rebellion brought titanic disaster to all their descendants.

It is significant and intensely interesting that most, if not all, primitive religious traditions have, in one form or another, a belief in such a catacylsmic event. The Fall permanently altered what previously was an idyllic relationship between God and man. Man is generally viewed as having intimate fellowship with his Creator. But ever since he offended Him he has suffered from God's displeasure as well as from the loss of fellowship that resulted from his estrangement. Even in primitive animistic societies, which worship many gods, there is belief in a high-sky God who is the creator. Since the passing of the golden age of intimate contact, this God is aloof from man. He now deals with human beings only through the lesser gods. All of these ideas seem to be echoes and reflections—distorted, faint, or mutilated by the passage of time—of the event, clearly described in the Bible (Gen. 3), which we call the Fall.

Personal Responsibility

The sin of Adam and Eve, as we have seen, was something for which they were personally responsible. They did not have sinful natures such as we have, so the temptation to sin must have come from outside them. The Bible describes this source as "the serpent" (Gen. 3:1), a term scripturally identified with Satan (Rev. 12:9). The Fall really explains how sin entered the human race, rather than how evil got into the world.

The ultimate answer to the profound question of the origin of evil is wrapped in the mysteries of God's counsels. Why did God not prevent evil from entering the universe, since He knew in advance what would happen? Why did He not make man incapable of sinning? He *could* have, but had He done so, we would not be human beings with freedom of choice. We would be robots, or "chatty dolls" that always speak the same word when someone pulls the string.

Though we have no final answers to sin's origin, God knew what would happen and, as someone has said, "thought it was worth the risk." C. S. Lewis observes that it is useless to speculate endlessly about the *origin* of evil. Each of us, however, faces the *fact* of evil, and the whole of God's redemptive program has to do with combatting it. God is not the Author of sin. Had our first parents not disobeyed Him, sin would never have entered the human race.

The several facets of sin are clear in the progression which is described in Genesis 3. Adam and Eve are first tempted to *doubt* God's Word, "Yea, hath God said?"; then led on to *disbelieve* it, "Ye shall not surely die"; and finally to *disobey* it, "They did eat."

The results of man's disobedience were immediate and obvious —separation from God and awareness of guilt. The curse which God pronounced involved, for mankind, both physical and spiritual death, hard physical labor, and sorrow. Man's fall involved the whole natural creation as well (cf. Rom. 8:21-22).

As a result of the Fall, the image of God in man was badly marred in both its moral and its natural dimensions. Man lost his original inclination toward God and became a perverted creature, inclined away from his Creator. His personality was sadly marred. His intellect became bound, his emotions corrupted, and his will enslaved. He lost his true manhood. Men speak about man as *evolving* from a primitive condition, but the Bible (Rom. 1:18-32) graphically portrays his *descent* rather than *ascent*.

"Total Depravity"

The result was "total depravity." This expression of man's condition after the Fall has been widely misunderstood, with the result that the Christian position regarding man's sinful nature has sometimes been unjustly caricatured. The doctrine of depravity "was never intended to convey the meaning that man is as bad as he possibly can be and that every trace of moral rectitude has been lost in fallen man. 'Total depravity' is intended to indicate that the evil principle . . . has invaded each part of human nature, that there is no part of it which can now invariably perform righteous acts or invariably think righteous thoughts." [4] In other words, man's total depravity means that *every area of his life* is blighted—not that everything about him is *totally bad*. His depravity is also total in that apart from God's grace he is forever lost.

The tragedy of the Fall went far beyond Adam and Eve. It was race-wide in its effect: "Wherefore as by one man sin entered into the world, and death by sin, . . . death passed upon all men, for all have sinned" (Rom. 5:12).

Men have held to three kinds of appraisals of the effect of the Fall on the human race:

1. The British monk, Pelagius, said that all men could be sinless if they chose, and that some men have lived free from sin. Pelagius reasoned that since a man can live free from sin, he must have been born into the world free from sin. Consequently, Adam's sin must have affected only Adam. In other words, Pelagius denied "original sin." Carrying his line of thinking further, he asserted that man has no need of supernatural help to live a righteous life.

Pelagius did, however, recognize sin's force of habit and its harmful example to others.

2. Augustine, the great bishop of North Africa, rose to do battle with Pelagius' heretical view, and it is with his name that the *second* view of the Fall is connected. Augustine insisted that Adam transmitted to his posterity, because of the unity of the human race, both his guilt and the corruption belonging to it. The nature that man now has, said Augustine, is like the corrupted nature of Adam. Man has lost his freedom not to sin. He is free to carry out the desires of his nature—but since his nature itself is corrupt, he is really free only to do evil. Augustine used the phrase "the will is free, but not freed." Though he has a free choice, man *chooses* a perverse course.

3. Roman Catholics hold a halfway position, called semi-Pelagianism—that in the Fall man lost the supernatural gift of righteousness which was not his by nature anyway, but had been added by God. In the Fall, man reverted to his natural state, without this righteousness that God had given him. So he is only *half* sick. Man, according to this view, still has a special gift of the Spirit which is sufficient to enable him to be righteous if he allows his will to cooperate with God's Spirit.

The Scripture is clear that though there may be a difference between men in their *degree* of sin, there is no difference in the *fact* of sin (cf. Rom. 3:9-10, 22-23; Isa. 53:6). The whole world is under judgment (Rom. 3:19), and because all men are apart from Christ, they are rebels against God, "children of disobedience," subject to His wrath (Eph. 2:2-4).

History and experience bear testimony to the universality of sin. The Augustinian view is closest to the biblical view—that man inherits a tendency to sin which always, to some extent, makes itself manifest. "And God saw that the wickedness of man was great in the earth and that every imagination of the thoughts of his heart was only evil continually. . . . The imagination of man's heart is evil from his youth" (Gen. 6:5; 8:21). When David said, "Behold, I was shapen in iniquity, and in sin did my mother conceive me" (Ps. 51:5), he was not speaking of the act of conception as sinful, but of the inherited bias to sin that is transmitted at conception.

Anyone who has ever had children recognizes clearly that self-centeredness shows up in the next generation at a very early age. You don't have to teach a child to be selfish. A great deal of effort, on the part of Christian parents, goes toward trying to overcome this tendency. The only one who has ever escaped this inherited bias toward sin is our Lord Himself.

Adam Our Representative

The Bible clearly teaches that Adam was our representative when he sinned (Rom. 5:12-19). Adam represented us just as, when our government declares war, it represents, affects, and involves us. As a result of Adam's sin, all who are in Adam die. This includes each of us. We tend to think that things might have turned out differently if we had been in Adam's place. But each of us, by doing as Adam did, has ratified the decision our first parents made to rebel and disobey God. Who would claim he had never sinned? And so we are justly condemned today not only for Adam's sin, but for our own sins.

But believers are also represented in Christ. The Bible teaches that as in Adam all die, so in Him all (believers) will be made alive (Rom. 5:19). The glory of the Gospel is that God did something for us in Christ that we could not do for ourselves. Because Adam's original sin is charged to us, we inherit a corrupt nature. Through Christ, the second Adam, we inherit a *new* nature. From Adam we received sin and guilt. From Christ we receive forgiveness and righteousness.

Sin, it is important to realize, does not begin with overt acts, nor is it limited to them. The acts proceed out of a corrupt heart and mind. In other words, we are not sinners because we sin—we sin because we are sinners. An apple tree is not an apple tree because it bears apples; it bears apples because it has the nature of an apple tree. Sins are the acts (or the apples); sin is our corrupt nature (the nature of the apple tree).

Through Christ we are not only forgiven our individual acts of sin, but we receive a new nature. The Gospel solution is radical, not merely one of outward reform. Someone has said, "Christ puts a new man in the suit—not just a new suit on the man." When the man himself is changed, his clothing (his particular actions) will tend to change as well.

Why We Are Responsible

But how can we be responsible for being sinners if God gave us a hopeless start in life? How can He then condemn us? The answer is twofold. First, as we have seen, we share Adam's sin. But beyond that, God has made full provision, through the sacrifice of Christ, for us to escape judgment. Scripture emphasizes man's ability to receive Christ if he wants to. As Jesus told Nicodemus, *"This* is the judgment: that light is come into the world, and man loved darkness rather than light"* (John 3:19). It has been said that the entrance to hell is guarded by a cross. No one comes into hell without walking past it. In other words, at Calvary God did everything necessary to keep man from judgment. If he refuses God's provision, man must himself bear responsibility for judgment.

But isn't it true, many people ask, that men are not all equally bad? Of course this is true. That "all have sinned" does not imply that all are as bad as they might be. But in relation to God's standard of holiness, all come short. You probably know honest, kind, and upright people who are not to be compared with the derelicts of Skid Row or with vicious criminals behind bars. Humanly, there are great differences.

But suppose we were to put one person in Death Valley, 280 feet below sea level; one in Denver, the mile-high city; and one on the peak of Mount Everest, altitude 29,000 feet. Let's suppose that the person in Death Valley represents the dregs of society and the kind of life such people live. The person in Denver is the *average man,* and the one on Mount Everest is the best person you can imagine. The enormous differences in their altitude, or elevation, are apparent. But let's suppose God's standard of holiness is represented by the distance to the moon. Recently we have had an opportunity to see how Mount Everest, Denver, and Death Valley look from the moon. They're all the same!

From our human standpoint, there are great differences in men's sinfulness, but—contrasted with the infinite holiness of God—all men are equally lost.

Sin Is Against God

Sin is always primarily directed against God. It is more than mere self-centeredness. David, though he had wronged Bathsheba in adultery, and had murdered Uriah, cried out, "Against Thee, *Thee only,* have I sinned, and done this evil in Thy sight" (Ps. 51:4).

The Bible defines sin variously as "transgression of the Law" (1 John 3:4), as falling short of the mark (Rom. 3:23), and as failure to do the good we know we should do (James 4:17). Sin has both an active, overt aspect (transgression of the Law) and a passive aspect (failure to do good). There are sins of commission and sins of omission. The *Book of Common Prayer* adequately summarizes, in its General Confession, "We have done those things we ought not to have done, and we have left undone those things we ought to have done."

The first sin was the prototype of all other sins. The seriousness of the first sin lies in the fact that Adam and Eve broke a commandment of God that showed His authority, goodness, wisdom, justice, faithfulness, and grace. In their transgression, they rejected His authority, doubted His goodness, disputed His wisdom, repudiated His justice, contradicted His truthfulness, and spurned His grace. Then and now, sin is the opposite of God's perfection.[5]

The seriousness of sin is based on man's alienation from and broken fellowship with God. It brought disastrous consequences to Adam, and to humanity and society in general. The root problem in the world today is not ignorance or poverty, as great as these are. The root problem is sin. Man is alienated from God, and hence is self-centered. The tensions between racial groups, economic classes, and nations are nothing more than the self-centeredness of the individual blown up on a wide canvas to include all men.

The Good News

If no power is strong enough to change human nature, there is no hope for man. But the good news of the Gospel is that there IS such power—in Christ. "Where sin abounded, grace did much more abound" (Rom. 5:20).

Unless we understand what the Bible teaches about the nature of man in creation and the devastating effects of the Fall, we cannot understand the grandeur of the grace of God. Many problems in understanding God's grace stem from an inflated view of man and his character and a shrunken view of God and His holiness.

These issues are matters of life and death. Man does not live and die like an animal. Death does not end man's existence. The soul and spirit survive the body. Jesus Himself spoke clearly of this continued existence for both the saved and the lost: "I am the Resurrection and the Life; he that believeth in Me, though he were dead, yet shall he live; and whosoever liveth and believeth in Me shall never die" (John 11:25-26). In the story of the rich man and Lazarus (Luke 16:19-31), Christ clearly taught the continued conscious existence of the unjust. The whole teaching of the New Testament about future judgment rests on the assumption that the soul survives after death. "It is appointed unto men once to die, but after this the judgment" (Heb. 9:27; cf. Rom. 2:5-11; 2 Cor. 5:10).

The Resurrection applies not only to those who will be raised to be with Christ forever (1 Thes. 4:16), but also to the wicked, who will be raised for judgment. Jesus said clearly, "The hour is coming in the which *all* that are in the graves shall hear His voice and shall come forth; they that have done *good* unto the resurrection of life, and they that have done *evil* unto the resurrection of damnation" (John 5:28-29).

The sobering truth that we exist forever makes it imperative that we give thought to our nature, condition, and destiny while we are still able to do what is needful.

In answer to the question "Who am I?" the Bible clearly answers that each of us is a personality created purposefully by God in His own image. It teaches that we have eternal significance and that our souls are worth more than the whole world (Mark 8:36). God Himself says that He has a plan and a purpose for each life, that we are morally responsible to respond to Him, and that we *can* respond in faith. We have an eternal destiny—either in His presence forever, or in everlasting separation from Him.

The Bible is the most realistic book ever written. It not only describes God as He really is, but us as we really are. It gives us a clear vision of our own nature and destiny, and that of the human race.

For Further Reading

Laidlaw, J. *The Bible Doctrine of Man*. Edinburgh: T. & T. Clark, 1905.

Leitch, Addison H. *The Creation of Matter, Life, and Man,* fifth in the "Fundamentals of the Faith" series. Washington: *Christianity Today,* Sept. 16, 1966.

Machen, J. G. *The Christian View of Man*. London: Banner of Truth, 1965.

Orr, James. *God's Image in Man*. Grand Rapids: Eerdmans, 1948.

SIX

THE HOLY SPIRIT

Of the three persons in the Godhead—Father, Son, and Holy Spirit—the Holy Spirit seems to be least known and understood today. Yet He is most vitally and intimately involved in our initial conversion and birth into the family of God, as well as in the on-going development of our Christian lives. Knowledge of and intimate relationship with the Holy Spirit bring us power, joy, and hope. When we neglect Him, through ignorance or indifference, we insure spiritual poverty.

God the Holy Spirit is as much a *person* as God the Father and God the Son. Many Christians are inclined to speak of Him as an impersonal *it*. They give the impression that the Holy Spirit is no more than an influence. Perhaps this is partially due to the fact that we use the term *spirit,* in casual conversation, in this sense. We speak of the *spirit* of the times or say that "a spirit of expectancy swept the crowd as they awaited the arrival of the president."

Misunderstanding may partially stem also from the fact that the work of the Holy Spirit is not as visibly prominent as that of the Father and of the Son. His work is never to call attention to Himself. Jesus, in speaking of the gift of the Spirit, said, "He shall not speak of Himself, but whatsoever He shall hear, that shall He speak. And He will show you things to come. He shall glorify Me: for He shall receive of Mine, and shall show it unto you" (John 16:13-14).

Some of the names and symbols by which the Holy Spirit is called may seem to suggest that He is not a personal being. Both the Hebrew and Greek words translated *spirit* mean, basically, *breath* or *wind*. The Greek word is in the neuter gender, which is why the King James version—adding to the confusion—translates "the Spirit *itself*" (Rom. 8:16, 26). Later versions read *Himself*.

Impersonal Symbols

Then, too, the symbols used in Scripture to describe the influence of the Spirit include oil, fire, and water—all of which are impersonal. To a superficial student, these symbols could imply that the Spirit is merely an influence. Yet the Father and the Son are described in similar figurative ways—as light, bread of life, living water, etc.

When we speak of the personality of the Holy Spirit, however, we must remind ourselves of the significance of this term as applied to God. As we have observed, God was not made in the image of man, but man in the image of God. *Personality* is not a perfect term for God, but it is descriptive of the Spirit's nature. The Holy Spirit has a mind, feelings, and a will, as God the Father does. He is a *person* in this sense.

It is impossible to explain many biblical references to the Holy Spirit apart from the fact that He is equal, in His personal nature, to the Father and the Son.

Jesus gave some of the clearest scriptural teaching about the Holy Spirit. He called the Spirit the Comforter, or Counselor, "whom the Father will send in My name; He shall teach you all things and bring all things to your remembrance, whatsoever I have said unto you" (John 14:26). These titles clearly imply personality. The terms *Comforter,* or *Counselor,* convey the idea of a person, such as a lawyer, on whom one calls for help.

In John 16:7, as in the previous reference, the emphasis is on Christ's going away and the Holy Spirit's being sent by the Father to replace our Lord Himself. This change, Jesus said, would be beneficial for His disciples. An impersonal force could hardly improve on the personal presence of Jesus Christ.

Repeatedly (John 16:7-15), Jesus used the masculine personal pronoun *He* when referring to the Spirit. As we have pointed out, the Greek word translated *spirit* is the same as that for *breath,* and is neuter in gender. Jesus used the masculine pronoun deliberately, intending it to indicate personality and intimacy.

Though the Holy Spirit is not mentioned with the Father and the Son in New Testament greetings and salutations (e.g., 1 Cor. 1:3; Gal. 1:3), He is mentioned in the baptismal formula. The Lord told the disciples, "Go ye therefore and teach all nations, baptizing them in the name of the Father and of the Son and of the Holy Spirit" (Matt. 28:19). The Spirit is also included in the Pauline benediction. "The grace of the Lord Jesus Christ, and the love of God, and the communion of the Holy Spirit be with you all" (2 Cor. 13:14). Association of the Holy Spirit with the other two Persons of the Trinity also appears in 1 Peter 1:1-2 and in Jude 20-21.

We can *treat* the Spirit as a *person.* Ananias was struck dead for lying to the Holy Spirit (Acts 5:3). The Spirit may be *grieved* (Eph. 4:30) and *sinned against* by unforgivable blasphemy (Mark 3:29). None of these things would be true of an impersonal force.

The Holy Spirit *does* things which only a person could do. He *speaks:* "The Spirit said unto Philip, 'Go near' " (Acts 8:29). He *strives:* "My Spirit shall not strive with man forever" (Gen. 6:3). "The Spirit also helpeth our infirmity . . . [and] *maketh intercession* for us" (Rom. 8:26). He *reveals, searches,* and *knows:* "But God hath revealed them unto us by His Spirit; for the Spirit searcheth all things . . . the things of God knoweth no man but the Spirit of God" (1 Cor. 2:10-11). He distributes spiritual gifts "to every man severally as He will" (1 Cor. 12:11). None of these verbs could rightly be used of a mere influence.

Identified with Believers
The Holy Spirit is identified with the thinking of believers. At the Council of Jerusalem the disciples declared, "It seemed good to us *and* to the Holy Spirit" (cf. Acts 15:28).

The Holy Spirit is not only a person—He is Deity. He is specifically called "God" in the Ananias incident (Acts 5:4). Paul says, "For the Lord is that Spirit" (2 Cor. 3:17; cf. v. 18), and again, "Ye are the temple of God . . . the Spirit of God dwelleth in you" (1 Cor. 3:16).

Our Lord says that blasphemy against the Holy Spirit is worse than blasphemy against the Son of man. This can only mean that blasphemy against the Spirit maligns and discredits God.

The Holy Spirit possesses attributes which belong only to deity. He is *eternal:* "Christ, who through the eternal Spirit offered Himself" (Heb. 9:14). He is *omnipresent:* "Whither shall I go from Thy Spirit? or whither shall I flee from Thy presence?" (Ps. 139:7). He is the "Spirit of *life*" (Rom. 8:2) and the "Spirit of truth" (John 16:13).

The Spirit does God's work. He was involved in *creation:* "the Spirit of God moved upon the . . . waters" (Gen. 1:2). He is involved in *regeneration,* the new birth: "So is everyone that is born of the Spirit" (John 3:8). Jesus cast out demons by the Spirit: "I cast out [demons] by the Spirit of God" (Matt. 12:28). The Holy Spirit participates in *resurrection:* "But if the Spirit of Him that raised up Jesus from the dead dwell in you, He . . . shall also quicken your mortal bodies by His Spirit that dwelleth in you" (Rom. 8:11).

The New Testament quotes many Old Testament passages in which the speaker is Jehovah, the Lord. In the New Testament, such messages are often attributed to the Holy Spirit. For instance,

Isaiah heard the voice of the Lord saying, "Hear you indeed but understand not" (Isa. 6:8-9). But Paul said, "Well spoke *the Holy Spirit* by Isaiah the prophet unto our fathers, saying . . . 'Hearing you shall hear and shall not understand' " (Acts 28:25-26).

Just as the truth of the Trinity is hinted at in the Old Testament but awaits its fullest expression in the New, so with truth about the Holy Spirit. His personality and deity are evident in the Old Testament, but the full expression of His activity is given only in the New Testament.

Old Testament Teaching

Five differing aspects of the work of the Spirit are discernible in the Old Testament: [1]

1. *The work of the Spirit in the creation of the universe* (Gen. 1:2) *and of man*: "The Spirit of God hath made me, and the breath of the Almighty hath given me life" (Job 33:4).

2. *The work of the Spirit in equipping for service:* He conferred power on judges and warriors. For instance, "The Spirit of the Lord came mightily upon [Samson]" (Jud. 14:6). The Israelites cried out to God and He gave them Othniel, "and the Spirit of the Lord came upon him, and he judged Israel and went out to war" (Jud. 3:10).

Wisdom and skill for particular jobs, including those of a non-spiritual nature, were imparted to various individuals by the Spirit. Bezaleel was filled with the Spirit to work in gold, silver, and brass for the tabernacle (Ex. 31:3-5).

3. *The work of the Spirit in inspiring the prophets:* Usually they began their message with, "Thus saith the Lord." At times, however, they also attributed their message to the Holy Spirit: "And the Spirit entered into me when He spake unto me, and set me upon my feet" (Ezek. 2:2). And Moses exclaimed, "Enviest thou for *my* sake? Would God that all the Lord's people were prophets and that the Lord would put His Spirit upon them!" (Num. 11:29)

Moral Living

4. *The work of the Holy Spirit in producing moral living:* David, in agony of repentance for his dual sin of adultery and murder, pleaded for God to create a clean heart in him, and begged, "Take not Thy Holy Spirit from me" (Ps. 51:11). The Spirit, David knew, is good, and He leads men to do God's will (Ps. 143:10). Because of the presence of God's Spirit, which David sensed is inescapable, he pleaded for a searching of his heart and for clear leading in the eternal way (Ps. 139:7, 23-24).

5. *The work of the Spirit in foretelling the coming of the Mes-*

siah: First are those which prophesy a direct indwelling of the Spirit in one messianic figure: "The Spirit of the Lord God is upon Me, because the Lord hath anointed Me to preach good tidings" (Isa. 61:1). Jesus read this passage in the synagogue at Nazareth and uttered the electrifying words, "This day is this Scripture fulfilled in your ears" (Luke 4:21; cf. Luke 4:18; Isa. 9:2-9; 42:1-4).

The second way the Holy Spirit anticipated Christ was in the more general way of speaking about the new covenant people of God. "A new heart also will I give you, and a new Spirit will I put within you" (Ezek. 36:26; cf. v. 27). Both this prophecy and the comprehensive promise to Joel speak of the Spirit being given to all classes: "And . . . I will pour out My Spirit upon all flesh" (Joel 2:28; cf. v. 29).

Equips for a Task

The Old Testament's earlier teaching on the Holy Spirit emphasized the coming of the Spirit to equip a person to perform a certain task. The Scripture suggests that out of this bestowal of the Spirit, men grew more conscious of their inner need for God's help if they were to be morally pure enough to serve the Lord. Later in the Old Testament period, some scholars detect an awareness, on the part of believers, that the human government of Israel would never succeed in achieving the purposes of Jehovah, and a growing realization that, in time, the Spirit would be given to all God's people.[2]

Glimpses of the person and work of the Holy Spirit in the Old Testament are numerous and clear. However, the Old Testament period could not be called "the age of the Spirit" as our age, since the coming of the Holy Spirit in fullness on the Day of Pentecost, is called. Before Pentecost the Spirit came on particular people for particular tasks. While men could have an intimate relationship with Him, as shown by David's experience, the fellowship was not as personal or as permanent as is possible since Pentecost. The Spirit came upon individuals temporarily and then, when the occasion for His coming was over, withdrew. Samson's tragic downfall resulted from the Spirit's withdrawal. Samson had become so insensitive that he was not even aware that the Spirit had left him (Jud. 16:20). Nor was the experience of the Spirit in that era as widespread or universal as it is now, when He indwells everyone who is in the church of Jesus Christ by the new birth. It is emphatically true that "if any man have not the Spirit of Christ, he is none of His" (Rom. 8:9).

Our Lord's words to the disciples in this connection are instructive: "[The Spirit] dwelleth *with* you and shall be *in* you" (John

14:17). Just as there was a dispute in the church, during the Arian controversy, over the Trinity and whether or not the Son of God had existed eternally or was the first of God's creatures, so there was also conflict concerning the Holy Spirit. In the Nicene Creed He is called, "The Lord, the Life-Giver, that proceeds from the Father, that with the Father and Son is together worshiped and together glorified." This formula was finally adopted by the Council of Chalcedon in A.D. 451.

"Procession" and "Generation"

The phrase "proceeds from the Father" is taken from the Gospel of John: "But when the Comforter is come, whom I will send unto you from the Father, even the Spirit of truth, which proceedeth from the Father, He shall testify of Me" (15:26). This and other statements (e.g., John 14:16; 16:7; 20:22; etc.) imply a type of subordination of the Spirit to the Father and Son. This is only a subordination of relationship, not of deity.

Neither "generation" nor "procession" indicate a lack of equality within the Godhead, nor do they imply a creation or beginning of existence. Rather, they imply an eternal relation to the Father. They are "not a relation in any way analogous to physical derivation, but a life-movement of the divine nature, in virtue of which Father, Son, and Holy Spirit, while equal in essence and dignity, stand to each other in order of personality, office, and operation, and in virtue of which the Father works through the Son, and the Father and Son through the Spirit" [3]

In the year A.D. 589 the words, "and from the Son" were added to the Nicene Creed. This addition created tremendous controversy. The Western Church insisted on the addition to insure the preservation of the scriptural teaching that the Holy Spirit is the Spirit of Christ as well as of the Father. The Eastern Church refuses this insertion, feeling that it weakens the doctrine of subordination and makes our Lord a separate source of deity. But "the union of the Father and the Son in 'sending' the Spirit really works against any idea of differentiation which would mar the inner harmony of the divine Triad. . . . Scripture seems clearly to state that while the Spirit proceeds from the Father, He was also 'given' by the Son to His church, and that He is as much the Spirit of Christ as the Spirit of God" [4]

Some of the references that clarify and reinforce the concepts of the Spirit's deity and personality are: "The Spirit of God dwelleth in you" (1 Cor. 3:16); "the Spirit of Christ" (Rom. 8:9); and "God hath sent forth the Spirit of His Son into your hearts" (Gal. 4:6).

His Other Titles

Other descriptive titles of the Holy Spirit include "the Spirit of grace" (Heb. 10:29); "the Spirit of truth" (cf. 1 John 5:6); "the Spirit of wisdom and understanding, the Spirit of counsel and might, the Spirit of knowledge and of the fear of the Lord" (Isa. 11:2). He is the "Spirit of promise," that is, the One who came in fulfillment of Christ's promise (Eph. 1:13). He is also "the Spirit of glory" (1 Peter 4:14).

The Holy Spirit, then, is completely personal and completely God. He is coequal and coeternal with the Father and the Son.

We have already seen glimpses of the Spirit's work. We shall now look at it more closely. Though the Holy Spirit is self-effacing, His is the direct work of God and vitally affects each of us as individuals. He is active at various levels. In general, the Holy Spirit functions as the Executor of the purposes and plans of the Godhead. He is the One who carries out God's purposes—creation, conviction, regeneration, enlightenment, sanctification, and glorification.

In relationship to the world, the Spirit took part in the creation of the universe, as already mentioned in our review of His Old Testament activities. He is also referred to as the Preserver of nature: "Thou sendest forth Thy Spirit [the fish] are created: and Thou renewest the face of the earth" (Ps. 104:30; cf. Isa. 40:7).

Jesus outlined the work of the Spirit so far as humanity as a whole is concerned. He convicts the world of sin, of righteousness, and of judgment (John 16:8-11). As we saw in Chapter 1, the Holy Spirit is the Author of the Scriptures, the One who inspired them (2 Peter 1:20-21). He is also the One who interprets them and applies them to our hearts at a particular time. He is the Spirit of wisdom and revelation (Eph. 1:17), and He interprets the mind of God (1 Cor. 2:9-14). It has been rightly observed that this "illuminating" work of the Holy Spirit never becomes so mystical and subjective that grammatical and historical consistency are abandoned. By misunderstanding the role of the Holy Spirit in interpreting the Word, some have made the Bible almost a magical book, equating their subjective feelings with the authority of the Spirit.

The Spirit and Christ

The Holy Spirit had a particularly intimate relationship with the Lord Jesus Christ, who in His humanity was completely dependent on the Spirit. He was *conceived* by the Holy Spirit and *born* of Him (Luke 1:35). Jesus was *led* by the Spirit (Matt. 4:1). He was *anointed* for His ministry by the Spirit in a special way at His baptism (Matt. 3:13-17). He *offered* Himself as a sacrifice through the Spirit (Heb. 9:14), and He was *raised* from the dead by the power of the Spirit (Rom. 1:4). He gave *commandments* to the apostles whom He had chosen, and through them to the church, by the Spirit (Acts 1:2).

In the church, the Holy Spirit administers spiritual gifts for the good of the whole body: "But the manifestation of the Spirit is given to every man to profit withal" (1 Cor. 12:7; cf. entire chapter). He is the dynamic power which was promised the church before Pentecost: "Ye shall receive power, after that the Holy Spirit has come upon you" (Acts 1:8). Because of the phenomenal exploits of the early church, which turned the Roman world upside down, The Acts has been called "The Acts of the Holy Spirit."

Through the work of the Holy Spirit in the individual Christian, a believer comes into the most intimate personal contact with God.

The Holy Spirit is the One who brings conviction of sin to an individual (John 16:8). Whenever a person comes to a sense of his own sinfulness, whether by the preached, written, or personally spoken word, the Spirit of God has been at work.

The Spirit's Sealing

As soon as a person puts his trust in Christ He is *sealed* by the Holy Spirit (Eph. 1:13). A seal is a symbol of a finished transaction, of ownership, and of security. Because we are sealed by the Spirit, we can have certainty and assurance of salvation. "The Spirit Himself beareth witness with our spirit that we are the children of God" (Rom. 8:16).

The Spirit indwells each individual Christian, whose body is the Spirit's temple. Along with the Incarnation and Resurrection, here is another indication from Scripture that the human body is not inherently evil or sinful. It also reminds us that we are to take our bodies seriously. They are never to be in any way mutilated, abused, or neglected. There is no place in the Scripture for the kind of asceticism which punishes the body in the interests of *spirituality*. Extreme forms of such self-affliction occurred at different periods of church history, particularly in medieval times, and more sophisticated forms are with us even today.

We are sealed and indwelt by the Holy Spirit at the time we are baptized by the Spirit "for by one Spirit we are all baptized into one body, whether we be Jews or Gentiles, whether we be bond or free, and have been all made to drink into one Spirit" (1 Cor. 12:13). This baptism, with its attendant sealing and indwelling by the Spirit, takes place at the time of conversion. This participation in the Spirit is shared by *all* believers, despite their varying degrees of maturity, strength, and devotion.

Some Christians, however, apply the term *baptism* to one's first experience of being *filled* with the Spirit, which experience is part of God's purpose for us (Eph. 5:18).

Filled with the Spirit
This being filled with the Spirit is not a once-for-all experience, but one that may be repeated. On the Day of Pentecost the disciples were filled with the Spirit (Acts 2:4). A few days later, in a dramatic prayer meeting, they had such an experience again (4:31).

The filling of the Spirit implies being given power and boldness for God's service, and strength to meet particular crises. It is possible, and it sometimes happens, that the baptism of the Spirit and the infilling of the Spirit take place at the same time. They need not be separated in experience. But the filling of the Spirit is an experience to be repeated as necessary in the life of each believer. We are, literally, to "keep on being filled" (Eph. 5:18).

The Holy Spirit is not a substance, but a Person. The fullness of the Spirit is not a matter of our receiving more of Him. Rather, it is a matter of relationship. To be filled with the Spirit means we allow Him to occupy, guide, and control every area of our lives. His power can then work through us, making us effectively fruitful for God and flooding our hearts with His joy. This filling applies not only to our outward acts but to our inner thoughts and motives. When we are filled with the Spirit, all we are and have is subject to His control.

The test as to whether or not you are filled with the Spirit is not, "Have you received an external sign or been given a particular gift of the Spirit?" Rather, "Have you given yourself wholly and without reservation to God?" (Rom. 12:1) Are you genuinely willing that He should control, absolutely and entirely, your life? Many believers come to a point of utter frustration in their service for the Lord simply because they fail to realize the need to be filled with the Spirit if they are to act in God's power. Just as we cannot *save* ourselves apart from the work of the Holy Spirit, neither can we *live* the life of victory or serve the Lord effectively without the Spirit. When we learn to trust Him fully, allowing Him to work through us, we are freed from the frustration of trying to accomplish spiritual and eternal results solely through our human ability —or, more properly, inability.

It is the Holy Spirit who delivers us from the power of sin. "For the law of the Spirit of life in Christ Jesus has made me free from

the law of sin and death" (Rom. 8:2). The Holy Spirit changes
the *pattern* of our life so that we *can* overcome sin. He does not
make us sinless (1 John 1:8), but in Him we are able to start
fulfilling the righteousness of the Law (Rom. 8:4). Such holy
living is a work of the Spirit and a *result* of salvation; it is not in
any way the *basis* for our being saved.

The Spirit's Fruit

When the Holy Spirit produces His fruit in us, we find that "love,
joy, peace, patience, gentleness, goodness, faithfulness, meekness,
and self-control" (Gal. 5:22-23) come naturally to us instead of
our having to labor strenuously to cultivate these traits.

The Holy Spirit is also a guide to the individual Christian. We
are instructed to "walk in the Spirit" (Gal. 5:16). His leadership
is one of the signs that an individual is really a child of God: "For
as many as are led by the Spirit of God, they are the sons of God"
(Rom. 8:14). The Holy Spirit clearly led and guided the early
Christians, as we read in The Acts, and He does the same today
if a Christian is open and sensitive to His control.

The Holy Spirit prays for us (Rom. 8:26). What a wonderful
thing to realize, especially when *we* don't know how to pray, that
the Spirit of God makes intercession for us!

The opposite of this intimate, loving, dynamic relationship with
the Holy Spirit is experienced when we offend Him. We are not to
grieve the Spirit (Eph. 4:30). To grieve is to make sad. In the
verses immediately following this command, some of the things
that grieve the Spirit are enumerated. They have to do with attitudes, thoughts, words, and actions. Other things also grieve God's
Spirit—idolatry, hatred, strife, heresy, envy, etc. (Gal. 5:18-21).
To withhold anything from Him is to grieve Him. It is a solemn
thing to realize that even as *we* can be grieved, we can also, in a
much more profound way, grieve God's Holy Spirit.

We are commanded, "Quench not the Spirit" (1 Thes. 5:19).
Because the figure of quenching suggests the idea of fire, some
believe that this sin is more related to outward service than to
motives and attitudes. In the scriptural context it suggests both.
The verse follows a call to rejoice, pray, and give thanks. It precedes a warning not to despise whatever claims to be of God, but
to test it. We may not only quench the Spirit in ourselves, but,
by sinful living, confused beliefs, and unconcern may quench His
work in and for others as well. On the other hand, the Spirit may
well use others to correct, enlighten, and encourage *us*. To fail to
receive God's Word through another person simply because he, like
us, is imperfect, is to quench God's own Holy Spirit.

Through the Holy Spirit we *come* to know Christ, and by the Holy Spirit's power we *live* and *grow* in Christ, in the service of the King and in the fellowship of His church.

For Further Reading

Morgan, G. Campbell. *The Spirit of God.* London: H. E. Walter, 1953.

Morris, Leon. *Spirit of the Living God.* Downers Grove, Ill.: Inter-Varsity Press, 1960.

Ryle, J. C. *Holiness.* Edinburgh: James Clarke, 1952.

Thomas, W. H. Griffith. *The Holy Spirit of God.* Grand Rapids: Eerdmans, 1955.

SEVEN

THE CHURCH

A great many ecclesiastical leaders today are admittedly uncertain as to just what the church is. One modern theologian has written a book whose title sums up what is in the minds of many people: *The Misunderstanding of the Church.* Small wonder, then, that confusion about the church is common in the minds of "ordinary" Christians, especially in view of the increasing extent to which "the church" is in the news. The ecumenical movement is increasingly influential, and denominational mergers are occurring with more frequency than had been thought possible.

Among (and sometimes even *within*) the various groups of "Christians," there is considerable difference of opinion about matters of form, church government, mode of baptism, essential doctrines, etc. Some competing groups profess to be "the *one* 'true' church." It is especially important, in view of all the conflicting voices heard today, that every Christian know what the Bible teaches about the church.

In the New Testament, the Greek word *ekklēsia,* translated "church," means a *called out* group, or *assembly*—not necessarily a religious one. The Ephesus town clerk, trying to quell a near-riot, said, "If ye enquire anything concerning other matters, it shall be determined in a lawful assembly [*ekklēsia*]" (Acts 19:39).

Applied to Christians, "the church" means those who have been called out to Jesus Christ. In the New Testament it "mostly means a local congregation of Christians, and never a building. . . . Although we often speak of these congregations collectively as the New Testament church, or the early church, no New Testament writer uses *ekklēsia* in this collective way. Its commonest use was for the public assembly of citizens duly summoned, which was a feature of all the cities outside Judea where the Gospel was planted." [1] The term also applied to the universal church, the body of Christ: "[God] hath put all things under [Christ's] feet, and gave Him to be head over all things to the *church,* which is His body" (Eph. 1:22-23).

The New Testament church, then, is defined in two ways. First, it is "the whole company of regenerate persons . . . in heaven and on earth" (Matt. 16:18; Eph. 5:24-25; Heb. 12:23).[2] This is the universal invisible church. It is universal in that it includes all true believers in every place, and those who have gone on as well as those still alive. It is invisible in that it is not apparent in its entirety at any given time or place.

Second, there is also the individual local group, or church, through which the universal church is evident. "The individual church may be defined as that smaller company of regenerate persons who, in any given community, unite themselves voluntarily together in accordance with Christ's laws, for the purpose of securing the complete establishment of His kingdom in themselves and in the world." [3]

People in View

In both definitions, *people* are in view—not buildings. Today we use the word "church" in several additional ways. In answer to the question, "Where is your church?" we are more likely to answer, "At 18th and Green Streets" than "At County Hospital, Joe's Texaco Station, Motorola, and Circle Campus." A church is where its members are at any given time. Part of our problem, in reaching the world today, results from our "building" mentality. When we think of the activities of the church we tend to think only of what goes on within the four walls of the church building, rather than what takes place *in the world* through what believers say, do, and *are.*

God has always had His people. From the time of the Fall, when God gave Adam and Eve His promise of the Redeemer (Gen. 3:15), all who have believed His promises have been His people. God called Abraham and promised him, "I will bless them that bless thee, and curse him that curseth thee: and in thee shall all families of the earth be blessed" (Gen. 12:3). He established an eternal covenant with the nation of Israel as His "chosen people." They were not chosen because of inherent superiority over other racial or ethnic groups. "The Lord did not set His love upon you, nor choose you, because ye were more in number than any people, for ye were the fewest of all people, but because the Lord loved you, and because He would keep the oath which He had sworn unto your fathers" (Deut. 7:7-8).

Merely being born into the nation of Israel did not make a person one of God's people spiritually: "For he is not a Jew, which is one outwardly; neither is that circumcision which is outward in the flesh; but he is a Jew which is one in the Spirit, and not in the letter" (Rom. 2:28-29). Many who were not Jews physically became Jews spiritually by recognizing Jehovah as the true and living God and turning from idols to Him. Perhaps the most dramatic example of conversation to Judaism was in the days of Esther, after the Jews' deliverance from Haman. "In every province and in every city, whithersoever the King's commandment and his decree came, the Jews had joy and gladness, a feast and a good day. And many of the people of the land became Jews" (Es. 8:17). The occasion is still celebrated today in the Feast of Purim.

Members of the church are to have an intimate relationship with each other as well as to Christ. Therefore what hurts one member will hurt all, and when one member is honored, all the others will rejoice with him (1 Cor. 12:26).

The church was first mentioned by Jesus: "Upon this rock I will build My church; and the gates of hell shall not prevail against it" (Matt. 16:18). On another occasion He described the simplest form of a church, saying, "Where two or three are gathered in My name, there am I in the midst of them" (Matt. 18:20).

Began at Pentecost

The Christian church, as such, came into being with the coming of the Holy Spirit on the Day of Pentecost. After Peter's sermon on that occasion, "they that received his word were baptized; and there were added unto them in that day about three thousand souls. And they continued steadfastly in the apostles' teaching and fellowship, in the breaking of bread and the prayers. . . . And the Lord added to them day by day those that were being saved" (Acts 2:41-42, 47, ASV, marg.). The church was born in Jerusalem. It at first consisted mainly of Jews who recognized Jesus as the Messiah. Many of them were Hellenists—that is, Greek-speaking Jews—who had been scattered all over the empire. Many came to Jerusalem regularly as pilgrims.

The church was at first considered a sect within Judaism. One of Paul's accusers referred to him "as a mover of sedition among all the Jews throughout the world, and a ringleader of the sect of the Nazarenes" (Acts 24:5). The Roman government gave Christians the same exemption from military service it gave the Jews. The first Jewish Christians in Jerusalem continued to recognize their obligations to the Mosaic Law and still participated in the worship services of the temple or synagogue.

Increasingly, however, Jewish proselytes (Gentiles who had embraced Judaism) believed the Gospel and came into the church.

Philip preached the good news in Samaria and later baptized an Ethiopian to whom he had witnessed (Acts 8). Only after a vision from the Lord did the universal scope of the Gospel finally get through to reluctant Peter (Acts 10:9-16). He later explained to Cornelius, a Gentile, that it had been "an unlawful thing for a man that is a Jew to keep company or come unto one of another nation; but God hath showed me that I should not call any man common or unclean" (v. 28).

On hearing Cornelius' declaration of faith, Peter uttered the historic words, "Of a truth I perceive that God is no respecter of persons; but in every nation he that feareth Him and worketh righteousness is accepted with Him" (v. 34-35). As if to vouch for the truth of what Peter was saying, the Holy Spirit came on his listeners, most of whom were Gentiles, as he spoke. The Jews with Peter were amazed that Gentiles also received the Holy Spirit, but Peter baptized them.

Other Christian Jews preached the Gospel in Antioch, where a mixed church of Jews and Gentiles came into existence (Acts 13:1). It was here that believers were first called Christians (Acts 11:26), or "Christ's men."

What relationship Gentile converts should have to the Law and circumcision was the first great question the early church had to decide. A council held in Jerusalem made the momentous declaration, "For it seemed good to the Holy Spirit and to us to lay upon you no greater burden than these necessary things; that ye abstain from meats offered to idols, and from blood, and from things strangled, and from fornication, from which if ye keep yourselves ye shall do well" (Acts 15:28-29).

New Testament Figures

The figures used in the New Testament to describe the church are instructive. One is the "body of Christ." Christ is the Head of the body. Every member functions under His leadership and in dependence on each other member. "For as the body is one, and hath many members, and all the members of that one body, being many, are one body, so also is Christ" (1 Cor. 12:12; cf. Eph. 4:4; Col. 3:15).

Christ leads the church, and it is to be subject to Him (Eph. 5:23-24). He is the source of its unity—"for ye are all one in Christ Jesus" (Gal. 3:28). Some Christians make few practical applications of this unity.

The church is also compared to a building: "Ye [believers] also, as living stones, are built up a spiritual house, an holy priesthood" (1 Peter 2:5). This household of God is "built upon the foundation of the apostles and prophets, Jesus Christ Himself being the chief Cornerstone" (Eph. 2:20). This building, or temple, is the dwelling place of the Holy Spirit; it is comprised of all individuals indwelt by the Holy Spirit (1 Cor. 6:19 ff.). God Himself dwells within the church, so whoever attacks the church attacks God. In criticizing the church, we must be careful we are not criticizing God.

The church is called the bride of Christ. Marriage illustrates Christ's relationship to the church (Eph. 5:25-27, 31-32; cf. 2 Cor. 11:2; Rev. 19:7; 22:17). This figure powerfully displayed Christ's intense love for His church and His total commitment to her.

The church in the New Testament apparently was relatively simple. There were no denominations, though Paul rebuked party spirit among the Christians in Corinth (1 Cor. 3:3-8). How, then, have we come to the complex situation in which we find the church today?

There are, of course, numerous historical reasons, such as persecutions, heresy, and formation of national churches. But part of the reason for the development of differing groups of believers is the fact that the New Testament gives only limited instruction about church organization and practice. Sincere Christians, all claiming scriptural authority, have always differed in the interpretation of certain passages and teachings of the New Testament. It is important, therefore, to trace the discernible lines of the New Testament church pattern and to understand some of the major interpretations of them.

Membership Requirements

Requirements for church membership are implicit in The Acts. The first was belief in the Lord Jesus Christ (Acts 2:38). Faith in Christ, which normally includes repentance for sin, is the spiritual prerequisite to new life and membership in the body of Christ. When people asked Jesus the question, "What shall we do, that we might work the works of God?" He answered, "This is the work of God, that ye believe on Him whom He hath sent" (John 6:28-29).

Baptism was to follow faith, as an open confession of trust in Christ, though some earnest Christians believe that the "one baptism" (Eph. 4:5) is the baptism of the Holy Spirit, and that water baptism is not God's purpose for Christians today.

Adherence to revealed truth, among early Christians, was the standard. "And they continued stedfastly in the apostles' doctrine and fellowship, and in breaking of bread and in prayers" (Acts 2:42). Paul warns of false teachers arising within the church

(Phil. 3:2), and Peter echoes the same solemn theme. Throughout the New Testament there is emphasis on doctrinal purity and holiness of life. Doctrinal and moral impurity are to be purged from the church (1 Cor. 5:7).

God's "called out" people were designated "saints" (Eph. 1:1; 1 Cor. 1:2; Phil. 1:1). They met together for worship and mutual upbuilding of spiritual life (1 Cor. 14:3, 5, 19; Col. 3:16). The church was an evangelizing fellowship whose purpose was the communication and preservation of the Gospel message throughout the whole world (Matt. 28:19-20; Acts 1:8). Paul's letters placed little stress on evangelism, possibly because early believers were naturally and effectively evangelistic. He wrote to the Thessalonians, "For from you sounded out the word of the Lord not only in Macedonia and Achaia, but also in every place your faith toward God is spread abroad, so that we need not to speak anything" (1 Thes. 1:8, sco).

Christian were to be servants, meeting the physical and spiritual needs of both believers and unbelievers. "As we have therefore opportunity, let us do good unto all men, especially unto them who are of the household of faith" (Gal. 6:10). Christ Himself was the example; He "went about doing good" (Acts 10:38).

As Leon Morris puts it, "During the history of the church there have been many variations from the New Testament pattern. Indeed, there are so many gaps in our knowledge of what went on in New Testament times that we cannot be quite sure what constituted that pattern. Even those groups who claim to model their polity exactly on the New Testament cannot be certain they have succeeded. . . . No attempt seems to have been made to fasten any pattern on succeeding generations, for no authoritative directions were given as to the mode and perpetuation of the ministry. Ministerial forms have evolved in a variety of ways." [4]

That there was some organization at the local level in New Testament times seems clear. There were stated meetings (Acts 20:7); elected deacons (Acts 6:5-6); membership discipline (1 Cor. 5:13); letters of commendation (Acts 18:27); and lists of widows for support (1 Tim. 5:9).

God gave spiritual gifts to the church. "He gave some, apostles; and some, prophets; and some, evangelists; and some, pastors and teachers; for the perfecting of the saints for the work of the ministry, for the edifying of the body of Christ" (Eph. 4:11-12). The purpose of these gifts is "the perfection of the saints for the work of the ministry." There is no clear distinction between the clergy and the laity, either in terms of church government or spiritual ministry.

Periods of Ministry

Hammond outlines the three periods in the New Testament ministry: [5]

1. *The first period.* (a) Our Lord's ministry with the 70 whom He commissioned; (b) the apostolic ministry of those who had specially delegated authority from the Lord to give authoritative leadership in the church after Pentecost; and (c) the ministry of deacons, elders, and bishops. The three pastoral epistles (1, 2 Tim.; Titus) give the principles of and qualifications for the ministry.

2. *The transitional period.* During most of the lifetime of the apostles, and until the New Testament had been circulated to the various Christian communities, there were special gifts, such as prophecy, in the church. The object of these was to enable the local community to receive the New Testament revelation of Christ direct from the Spirit of God. When the apostles had completed their work, some of these "gifts" ceased. For instance, there was not an unending succession of apostles and prophets (cf. Eph. 2:20; 3:5; 4:11).

3. *The permanent ministry.* A bishop, or elder, was to teach spiritual truth and exercise rule and discipline in the local church (1 Tim. 5:17; Heb. 13:7). "Remember them which have the rule over you, who have spoken unto you the Word of God: whose faith follow, considering the end of their manner of life" (Heb. 13:17; cf. 1 Tim. 5:17).

Deacons helped in administering the business of a church (Acts 6:1-6; 1 Tim. 3:8-12), though it is clear there are spiritual overtones to their activity.

In view of the many denominations and sects throughout church history, it is surprising that all forms of church government and views of the ministry fall generally into one of three groupings: the episcopal, the presbyterial, or the congregational. [6] (These terms refer to systems of church government rather than to denominations.)

Episcopalianism

In the episcopalian system, the church is governed by bishops, but there are also presbyters (or priests) and deacons. The only one in this system who has power to ordain is the bishop. The bishops trace their office back many centuries. Some, in fact, claim to trace the line back to the apostles—hence the term so often used—*apostolic succession.* Among other groups, the Roman Catholic, Orthodox, Anglican, Episcopal, Methodist, and some Lutheran churches have the episcopal form of government.

This system is admittedly not found in the New Testament. A

full episcopalian system had not yet developed. Those who hold to this type of church government, however, feel that it was a natural development in the second century church. They see, in the work of some New Testament figures, a transition between the itinerant ministry of the apostles and the more settled ministry of the later bishops. Timothy and Titus had a good deal of authority over a number of churches, yet lacked the wide apostolic authority of Paul. James of Jerusalem was, it is felt, an example of an apostle who had a localized ministry but was more like a later bishop than like Paul. The development of episcopacy is traced through the early church fathers.

It is significant, many feel, that there is no trace of a struggle to establish the episcopalian system. If a divinely established presbyterial or congregational system had been overthrown, it is argued, a bitter conflict between the two factions would have been inevitable. By the second century, however, without any such conflict, the episcopal system predominated throughout the whole church.

Presbyterianism

In presbyterianism, the church is governed by elders. Presbyterians recognize that in the New Testament the term *elder* and *bishop* are used interchangeably and that they are clearly the most important element in the local ministry. In each local church, it would seem, a number of elders formed a kind of committee to handle church affairs. Elders in New Testament times acted with the apostles (Acts 15)—an indication of their importance. When the apostles passed from the scene, elders were the leading officers.

The local congregation seems also to have had a voice in the selection of men for the ministry. They chose the seven deacons (Acts 6:1-6) and apparently had a hand in setting aside Paul and Barnabas for missionary work (13:1-3). Presbyterians believe in the equality of elders, in the right of the people to take part (through their representatives) in the government of a church, and in the unity of the church through a graduated series of church courts which express and exercise the common authority of the church as a divine society.

John Dall distinguishes presbyterianism from the other two systems as follows: "As opposed to prelacy, the presbyterial type of government rests upon the equality of ministerial status and seeks to give ecclesiastical power to the members of the church instead of to clerical individuals or councils; as opposed to congregationalism, it seeks to realize the unity of the church by entrusting to a carefully devised system of graded church courts legislative, executive, and judicial—not merely advisory—powers." [7]

Presbyterians usually make a distinction between teaching and ruling elders (1 Tim. 5:17). The teaching elder is the principal order of ministry. He is ordained by the laying on of the hands of other elders. This is, in the presbyterial view, ordination to the universal church and not to some small section of it.

Ruling elders are chosen by the congregation and admitted to their office by ordination. They may not preach, baptize, or administer communion, but they assist in the government of the church and in the exercise of discipline. They also have responsibility for the financial affairs of the church. Some presbyterians feel that the office of ruling elder is the same as that of teaching elder, but others regard ruling elders as laymen.

Presbyterians account for the development of a universal episcopal system by saying that *monarchial* bishops gained the supremacy over presbyters in the church just after the apostolic age. They explain that church problems involving persecution and heresy could more easily be met by such a central authority. But this development, presbyterians maintain, was not in harmony with the essential nature of the ministry as revealed in the New Testament. They also believe that their system preserves the *episcopacy* through its *moderators* and general assembly, and that this preservation is not at the expense of ministerial equality.

Congregationalism

The third basic form of church government is congregationalism. Every group whose emphasis is on the autonomy of the local congregation would be included here. Such groups include Baptists, the Open Brethren, Christians (Disciples), Evangelical Free Churches, and some Bible and other independent churches. Followers of this polity hold that no man or group of men should exercise authority over a local congregation of Christ's church. With some exceptions, these churches have two types of ministers —pastors and deacons. Pastors have oversight of the congregation. They are usually ordained or set apart in a service attended by representatives of other similar congregations, though neither their participation nor approval is necessary. Deacons (or, sometimes, elders) are generally assigned the responsibility of watching over the spiritual and material needs of the local congregation. Their office is usually regarded as purely local. Congregationalists, as most other Protestants, deny that ordination imparts special grace to a man.

Two basic ideas are behind the congregational view of the ministry. One is that Christ is the Head of His church and, as such, is in living and vital contact with it. As our physical heads need no intermediary to control our bodies, so it is with the Head of the church and *His body*. It is not two or three officials, but two or three *believers*, gathered together in His name, in whose midst Christ promises to be (Matt. 18:20).

The second basic idea, common to most other Protestants as well, is the priesthood of all believers (1 Peter 2:9). Strictly speaking, there are no laymen in the church. All believers are priests (1 Peter 2:9)—that is, representatives of God to witness and minister to men in His name and power.

Further, the emphasis in the New Testament seems to be on the local church. There is no evidence of presbyterial or episcopal control of the church as a whole. Bishops and elders appear to have exercised their control within a local congregation, but not beyond it. The episcopal system did not appear until the second century.

Almost all churches fit into one of the above three groupings so far as polity is concerned.

Church Ordinances

There are numerous differences of opinion about the number and nature of *ordinances* in the church. Ordinances—some call them *sacraments*—are outward rites that signify or represent spiritual grace or blessing. The Roman Catholic Church has seven sacraments: baptism, the Lord's Supper, confirmation, penance, orders, matrimony, and extreme unction. Protestants maintain, however, that Scripture recognizes only two ordinances—baptism and the Lord's Supper.

Roman Catholics teach that objective merit or grace is conferred by the sacraments. In contrast to this mechanical, almost magical, view, most Protestants emphasize faith and the working of God directly in the believer.

The meaning of baptism is perhaps most fully explained in Romans 6:1-4 (though some Christians insist that this chapter does not have baptism with water in view). Baptism has been called "an outward sign of an inward grace," a declaration and public identification with Christ in His death, burial, and resurrection. Protestants are divided on whether baptism should be administered only to those who are believers, who in it make a public profession of faith, or whether infants also should be baptized. Episcopalians, Presbyterians, Lutherans, Methodists, and others practice infant baptism. Baptists, Disciples, and a great number of independent churches, hold to believers' baptism only. The former group use various modes of baptizing; the latter use immersion.

Most Christians agree on their obligation to observe the Lord's request. "This do in remembrance of Me." The Lord's Supper was to be a memorial and a "showing forth," or declaration, of His death till He returns (1 Cor. 11:23-26).

Roman Catholics teach that in the Lord's Supper the bread and wine become the *actual* body and blood of our Lord, though their appearance remains the same. This view is called *transubstantiation*. They further teach that the body and blood of Christ are offered every time a mass is observed. Scripture, however, emphatically contradicts such ideas. Christ's death on the cross was a complete and fully effective sacrifice, and He died once for all (Heb. 10:10; cf. 7:27; 9:12).

Lutherans believe in *consubstantiation*. In this view Christ is present *with* the unchanged substance of the bread.

Most Protestants, however, believe either that the elements are only a symbolic memorial or that by faith the believer, in the communion, enters into a special spiritual union with the glorified Christ.

Though participation in neither of these ordinances is necessary for salvation, every true believer should want to show his devotion to Christ by following Him in baptism and by remembering Him in the Lord's Supper.

Each genuine Christian, regardless of denomination, is spiritually one with every other believer. All are in the church universal. We are united in Christ, who is our life. There is no such thing as "lone-wolf" Christianity. If we are obedient to our Lord, we will identify with and join other believers for worship and service. In so doing, we not only contribute our own unique gifts to the fellowship, to be used by God to help bless others, but are ourselves blessed.

For Further Reading

Bainton, Roland H. *The Church of Our Fathers* (revised ed.). New York: Charles Scribners, 1950.

Bruce, F. F. *The Spreading Flame.* Grand Rapids: Eerdmans, 1953.

Flew, R. Newton: *Jesus and His Church* (new ed.). Naperville, Ill.: Allenson, 1956.

Latourette, Kenneth S. *Christianity Through the Ages.* New York: Harper, 1965.

EIGHT

ANGELS, SATAN, AND DEMONS

"Guardian angel" is a common expression, often used quite seriously and sincerely. In San Francisco there is a Church of Satan, with a minister who calls himself a high priest of Satan. Primitive peoples are often dominated by demons.

Are angels, the devil, and demons the result of ignorant superstition, or are they objective realities? The Bible speaks clearly about each of these types of spiritual beings. They can affect a Christian, and he is well advised to understand clearly who and what they are. Otherwise he is in danger of being victimized by popular ideas that may be totally erroneous and harmful.

Angels

Angels are mentioned in both the Old and the New Testaments. Jesus Himself referred to them many times. Speaking about "little ones," Jesus said, "In heaven their angels do always behold the face of My Father" (Matt. 18:10). Concerning His return to earth in the last days, He said, "But of that day and that hour knoweth no man, no, not the angels which are in heaven" (Mark 13:32). Other references He made to angels are recorded in Mark 8:38; Matthew 13:41; 26:53.

Angels are created beings. "For by Him were all things created that are in heaven, and that are in earth, visible and invisible, whether they be thrones, or dominions, or principalities, or powers; all things were created by Him and for Him" (Col. 1:16). Angels probably preceded man in creation; Satan, presumably a fallen angel, visited the Garden of Eden to tempt man. The words, "In the beginning God created the heaven and the earth," probably include the creation of angels, though they are not specifically mentioned.

Unlike man, who is composed of body and spirit, angels are incorporeal (purely spirit) beings. "Are they not all ministering spirits?" (Heb. 1:14) They at times take bodily form, as when two angels came to Lot in Sodom (Gen. 19:1), and sometimes they become visible, as at the Resurrection (John 20:12). Such appearances, however, were exceptions rather than the rule.

Though the masculine gender is always used with the word "angel," there is no distinction of sex with these beings. Jesus referred to this truth when He said of resurrected believers, "They neither marry nor are given in marriage, but are as the angels of God in heaven" (Matt. 22:30).

Angels are eternal; they never die. They are not subject to aging, and in heaven we shall be like them in this respect. "Neither can [the saved in heaven] die anymore; for they are equal unto the angels" (Luke 20:36).

In God's order of creation, angels are higher than man. God has made man a little lower than the angels (Ps. 8:5). But redeemed man, as part of the new creation, is higher than the angels and will have authority over them. "Know ye not that we shall judge angels?" (1 Cor. 6:3)

The intelligence and power of angels are greater than man's, though they are limited or finite. This truth is implied in our Lord's statement that the angels, though they are in heaven, do not know the day or the hour of the end time (Mark 13:32). The Gospel and salvation are things the angels "desire to look into" (1 Peter 1:12), which implies that they do not fully understand them. Angels are also referred to as greater in power and might than men (2 Peter 2:11). They excel in strength (Ps. 103:20). One angel killed 185,000 Assyrians in one night (Isa. 37:36). The angels' power is not theirs inherently, but comes by delegation from God. The Greek term translated *angel* means, literally, "messenger." Angels are, basically, messengers or servants of God. They are messengers of His might (cf. 2 Thes. 1:7).

Angels stand in the very presence of God. Jesus said they "behold the face of My Father" (Matt. 18:10). They are higher than men in this respect, and they continually worship God (cf. Rev. 5:11-12; Isa. 6:3). They also take pleasure in His works and grace, and show awareness of and interest in individual human beings. "There is joy in the presence of the angels of God over one sinner that repents" (Luke 15:10).

Angelic Activity
The activity of angels on earth has a number of facets, though essentially it is concerned with the doing of God's will: "Ye His angels . . . that do His commandments . . . that do His pleasure" (Ps. 103:20-21).

Angels punish the enemies of God and execute His judgment, as Herod discovered when "the angel of the Lord smote him, because he gave not God the glory" (Acts 12:23). God sent an angel to destroy Jerusalem in David's time (1 Chron. 21:15).

A more comforting truth is the relationship of angels to individual believers. Angels protected Daniel because of his faithfulness to God. To the amazed Darius, who appeared at the lion pit expecting to find him dead, Daniel said, "My God hath sent His angel, and hath shut the lions' mouths, that they have not hurt me" (Dan. 6:22). An angel provided for distraught and hungry Elijah: "An angel touched him and said unto him, 'Arise and eat' " (1 Kings 19:5). Peter was twice released from prison by an angel (Acts 5:19; 12:8-11). From these instances and others, we see how angels defend, protect, and deliver God's servant when it is in His providence to do so.

Angels may guide Christians to witness to a certain unbeliever, as an angel led Philip to the Ethiopian (Acts 8:26). Angels may also guide an unbeliever to a Christian, as when Cornelius and Peter were brought together.

In the midst of a shipboard crisis, Paul was cheered by an angel in the night (Acts 27:23). During His agony in the garden, our Lord Himself was strengthened by an angel (Luke 22:43).

Angels are also concerned with the church and its activity. Paul charged Timothy, concerning his ministry: "Before God and the Lord Jesus Christ and the elect angels . . . observe these things" (1 Tim. 5:21). Women were enjoined to wear veils on their heads "because of the angels" (1 Cor. 11:10), who presumably would be offended by any show of immodesty or indecorum.

Angels will accompany Christ when He comes in glory and in judgment. "The Son of Man shall come . . . and all the holy angels with Him" (Matt. 25:31).

No number of the angels is given in Scripture, but it is clear that they are many. Daniel, of his vision of God, said, "A thousand thousands ministered unto Him, and ten thousand times ten thousand stood before Him" (Dan. 7:10). John reported, of *his* vision, "I heard the voice of many angels round about the throne . . . and the number of them was ten thousand times ten thousand, and thousands of thousands" (Rev. 5:11).

Among this vast number of angels there is organization and rank. Jesus said that had He so desired He could summon more than 12 legions of angels (Matt. 26:53). References to the hosts of heaven in the Old Testament imply organization. Micaiah said, "I saw the Lord sitting on His throne, and all the host of heaven standing by Him on His right hand and on His left" (1 Kings 22:19).

The statement about "thrones or dominions or principalities or powers" (Col. 1:16) seems to indicate ranking. These orders of heavenly beings are viewed as good, being God-ordained. Evil beings seem to have similar organization and ranking: "principalities . . . powers, . . . the rulers of the darkness of this world, against spiritual wickedness in high places" (Eph. 6:12).

Other Angelic Beings

Michael is the only archangel mentioned in Scripture. He is considered as a special guardian of Israel and as "one of the chief princes" (Dan. 10:13, 21). He contended with the devil for the body of Moses (Jude 9). It may have been Michael who spoke to Moses on Mount Sinai, or Horeb (Ex. 3:2). He led the battle in heaven against Satan (Rev. 12:7).

Apocryphal, Babylonian, and Persian sources mention seven archangels. That only one archangel is mentioned in the Bible indicates that the biblical doctrine of angels was not derived from secular sources, as some critics suggest.

The only other angel named in the Bible is Gabriel, renowned for blowing his horn. Presumably this association comes from 1 Thessalonians 4:16, where Christ's return is said to be accompanied by "the voice of the archangel and the trump of God." Gabriel appears in the Old Testament as the one commissioned to explain the vision of the ram and the he-goat to Daniel (Dan. 8:16) and to declare the prophecy of the 70 weeks (9:21-27). In the New Testament he announced two great births—of John to Zacharias and Elizabeth and of Jesus to Mary (Luke 1:19, 26). Gabriel evidently has high rank as one who continually stands in the very presence of the Lord (Luke 1:19). His function seems to be that of a messenger, while Michael's appears to be that of a warrior.

Angels are never mediators between man and God, and men are not to worship them. Certain ancient Greek philosophers developed a whole series of graded emanations or spirits through which men could make contact with God. These philosophers maintained that God is much too holy to have anything to do with material things in general, and with earth and man in particular. Ancient Zoroastrianism taught a similar belief. This sort of doctrine is totally foreign to the teaching of the Bible, however. Angels are God's messengers, but this in no way implies that He has no direct contact with men when He so chooses. It emphatically is not necessary for us to approach God through any medium other than Jesus Christ.

In most popular thinking and art, angels are winged creatures. There is little biblical warrant for this notion. In Scripture angels most often appear in manlike form. The only winged beings mentioned in Scripture are cherubim and seraphim (the singular forms are *cherub* and *seraph*). We do not have a great deal of information about either. God stationed cherubim at the east entrance of the Garden of Eden with a flaming sword to guard the tree of life (Gen. 3:24). In Ezekiel's vision (chaps. 1; 10), cherubim are called "living creatures." Each cherub is described as having four faces —of man, lion, ox, and eagle. Each has four wings; two are stretched upward and two downward to cover his body.

Seraphim are mentioned in Isaiah's vision of the heavenly temple. They have six wings and can fly (Isa. 6:2, 6). These beings apparently were human in form, apart from their wings, and were associated with the cherubim in guarding the divine throne. It is possible that the cherubim and seraphim are in some way related to the living creatures in heaven (Rev. 4; 5).

Contrary to a popular mythology, there is absolutely no scriptural warrant for the idea that a person becomes an angel after he dies.

The question often arises as to whether angels appear today as they did in biblical times. Experience does not indicate that such appearances are usual. There is, however, no biblical teaching that rules out this possibility. It would be wise, however, to maintain an attitude of healthy skepticism toward any story of an angelic appearance, unless the report were independently verified. Sometimes impressionable people have hallucinations, and sometimes they embellish their stories unwittingly in retelling them.

One story about angels which seems to be authentic has to do with the well-known missionary to the New Hebrides, John G. Paton. Since he had aroused the enmity of the local native chief by his successes in the Gospel, the chief hired a man to kill the missionary. The man went to the missionary's house, but instead of murdering Paton he returned in terror, saying he had seen a row of men, dressed in white, surrounding the missionary's home. The chief thought the man had drunk too much whiskey and encouraged him to try again. The next time others of the tribe accompanied him. That night they all saw *three* rows of men surrounding Paton's home.

When the chief asked the missionary where he kept the men in the daytime who surrounded his house at night, Paton knowing nothing of what had happened, disclaimed the whole idea. When the chief, in amazement, told his story, the missionary realized the natives had seen an angelic company which God had sent to protect him, and he related it to Psalm 34:7:

"The angel of the Lord encampeth round about them that fear Him, and delivereth them." The savages were powerfully impressed with the missionary's explanation, as well they might be.[1]

Evil Spiritual Beings

God created angels perfect, and they were originally uncorrupted in spirit. At the same time, they had free will and were susceptible to temptation and sin. How sin could have come into the experience of a perfect creature is a mystery, but that it actually happened is clear. Peter warns against apostasy on the basis of God's judgment on angels (2 Peter 2:4), and we read of angels that "kept not their first estate, but left their own habitation" (Jude 6). Some feel that this angelic fall took place after the Creation (Gen. 1:1) and that because of it the original creation became "without form and void" (v. 2). The cause of the angels' fall is not specified, but presumably is related to the fall of Satan.

The name *Satan* means "adversary" or opponent. Peter calls him "your adversary the devil" (1 Peter 5:8). Johua stood before the angel of the Lord, with "Satan standing at his right hand to resist him" (Zech. 3:1). Satan ("adversary") is the opposer and enemy of both God and His people.

It has been fashionable, in recent years, to consider belief in the existence and personality of Satan as primitive, naive, and even superstitious. It is suggested instead that Satan, if we must use the term, is only the personification of the evil in the world. This notion has resulted partly from reaction to extravagant ideas and poetic expressions about Satan that were prominent during the Middle Ages. But these distorted ideas have no basis in Scripture, our only source of authoritative information.

Nowhere does the Bible depict Satan as a red man with horns, a tail, and a pitchfork. Some suggest that these caricatures are part of Satan's wiles to persuade sophisticated twentieth century men that he doesn't exist. People's credulity makes his job that much less difficult.

Biblically, there can be no doubt as to the devil's existence and personality. He is presented as appearing before the Lord when God challenged him about Job (Job 1:6-12; 2:1-7). There is no mistaking Satan's reality in his temptation of our Lord in the wilderness. He spoke to Jesus and Jesus spoke to him. (Matt. 4:1-11).

Satan's Other Names

Satan's other scriptural names also indicate his reality and personality. The only other proper name given him is *Devil*. Other terms applied to him describe him and his work. He is *the tempter* (1 Thes. 3:5). He is the *wicked one* who snatches away the good seed of the Word of God out of people's hearts (Matt. 13:19). He is the *enemy* who sows tares among the good seed (Matt. 13:39). He is our *adversary* (1 Peter 5:8). Jesus calls him the *father of lies* and a *murderer* (John 8:44). He is the supreme *deceiver* (Rev. 12:9).

Belial (2 Cor. 6:15) and *Beelzebub* (Matt. 12:24) have obscure derivations, but are used as synonyms for Satan. They denote a wicked person.

The fall of Satan from his exalted position as a perfect angel is shrouded in mystery, as is that of the other angels who fell with him. Presumably they shared his attitudes and he became their leader. Many Bible students feel that two Old Testament passages give clues as to what led to Satan's rebellion and fall.

One of these passages is Ezekiel 28:12-19. Though the entire passage speaks of the "prince of Tyrus" (v. 12), it seems also to characterize a being who was more than a mere man. What is said of Tyrus could only be applied to the earthly king of Tyre in a graphic and figurative sense. But if we take what is said as applying to Satan, we learn that he was, as originally created, "full of wisdom and perfect in beauty" (v. 12). The passage also indicates that originally he was assigned by God to the earth. The statement, "Thou wast perfect in thy ways from the day that thou was created till iniquity wast found in thee," would indicate that though he was created perfect, he *became* sinful. Since this sin dates back to pre-Adamic times, Satan probably was the originator of sin. His sin was pride.

The second of the two passages is Isaiah 14:12-15, which, if we take it to refer to Satan, describes the nature of his initial sin. The passage refers specifically to the king of Babylon, but there are reasons for believing that Satan wants to identify with the leading political power in the world at any given period of history. If this is so, it is easy to see how he may be described as the king of Tyre at one time and as the king of Babylon at another. The Lord Jesus three times referred to him as "the prince of this world" (John 12:31; 14:30; 16:11). Scripture teaches that the affairs of nations and cultures are affected by both angels and demons.

If Isaiah 14 refers to Satan, we see that he may have felt that his assignment on earth was too trivial for his status, which may well have been that of archangel. He is called "Lucifer, son of the morning" (Isa. 14:12). The word Lucifer means "shining one," or "light bearer." As a created being and a servant of God, he perhaps was not fully aware of his Master's plan concerning the earth (cf. John 15:15), and therefore did not understand its importance as the sphere where God would display Himself both in His creature, man, and later in the incarnation of His Son.

In the five "I wills" attributed to Satan (Isa. 14:13-14), some see the root of all sin—the setting of a creature's mind and will against God's. In the Garden of Eden, Satan cast doubts on God's love and wisdom (Gen. 3:4-5), as though God either did not know what was best for man or was unwilling to give it to him. "God's will is always the highest good His wisdom can devise. In the Garden of Eden Satan succeeded in convincing man that he could do better for himself than God had planned for him; and this is a contemporary problem in the world today." [2]

There are similarities between the description in Isaiah, Jesus' statement ("I beheld Satan as lightning fall from heaven," Luke 10:18), and the vision of John on Patmos: "I saw a star fall from heaven unto the earth: and to him was given the key of the bottomless pit" (Rev. 9:1). These passages all refer to Satan and they further indicate his identification with Lucifer.

After being cast out of heaven, Satan continued his work of opposition to God in the Garden of Eden, where he succeeded in tempting Adam and Eve to sin. He has continued his diabolical work through man's history, and is actively prosecuting it to this day. He is "the god of this world, [who] hath blinded the minds of them that believe not" (2 Cor. 4:4). This is an important fact to remember in evangelism, which is not merely a contest of human wills or intellects. The opponent of Christian witness is "the *prince of the power of the air,* the spirit that now worketh in the children of disobedience" (Eph. 2:2). He heads a powerful kingdom whose earthly subjects only Christ can turn "from darkness to light and from the power of Satan unto God" (Acts 26:18).

Our Lord was accused of casting out demons by the power of "the prince of demons" (Matt. 9:34, ASV). Demons are most likely fallen angels. They carry out the same kinds of activity as Satan.

Demon Possession

In modern times, many theologians regard demon possessions as only a primitive, prescientific description of what we now call mental illness. Throughout history, undoubtedly, some victims of mental illness have been wrongly accused of demon possession, and so treated harshly. But we should guard against confusion of the two conditions.

Some people suggest that all sickness is initiated and caused by demons, but the New Testament makes clear distinctions: "They brought to [Jesus] all who were ill, taken with various diseases and pains, demoniacs, epileptics, paralytics" (Matt. 4:24, NASB). Here clear differentiation is made between ordinary diseases and demon possession, and between demon possession and lunacy.

On another occasion Jesus cast out a demon who had caused dumbness (Matt. 9:32-33). From this account it is clear that the results of demon possession are not exclusively mental or nervous. Nor does the Bible connect epilepsy and demon possession. The boy Jesus healed of fits (Matt. 17:15-18) seems to have been afflicted with more than epilepsy. The Gadarene maniac (Mark 5:1-20), and possibly the man who overpowered two sons of the exorcist, Sceva (Acts 19:16), in addition to being demon possessed, may also have been afflicted with mental illness.

Demon possession is seldom mentioned in the Old Testament, The Acts, or the epistles. The incidents of it centered around our Lord's ministry and may indicate a special attack on mankind by Satan during that period.

Demon possession is a worldwide phenomenon, however, with authenticated contemporary cases being reported in this country as well as in other parts of the world. It is apparently possible deliberately to open oneself to demons. Trifling with the occult or playing around the edges of the spirit world are dangerous practices and Christians should carefully avoid them.

We should never try to conquer demons by our own power. Even the disciples had some frustrating encounters with such spirits. Jesus said, "This kind can come forth by nothing but prayer and fasting" (Mark 9:29). Generally, evil spirits were exorcised by being commanded to come out in the name of Christ (e.g., Acts 16:18). It has been suggested that rather than attempt to exorcise a satanic spirit ourselves, even in the name of Christ, we should ask God to do so for us. Even Michael the archangel did this (Jude 9).

A demon-possessed person invariably acts in ways that are not natural and normal to him. He often speaks in a voice entirely different from his normal one, and sometimes displays superhuman strength. He may also have powers of telepathy and clairvoyance. It should be noted that possession, in every instance, is by demons or evil spirits, never by good spirits.

Despite the great power of Satan and his demons, however, a Christian need not fear them if he is in close fellowship with the Lord. The Holy Spirit's presence in us is a reality and insures our safety (1 John 4:4).

These truths are clear from scriptural teachings and their implications about Satan and demons.

First, Satan's power over a believer is limited. The devil could not touch Job without God's permission (Job 1:9-12; 2:4-6).

Demons had to ask permission of Christ to enter swine (Mark 5:12). Satan is *not* all-powerful.

Neither is the devil all-knowing. If he were, he would have known in advance the futility of his scheme to subvert Job, and he would surely have realized that it was useless for him to tempt the Lord in the wilderness.

Satan was conquered by Christ on the cross. There, "having spoiled principalities and powers, He made a show of them openly, triumphing over them in it" (Col. 2:15). We are told that "for this purpose the Son of God was manifested, that He might destroy the works of the devil" (1 John 3:8).

Satan is slated for final eternal judgment: "And the devil that deceived them was cast into the lake of fire and brimstone, where the beast and the false prophet are, and shall be tormented day and night forever and ever" (Rev. 20:10).

Because Satan has been overcome by Christ, Christians are encouraged by God's promise that if they resist the devil he will flee from them (James 4:7). But our resistance must be "steadfast in the faith" (1 Peter 5:9). We can best thwart Satan's designs on us by daily yielding ourselves to the Lord in prayer and by putting on the whole armor of God (Eph. 6:10-17).

We should avoid the extreme of trying to see Satan behind every misfortune, in this way evading our personal responsibility. Equally dangerous, however, is being so lulled by the sophistication of our age as to be unaware of Satan and his wiles against us in the spiritual battle in which every true believer is engaged.

For Further Reading

Koch, Kurt. *Christian Counseling and Occultism*. Grand Rapids: Kregel, 1965.

Lewis, C. S. *Screwtape Letters*. New York: Macmillan, 1947.

Peterson, Robert. *The Roaring Lion*. London: Overseas Missionary Fellowship, 1968.

Unger, Merrill F. *Biblical Demonology*. Wheaton, Ill.: Scripture Press, 1952.

NINE

SALVATION

From one point of view, salvation is very simple. It can be summoned up in Paul's words to the Philippian jailer: "Believe on the Lord Jesus Christ and thou shalt be saved" (Acts 16:31). At the same time, salvation is profound; it has the most pervasive and permanent impact possible on the one who experiences it. We do not, of course, have to understand all the aspects of salvation before we can receive it. We may understand very little when we first trust Christ. A great deal we will not understand until we see our Lord face to face. But studying God's Word and trying to understand more fully the truth of our salvation greatly enriches us spiritually.

Several theological terms are generally used in connection with salvation. Each contributes something and, taken together, they give a greater fullness of God's light and truth. None of these theological terms or truths can be isolated completely from the others. We should always study them in their contexts. We cannot always be dogmatic about the order, or sequence, in which an individual should experience these various aspects of salvation, for they often overlap and sometimes are simply different views of the same truth.

Repentance

John the Baptist began his ministry with a call to *repentance:* "Repent ye, for the kingdom of heaven is at hand" (Matt. 3:2). Jesus began preaching with the identical words (Matt. 4:17). He commanded His disciples that "repentance and remission of sins should be preached in His name among all nations, beginning at Jerusalem" (Luke 24:47). Peter took up this message on the Day of Pentecost (Acts 2:38). Paul points out that now God "commandeth all men everywhere to repent" (Acts 17:30; cf. 26:20). Acceptance of the Gospel, to both Jews and Greeks, consists of "repentance toward God, and faith toward our Lord Jesus Christ" (Acts 20:21).

The word used in the Old Testament for repentance means to turn or return. It implies a personal decision to turn away from sin and *to* God. In the New Testament, the terms *repent* and *repentance* that apply to man's relationship to sin and God have the basic meaning of a change of mind. They imply a change of mind about sin, and a turning to God. In a sense, they are the negative and positive aspects of the same truth. The two together are inseparable and complementary. Paul, in his defense before Agrippa, said he preached that both Jews and Gentiles "should repent and turn to God and do works meet for repentance" (Acts 26:20).

True repentance is not merely a feeling of remorse, such as Judas had after he betrayed the Lord. It involves the intellect, the emotions, and the will.

Repentance brings the mind to realize both the holiness of God's law and one's utter failure and inability to keep it. It may also involve a change of mind as to who Christ is, as was true with the Jews on the Day of Pentecost (Acts 2:14-40). They had formerly viewed Jesus as an imposter, but Peter called on them to accept Him as Messiah and Saviour.

The emotions are involved in repentance. "Godly sorrow," in contrast to one's being superficially sorry for sin, often precedes the change of mind. "The sorrow that is according to the will of God produces a repentance without regret, leading to salvation" (2 Cor. 7:10, NASB). Repentance involves a feeling of the awfulness of sin in its effect on man and his relationship to God. Emotion, however, is no gauge of the extent of one's repentance. The presence or absence of tears does not necessarily indicate genuineness or lack of it. But when we truly repent we are sure to experience some feeling about it.

Repentance involves the will. The prodigal son not only came to his senses intellectually, and felt a loathing for himself and what he had done, but he *acted:* "I will arise and go to my father. . . . And he arose" (Luke 15:18, 20). Repentance is deliberate, willful turning away from sin and following after God. True repentance *always* leads to a change in conduct or attitude.

Faith

Repentance, if it is genuine, will lead to *faith*. In fact, some Christians understand "faith" to *include* repentance, pointing out that for a person to receive Christ as his Saviour in faith is in itself evidence that he is aware of his need, as a sinner, for the Saviour. The term *faith*, in its noun, verb, and adjective forms, is used dozens of times in the Old Testament, but occurs several hundred times in the New Testament. Its most common meaning is confident trust in or reliance on.

Faith is central to the whole Christian experience. "Without faith it is impossible to please [God], for he that cometh to [Him] must believe that He is, and that He is a rewarder of them that diligently seek Him" (Heb. 11:6). Faith, in the New Testament, always has as its background the Person and work of Christ. He is the object of our faith, reliance, or trust. Whoever believes in Him will not perish, but has everlasting life (John 3:16). In and of itself, faith is meaningless. It always has an object to which it is directed and upon which it rests. If the object of our faith is worthless, we are a victim of superstition, no matter how intensely and sincerely we believe.

Saving faith consists of several elements. First are the *facts* about Christ—His deity, His death, and our need of Him. We must accept these facts as *true,* though mere mental assent to this truth does not save us. James makes this clear: "Thou believest there is one God; thou doest well; the demons also believe and tremble" (James 2:19, ASV). One could not possibly be a Christian without believing these basic facts, but saving faith goes beyond mere belief *about* Christ to complete commitment *to* and trust *in* Him. Such commitment involves the *will* as well as the mind and the emotions. One does not believe simply because of one's feelings—one *decides* to believe.

Faith is the instrument that links us to Christ. The New Testament emphasizes that we are saved by *faith* and not by *works.* "But to him that worketh not, but believeth on Him that justifieth the ungodly, his faith is counted for righteousness" (Rom. 4:5).

At first sight, the Epistle of James appears to disagree: "What doth it profit, my brethren, though a man say he hath faith and have not works. Can [such] faith save him? . . . Ye see, then, how that by works a man is justified, and not by faith only" (James 2:14, 24).

The "faith" James criticizes is "head belief"—mere intellectual assent to facts. Such "faith" does not lead to holy living and hence is worthless, or "dead" (James 2:20). It has no saving value. When we read about "faith" in the other epistles, whole-hearted trust in Christ is in view. This is the faith on the basis of which God credits a believer with righteousness and which leads its possessor to want a holy life.

When we read that we are saved by faith rather than by *works,* the works in view are the keeping of the Law in an effort to earn salvation. James (2:14, 18, 20) does not use the term *works* in this sense. His *works* are very much like "the fruit of the Spirit" of which Paul speaks (Gal. 5:22). "They are warm deeds of love springing from a right attitude to God. They are the fruits of faith. What James objects to is the claim that faith is there when there is no fruit to attest it." [1]

How does faith come about? "Faith cometh by hearing, and hearing by the Word of God" (Rom. 10:17). In the days of the apostles, "many of [the people] who heard the Word believed" (Acts 4:4). God uses His Word, both spoken and written, to produce faith. At the same time, "God hath dealt to every man the measure of faith" (Rom. 12:3), which implies that faith is a work of God.

In almost every phase of salvation there is a mysterious interplay between the divine and human sides. It is not always possible, though, to draw neat lines of distinction. For instance, we may think of *repentance* and *faith* as man's response to *regeneration,* which God produces.

Regeneration

"Regeneration, or the new birth, is the divine side of that change of heart which, viewed from the human side, we call conversion." [2] The term is used only twice in the New Testament—of the restoration of the world (Matt. 19:28) and of the renewal or rebirth of individuals: "Not by works of righteousness which we have done, but according to His mercy He saved us, by the washing of regeneration and renewing of the Holy Spirit" (Titus 3:5).

Sin is so serious that a sinner cannot even *see* the kingdom of God, let alone *enter* it, unless he is born from above, or born again (John 3:3)—as Jesus pointed out in His conversation with the Jewish leader, Nicodemus. God takes the initiative in regeneration, or rebirth, but man must actively respond in faith. "But as many as received Him, to them gave He power to become the sons of God, even to them that believe on His name, which were born not of blood, nor of the will of the flesh, nor of the will of man, but of God" (John 1:12-13). "God, who is rich in mercy . . . even when we were dead in sins, hath quickened us together with Christ" (Eph. 2:4-5).

The new birth results not in a change of personality as such, but in a whole new way of life. Before the new birth, self and sin are in control; but after it, the Holy Spirit is in control. A bornagain person shares in the very life of God. He becomes a "partaker of the divine nature" (2 Peter 1:4), and is described as a "new creation" (2 Cor. 5:17, NIV); he puts on "the new man, which after God is created in righteousness and holiness" (Eph. 4:24; cf. Col.

3:10). Regeneration is a decisive experience that happens once for all, though it has continuing results in the life of a Christian.

God wants "all men to be saved and come to a knowledge of the truth" (1 Tim. 2:4). That some men are not regenerated or reborn is not God's fault. The responsibility rests with men. Our Lord diagnosed this problem. When speaking to a typical group, He said, "Ye *will not* come to Me that ye might have life" (John 5:40). It wasn't that they *could* not have come, but that they *would* not. They deliberately refused.

How men actually come to faith in Christ is a profound question. Some, by approaching the problem entirely from man's side, have tended to eclipse the sovereignty of God. Others, by approaching it only from God's side, have seemed to obliterate man's freedom.

We need to understand several theological terms to avoid confusion and popular misconceptions. These terms are election, predestination, and foreknowledge.

Election

Election has to do with God's choice of certain groups and people to receive His grace. This choice is based on His sovereign pleasure and not on the value, goodness, or disposition of those chosen. In the Old Testament, God's election is illustrated in His choice of Abraham, with whom He made an everlasting covenant, and of Abraham's descendants, the nation of Israel, to have a special relationship with Himself (Gen. 11:31—12:7).

Election, as used in the New Testament, has to do with God's choice of particular individuals for salvation. Jesus said, "And then shall [God] send His angels and shall gather together His elect [chosen] from the four winds" (Mark 13:27). Christians are "elect [chosen] according to the foreknowledge of God the Father" (1 Peter 1:2). God has "chosen [elected] us in Him before the foundation of the world . . . having predestinated us unto the adoption of children by Jesus Christ to Himself according to the good pleasure of His will" (Eph. 1:4-5). Jesus Himself explicitly said, "Ye have not chosen Me, but I have chosen [elected] you and ordained you" (John 15:16).

Predestination and Foreknowledge

Closely allied to election are *predestination* and *foreknowledge*. Predestination is a term used only of Christians. It indicates that God's purpose for a believer—that he become Christlike—is sure to be fulfilled. "For whom He did foreknow, He also did predestinate to be conformed to the image of His Son. . . . Moreover, whom He did predestinate, them He also called; and whom He called, them He also justified, and whom He justified, them He also glorified" (Rom. 8:29-30). Foreknowledge, predestination, calling, justification, and glorification are all grouped together in one "package." A person who has *one* of them has them *all*. The sequence indicates that apart from the grace of God we cannot trust in Christ. Jesus said, "No man can come to Me except the Father that sent Me draw him" (John 6:44).

Like election, *predestination* is according to God's sovereign purpose and will. It is not based on any merits in those persons whom He has chosen.

It is important to realize that *all* men are sinners and are under the judgment of God. "God in sovereign freedom treats some sinners as they deserve . . . but He selects others to be 'vessels of mercy,' receiving the 'riches of His glory' (Rom. 9:23). This discrimination involves no injustice, for the Creator owes mercy to none and has a right to do as He pleases with His rebellious creatures (Rom. 9:14-21). The wonder is not that He withholds mercy from some, but that He should be gracious to any." [3]

The purpose of the Bible's teaching on election and predestination is to lead pardoned sinners to worship God for the grace they have experienced. They come to see, in unmistakable terms, that salvation is *all* of God and not at all of themselves. They also come to see that since they were chosen in Christ before the foundation of the world, their election is eternal and therefore certain. This inspires devotion and love to Christ in gratitude for God's unfathomable love.

The popular misconception of election and predestination as the arbitrary acts of a capricious tyrant is totally foreign and unfair to Scripture. The attitude often expressed by unbelievers is that if they are elect, they'll get into heaven anyway, and if they're not, there's no use in their trying. In either case, they reason, they needn't be concerned. This is a tragic misconception. No one in hell will be able to tell God, "I wanted to be saved, but my name was on the wrong list."

Election and predestination are always to salvation and its blessings—never to judgment. It is true that no one believes on the Saviour unless God the Holy Spirit convicts him, but it is also true that those who do not trust Christ *choose* not to believe. God never refuses to save anyone who wants salvation.

Some feel that the expression, "elect according to the foreknowledge of God" (1 Peter 1:2) means that God elects to salvation those whom He knows in advance will respond positively to the Gospel. But foreknowledge is not the same thing as foreordination or election.

Throughout church history, honest differences of opinion have arisen about these complex and not fully explainable doctrines. Each believer should be persuaded in his own mind about them, and should show a charitable spirit toward those who differ.

A conversation between Charles Simeon and John Wesley, on December 20, 1874, is helpful at this point. Simeon said, "Sir, I understand that you are called an Arminian; and I have sometimes been called a Calvinist; and therefore I suppose we are to draw daggers. But before I consent to begin the combat, with your permission, I will ask you a few questions. . . . Pray, Sir, do you feel yourself a depraved creature, so depraved that you would never have thought of turning to God if God had not first put it in your heart?"

"Yes," said Wesley, "I do indeed."

"And do you utterly despair of recommending yourself to God by anything you can do, and look for salvation solely through the blood and righteousness of Christ?"

"Yes, solely through Christ."

"But, Sir, supposing you were at first saved by Christ, are you not somehow or other to save yourself afterwards by your own works?"

"No, I must be saved by Christ from first to last."

"Allowing, then, that you were first turned by the grace of God, are you not in some way or other to keep yourself by your own power?"

"No."

"What then? Are you to be upheld every hour and every moment by God, as much as an infant in its mother's arms?"

"Yes, altogether."

"And is all your hope in the grace and mercy of God to preserve you unto His heavenly kingdom?"

"Yes, I have no hope but in Him."

"Then, Sir, with your leave I will put up my dagger again; for this is all my Calvinism; this is my election, my justification by faith, my final perseverance: it is in substance all that I hold, and as I hold it; and therefore, if you please, instead of searching out terms and phrases to be a ground of contention between us, we will cordially unite in those things wherein we agree." [4]

The experience of salvation, in relation to the divine and human factors, includes some ambiguities. The results of salvation, however, are very clear. There are three phases of salvation: past, present, and future. That we have *been* saved, that we are *being* saved, and we *shall* be saved are all true statements. Each refers to a particular aspect of salvation.

Justification

Justification has often been defined as meaning, "Just as if I'd never sinned." This aspect involves acquittal, but justification goes even farther by declaring a person to be *righteous*. When God justifies us, He does not merely forgive our sins, making us neutral—moral and spiritual ciphers. He sees us in Christ as having His perfect righteousness. Justification has to do with our standing before God, and is *objective*. It does not make one *personally* righteous, but it *declares* him righteous in a legal sense, and brings him into right relationship with God.

Paul, to whom justification is central in salvation, stresses that we cannot be justified by the works of the Law, "for by the Law is the knowledge of sin" (Rom. 3:20). Rather, we are "justified freely by [God's] grace through the redemption that is in Christ Jesus" (Rom. 3:24).

The *basis* or ground of our justification, or being declared righteous, is twofold. Christ's death as our Substitute satisfied the claims of God's holy law against our sin. "While we were yet sinners, Christ died for us. Much more then, being now justified by His blood, we shall be saved from wrath through Him" (Rom. 5:8-9).

The other basis of God's declaring us righteous is Christ's perfect obedience. "For as by one man's [Adam's] disobedience many [i.e., all men] were made sinners, so by the obedience of One [Christ] shall many [i.e., all who believe] be made righteous" (Rom. 5:19). Christ became identified with us when He was made sin for us on the cross; and we are identified with Him in His newness of resurrection life, and share His righteousness.

We are justified by faith. This truth burst upon the heart and mind of Martin Luther like a bombshell as he considered the words: "Therefore being justified by faith, we have peace with God through our Lord Jesus Christ" (Rom. 5:1). After long struggling in unsuccessful self-effort to win the favor of God, Luther suddenly realized it was not what *he* could do, but what *God* had done, that made justification and peace possible. The Protestant Reformation resulted from this discovery.

The fact that we have been justified becomes clear through the evidence of our changed lives, marked by obedience to God and desire to do His will. When we say that we *have been* saved, we are referring to our justification. Paul wrote to the Ephesians, "For by grace are ye saved through faith" (Eph. 2:8). Paul's certainty of a past event, based on what God has done, led him to overflow with assurance. "I am persuaded," he wrote, "that neither death, nor life, nor angels, nor principalities, nor powers, nor things present, nor things to come, . . . nor any other creature shall be able to separate us from the love of God which is in Christ Jesus our Lord" (Rom. 8:38-39). We, too, may enjoy such assurance, for our salvation is an accomplished fact if we are in Christ.

Sanctification

But we are also *being* saved. This process of becoming holy is called *sanctification*. Justification has to do with our standing before God and is instantaneous. Sanctification has to do with our character and conduct and is progressive. It continues as long as we live.

Basically, the word *sanctified* means "set apart." The term *saint* comes from the same root and means "a set-apart one." Another word with the same meaning is "holy."

Sanctify is used in two ways:

(1) To set apart, or declare holy, for God's use or service. Christians are called *saints* in this sense—God has set them apart for His service. Such *sanctification* is usually regarded as being instantaneous and as taking place at the time of one's conversion. "Ye are washed . . . ye are sanctified . . . ye are justified in the name of the Lord Jesus and by the Spirit of God" (1 Cor. 6:11).

(2) To make the personal life of an individual Christian holy, in the sense of moral and spiritual improvement. This is a lifelong process. We are to "grow in grace and in the knowledge of . . . Jesus Christ" (2 Peter 3:18), and as we mature spiritually we "are changed into the same image [that of Christ] from glory to glory, even as by the Spirit of the Lord" (2 Cor. 3:18).

Some feel that sanctification is a crisis experience, as is justification, and that one can experience "entire sanctification" in a moment of time. Differences of opinion on this question hinge almost completely on the definition of sin and on the standard of holy living meant. Sin is often defined as "any voluntary transgression of a known law," as Wesley put it. The *Westminster Shorter Catechism,* on the other hand, defines sin as "any want of conformity unto or transgression of the law of God." This definition includes sins of omission and also takes our sinful nature into consideration—as well as overt sins committed deliberately.

Another big question has to do with *how* God sanctifies us. Those who say the process is all of God tend to minimize human responsibility. On the other hand, those who tend to minimize sin exaggerate human responsibility in sanctification.

A key principle that recognizes both God's initiative and man's responsibility is expressed in the scriptural command, "Work out your own salvation with fear and trembling. For it is God who worketh in you both to will and to do of His good pleasure" (Phil.

2:12-13). It is because God works in him that man is able to work. On the other hand, although God enables, man must respond. He is to show neither supine passivity nor naive confidence in his own effort.

Justification, declaring us righteous, delivers us from the *penalty* of sin. Sanctification, involving the development of holiness of character, delivers us from the *power* of sin. But how does holiness become *real* in our daily experience? Paul portrays the personal struggle vividly (Rom. 7) and also gives the remedy for it. He says that Christ died so "that the righteousness of the Law might be fulfilled in us, who walk [live] not after the flesh, but after the Spirit" (Rom. 8:4). God's command is, "Walk [live] in the Spirit and ye shall not fulfill the lust of the flesh" (Gal. 5:16). The Holy Spirit gives us power to overcome sin and produces in us the fruit of the Spirit (Gal. 5:22-23). This *walk* is a life of daily faith in which we claim and live personally what has already been given us by God. Christ has been made to us "wisdom, righteousness, sanctification, and redemption" (1 Cor. 1:30).

As we depend on Christ, then, His patience, love, power, purity, etc., will begin to show in our attitudes and conduct. He does not dole out these qualities to us in "little packages"—we have all of them we need in Christ, who indwells us. "His divine power has given unto us *all things* that pertain to life and *godliness,* through the knowledge of Him that hath called us to glory and virtue" (2 Peter 1:3).

The key principle in sanctification, as in justification, is faith. We can be *saved* only by faith and we can *live effectively* as Christians only by faith. "As ye have therefore received Christ Jesus the Lord [by faith], so walk [live] ye in him" (Col. 2:6). God, in both instances, does what we cannot do. Our part is to respond in faith.

Glorification

But there is a sense in which salvation is also future: we *shall* be saved. We have been saved from the *penalty* of sin, we are being saved from the *power* of sin, and we shall be saved from the very *presence* of sin. We shall personally be perfect and free from all sin. "Beloved, now are we the sons of God, and it doth not yet appear what we shall be; but we know that when He shall appear, we shall be like Him, for we shall see Him as He is" (1 John 3:2). It is in this sense that we are appointed "to *obtain* salvation" (1 Thes. 5:9), and it is *this* salvation which is ready to be revealed in the last time and to which Paul refers when he says, "Now is our salvation nearer than when we [first] believed" (Rom. 13:11). This complete and final sanctification and deliverance from the very presence of sin are called *glorification*.

Salvation is God's great gift to man. Though in experience its aspects may not be separated, an understanding of its details gives a Christian deeper appreciation, greater love, and happier praise for the God who has saved him.

For Further Reading

Berkouwer, G. C. *Faith and Perseverance*. Grand Rapids: Eerdmans, 1958.

Macon, Leon M. *Salvation in a Scientific Age*. Grand Rapids: Zondervan, 1955.

Prior, K. F. W. *The Way of Holiness*. Downers Grove, Ill.: Inter-Varsity Press, 1967.

TEN

THINGS
TO COME

One of the most fascinating features of the Bible is that it tells what is ahead. Both Old and New Testaments contend that history is moving to a climax and that the sovereign God is in control. Helmut Thielecke, in his book, *The Waiting Father,* sums up this truth in a magnificent way: "When the drama of history is over, Jesus Christ will stand alone upon the stage. All the great figures of history—Pharaoh, Alexander the Great, Charlemagne, Churchill, Stalin, Johnson, Mao Tse-tung—will realize they have been bit actors in a drama produced by Another." [1]

Throughout the Old Testament, the prophets looked forward to "the Day of the Lord," the time when God would exercise final judgment on Israel and other nations for their wickedness. All judgments—whether by means of invasion, plague, or natural disaster—will come to full flower at the return of Christ.

The Old Testament contains two lines of messianic prophecy. One pictures the Messiah (Christ) as the Suffering Servant (e.g., Isa. 53). The other regards Him as a reigning King (e.g., Isa. 9:6). The first coming of Christ, as the Suffering Servant, answered the hope for God's coming to redeem His people. The second coming of Christ will bring consummation of that hope when He returns as reigning King.

In the meantime, though, Satan has been conquered by Christ—at the cross and in the Resurrection—so that "through death He might destroy him who had the power of death, that is, the devil" (Heb. 2:14). But Satan is, temporarily, still "the god of this world" (2 Cor. 4:4), and he is actively opposing Christ and His church.

The Antichrist
Satan's opposition will culminate in the appearance of a being called Antichrist. The "spirit of Antichrist" is to be abroad before this person appears. In fact, his presence was noted already in

apostolic times: "Little children, it is the last time; and as ye have heard that Antichrist shall come, even now are there many antichrists; whereby we know it is the last time" (1 John 2:18). Of this coming being it is asked, "Who is a liar but he that denieth that Jesus is the Christ? He is Antichrist that denieth the Father and the Son" (v. 22).

Though there is considerable difference of opinion among Bible scholars, some feel, because of the similarity of description given in Daniel 11:37 and 2 Thessalonians 2:4, that these passages refer to the same person. If these also refer to the same person as "the beast" (Rev. 13:3, 13, 16-17), several striking characteristics emerge. Satan, with a view to deceiving and persuading men, will inspire Antichrist and give him power to act supernaturally. As an ecclesiastical leader, he will manipulate religion for his own ends, so as to claim the worship due God. He will also demand political allegiance and will exercise economic pressure to force compliance (Rev. 13:16-17). Those who try to oppose him will face tribulation so great that unless God shortened the days no one would survive (Matt. 24:22-23).

Christ's Return

The coming of Christ will bring the rule of Antichrist to an end. It is the great event to which all Scripture looks forward. The Old Testament prophets spoke of it, though the first and second comings often merged in their thinking. Jesus Himself frequently referred to it: "I will come again and receive you unto Myself, that where I am, there you may be also" (John 14:3); and, "Immediately after the tribulation of those days . . . shall appear the sign of the Son of man in heaven. . . . And they shall see the Son of man coming in the clouds of heaven with power and great glory" (Matt. 24:29-30). As the disciples watched Jesus' ascension: "Two men stood by them in white apparel, which also said, 'Ye men of Galilee, why stand ye gazing up into heaven? This same Jesus . . . shall so come in like manner as ye have seen Him go into heaven'" (Acts 1:10-11). The epistles also emphasize it: "For the Lord Himself will descend from heaven with a shout, with the voice of the archangel, and with the trump of God; and the dead in Christ shall rise first" (1 Thes. 4:16).

The second coming of Christ is the great anticipation of the church. As Christians we should, with Paul, love to look for that "blessed hope and the glorious appearing of the great God and our Saviour Jesus Christ" (Titus 2:13). His coming is an incentive for holy living: "And now, little children, abide in Him; that when He shall appear we may have confidence, and not be ashamed before Him at His coming"; and, "Every man that hath this hope in Him purifieth himself even as He is pure" (1 John 2:28; 3:3).

Views of the Rapture

Bible scholars are not completely agreed as to whether the Second Coming is a single event or has two phases. Many evangelicals distinguish between Christ's coming *for* His saints in the "Rapture" and His coming *with* His saints in the revelation of His power.

Among premillennialists (who believe Christ will return *before* He reigns with His resurrected saints for a thousand years), there are three views, commonly known as the pre-, mid-, and posttribulation views of the Rapture.

Those who hold the pretribulation view believe that Christ will return *for* His church *before* the Great Tribulation, which, therefore, believers will not have to endure. After this period of turmoil and affliction on earth, Christ will return again *with* His church. He will rule as King during the Millennium. The Tribulation, it is believed, coincides with the 70th "week" mentioned in Daniel's prophecy: "And he [the prince that is to come, or Antichrist] shall confirm the covenant with many [i.e., with Israel] for one week; and in the midst of the week he shall cause the sacrifice and the oblation [in the temple at Jerusalem] to cease, and for the overspreading of abomination he shall make it desolate even until the consummation shall be poured upon the desolate" (Dan. 9:27; cf. v. 26).

By comparing the whole prophecy (Dan. 9) with parallel passages, it appears these "weeks" are "sevens" of *years,* not *days.* According to pretribulation interpretation, therefore, the Tribulation will be a literal seven-year period, ruled by Antichrist, just before his final defeat by Christ. Emphasis is laid, in the pretribulation Rapture view, on the fact that though the church, through the centuries, has known much persecution, the final Great Tribulation will not involve believers and will be unique in its awfulness (Matt. 24:21).

The midtribulation view holds that the Rapture will take place in the *middle* of the 70th "week," 3½ years after its beginning. The posttribulation view is held by premillenarians who believe that Christ's rapture (coming *for* His saints) and His revelation (coming *with* His saints) are one and the same event, occurring just *after* the Tribulation and just before the Millennium.

Is anything yet to happen before Christ can return for His own? Those holding the pretribulation view feel there is nothing to prevent the Rapture from happening at "any moment." This "perhaps today" awareness encourages many Christians as they try to live each day in the light of their Lord's imminent return. Most of those having mid- or posttribulation convictions believe, of course, that certain events (primarily the Tribulation, or the first half of it) must take place before Christ comes again.

The Millennium

Another related and important question has to do with whether or not the Millennium is literal. Premillenarians believe that Christ will have a literal thousand-year reign: "And I saw thrones, and [the saints] sat upon them, and judgment was given unto them; and I saw the souls of them that were beheaded for the witness of Jesus, and for the Word of God, and which had not worshiped the beast, neither his image, neither had received his mark upon their foreheads or in their hands; and they lived and reigned with Christ a thousand years" (Rev. 20:4). This reign will follow the binding and imprisoning of Satan (20:1-3) so that he may no longer deceive the nations.

Some view the Millennium as an extension and visible expression of Christ's reign in the hearts of His people on earth and in heaven. Others see it as a fulfillment of God's promises to Israel, involving the restoration of the Jews to their homeland as a nation and the reestablishment of a literal throne, king, temple, and sacrificial system.

Many Bible scholars feel that the idea of a literal Millennium cannot be harmonized with biblical eschatology (teaching about the last days). They view the Millennium as a symbol of the ideal church. Since these people do not believe in an actual millennium, they are called "amillennialists."

Still another amillennarian view says that the symbolic language of The Revelation represents God's working in history, and that the kingdom of God is to be realized through the preaching of the Gospel. The missionary task of the church, they claim, includes the ultimate Christianizing of society.[2]

Jesus Is Coming!

Whatever points of view expositors take on the Tribulation, the Rapture, and the Millennium, it is thrilling to realize that all agree on the great, glorious, and incontestable fact that *Jesus is coming again*. The details of His next appearance are interesting and important to study, but differences in interpreting these details should never obscure the central *fact* of His coming.

It is significant that neither our Lord nor the prophets and apostles mention the return of Christ for speculative purposes, but always as a motive for practical daily holiness. We could summarize the doctrine: "Since all these things are to be destroyed in this way, what sort of people ought you to be in holy conduct and godliness" (2 Peter 3:11, NASB).

Two Resurrections

Some momentous events will take place at the coming of Christ. The resurrection of the believing dead will then occur, and we who are still alive will be glorified (1 Cor. 15:52) and caught up to meet Him in the air (1 Thes. 4:17). The resurrection of the dead is emphasized in the New Testament, but it is taught throughout Scripture. Even Job said, "I know that my Redeemer lives, and at last He will stand upon the earth; and after my skin has thus been destroyed, then out of my flesh I shall see God; whom I myself shall see, whom my own eyes shall behold, and not another" (Job 19:25-27, BERK).

David anticipated this resurrection (Ps. 16:9) and Daniel mentioned it (Dan. 12:1-3). Jesus taught it repeatedly and emphasized that it will include *all* men: "The hour is coming, in the which *all* that are in the graves shall hear His voice, and shall come forth, they that have done good unto the resurrection of life, and they that have done evil unto the resurrection of damnation" (John 5:28-29).

That the resurrection is a physical rather than a merely spiritual event is proved by the resurrection of Lazarus (John 11:44) and by that of our Lord Himself (Luke 24:39).

The resurrection of the body is part of our total redemption (Rom. 8:23). A Christian should not long to be delivered from the body, with all of its weaknesses and problems, but for the body's redemption. "We sigh deeply while in this tent, not because we want to be stripped of it, but rather to be invested with the other covering, so that the mortal may be absorbed by the real life" (2 Cor. 5:4, BERK). Our resurrection bodies will not be identical with the ones we have now, but will be closely related to them.

Believers will be resurrected at the coming of Christ (1 Thes. 4:16). This will be the *first* resurrection (cf. John 5:28-29), of which Paul wanted to be part (Phil. 3:11). It is, literally, the resurrection "out of the dead." That is, the righteous will be raised from among the wicked.

There is clearly a time lapse between the resurrection of believers to glory and the resurrection of unbelievers to judgment. Though we cannot be dogmatic as to the *exact* length of this interval, there will be a lapse of at least a thousand years between the two resurrections: "I saw the souls of them that were beheaded for the witness of Jesus, and for the Word of God, and which had not worshiped the beast, neither his image, neither had received his mark upon their foreheads, or in their hands; and they lived and reigned with Christ a thousand years. But the rest of the dead lived not again until the thousand years were finished. . . . Blessed and holy is he that hath part in the first resurrection; on such the second death hath no power, but they shall be priests of God and of Christ and shall reign with Him a thousand years" (Rev. 20:4-6).

The Dead

What about the condition of the dead before they are resurrected? The Scriptures affirm the conscious existence of both the wicked and the righteous after death and before their resurrections, but give few details. It seems clear that the soul is without a body and that believers are in a condition of conscious joy. Unbelievers, however, await the resurrection in a state of suffering (Luke 16:23). Paul was willing "to be absent from the body and to be present with the Lord" (2 Cor. 5:8). He said, referring to death, that he preferred "to depart and be with Christ, which is far better" (Phil. 1:23). Dead believers are at rest: "Blessed are the dead which die in the Lord from henceforth . . . that they may rest from their labors" (Rev. 14:13).

Death is frequently described in the Bible as sleep. In the Old Testament the term *sleep* is applied to *all* the dead, but in the New Testament it applies mostly to the *righteous* dead. Paul used the word only of believers. This term does not apply to the soul or spirit; it does not imply total unconsciousness until the resurrection. It rather implies unconsciousness with reference to *earthly life,* for which consciousness the body is necessary. The dead are *asleep* so far as this world is concerned, but this in no way implies that they are asleep or unconscious to the other world or that their spirits are totally unconscious.

Scripture clearly nowhere teaches "soul sleep." Passages quoted to prove this doctrine refer primarily to bodily, or physical, relations. All that we have said about the state of the righteous dead bears this out.

The consciousness of the unrighteous dead is also clearly taught. They are in prison (1 Peter 3:19), which would be unnecessary if they were unconscious. The story of the rich man and Lazarus (Luke 16:19-31), whatever else it may or may not teach, shows that the unrighteous dead experience conscious suffering and punishment.

No Purgatory

The passages cited clearly refute the doctrine of purgatory. A person dies either as one who has been redeemed or as one who is under judgment. After death there is no passing over from one condition to the other. Final judgment or redemption simply settles what has already begun at the time of death.

More is said about the condition of the dead than about their location. In the Old Testament the souls of all the dead are spoken of as going to sheol, which is translated "grave," "hell," or "pit." "Thou wilt not leave my soul in hell [sheol], neither wilt thou suffer thy holy one to see corruption" (Ps. 16:10). Sheol is a place of sorrow. "The sorrows of hell [sheol] compassed me about" (2 Sam. 22:6), said David. Hades, translated "hell" and "grave," is the New Testament equivalent of sheol. Other New Testament terms for the intermediate state include "paradise" (Luke 23:43) and "Abraham's bosom" (16:22).

The Judgments

But the intermediate state will be succeeded at last by the final judgment, toward which all history is heading. God is the Ruler of all men, the Lawgiver, and the final Judge. Sometimes the Bible mentions God (the Father) as judge: "God the Judge of all" (Heb. 12:23); and sometimes it mentions Christ: "The Lord Jesus Christ . . . shall judge the quick and the dead at His appearing and His kingdom" (2 Tim. 4:1). The relationship of the Father and the Son in judgment is made clear: "He [God the Father] hath appointed a day in the which He will judge the world in righteousness by that Man [Christ] whom He hath ordained, whereof He hath given assurance unto all men, in that He hath raised Him from the dead" (Acts 17:31).

God is judging men and nations continually, but there will be a final judgment which all previous judgments foreshadow. It will be an extension of past and present judgment. An unbeliever "*has been judged* already because he has not believed in the name of the only begotten Son of God" (John 3:18, NASB). A believer, on the other hand, "*has* [present tense] eternal life, and does not come into judgment, but has passed out of death into life" (John 5:24, NASB).

The purpose of final judgment will not be to *ascertain* the quality of an individual's character, but to *disclose* his character and to assign him to the eternal place corresponding to what he is because of his trust or lack of trust in God.

Several future judgments are mentioned in Scripture. The judgment of the living nations (Matt. 25:31-46), according to premillennialists, will take place at the return of Christ with His saints. It will lead to the setting up of the millennial kingdom.

Believers will be judged, but not with unbelievers: "We must all appear before the judgment seat of Christ, that every man may receive the things done in his body, according to that he hath done, whether it be good or bad" (2 Cor. 5:10). It is clear that this judgment does not decide a believer's salvation, but appraises his works. A Christian, in this judgment, can suffer loss of reward. "This is a judgment, not for destiny, but for adjustment, for reward or loss, according to our works, for position in the Kingdom: every man according as his work shall be." [3]

The final judgment of the unsaved will be at the great white throne of God. John describes it: "I saw a great white throne and Him that sat on it, from whose face the earth and the heaven fled away; and there was found no place for them. And I saw the dead, small and great, stand before God; and the books were opened; and another book was opened, which is the Book of Life; and the dead were judged out of those things which were written in the books, according to their works. And the sea gave up the dead which were in it, and death and hell [hades] delivered up the dead which were in them; and they were judged every man according to their works. And death and hell were cast into the lake of fire. This is the second death. And whosoever was not found written in the Book of Life was cast into the lake of fire" (Rev. 20:11-15).

The final judgment of Satan will occur just before that of the Great White Throne: "The devil that deceived [men] was cast into the lake of fire and brimstone" (Rev. 20:10). Presumably Satan's angels will be judged at the same time, for Jesus spoke of "everlasting fire prepared for the devil *and his angels*" (Matt. 25:41).

Hell

The final destiny of the wicked is hell. This awesome place is described in various ways. It is a place or state of unquenchable (Mark 9:43) and everlasting (Matt. 25:41) fire. It is spoken of as a lake of fire and brimstone (Rev. 20:10). That figurative language is used in these descriptions may be indicated by the fact that death and hell will be cast into it.

Hell is conceived of as outer darkness (Matt. 8:12). It is described as a place of eternal torment and punishment (Rev. 14:10-11). If figurative language is involved, it is obviously symbolic of something so awful no one in his right mind could be indifferent to avoiding it. Hell "is the loss of all good, whether physical or spiritual, and the misery of an evil conscience banished from God and the society of the holy and dwelling under God's positive curse forever." [4]

Nowhere in Scripture is there any trace of the idea that hell is a kind of "Jolly Boys' Club," absence from which would cause us to miss our friends. This flippant notion is Satan's lie. Hell is "the blackness of darkness forever" (Jude 13)—utter aloneness. C. S. Lewis once spoke of hell as "nothing but yourself for all eternity"! This is not the whole truth about hell, but it describes one of its most hideous aspects.

The future punishment of the wicked is not annihilation. "In support of the doctrine of conditional immortality [that the lost ultimately cease to exist] it has been urged that other terms descriptive of the fate of the condemned, such as 'perdition,' 'corruption,' 'destruction,' and 'death' point to a cessation of being. This, however, rests on an unscriptural interpretation of these terms, which everywhere in the Old and New Testaments designate a state of existence with an undesirable content—never the pure negation of existence—just as 'life,' in Scripture, describes a positive mode of being, never mere existence as such. Perdition, corruption, destruction, and death [refer to] the welfare of the ethical, spiritual character of man, without implying the annihilation of his physical existence." [5]

There is no biblical evidence for believing in the final restoration of the lost or in the universal salvation of all men. Perhaps the clearest disproof of these notions, as well as of final annihilation, is the fact that *the same word* is used to describe both punishment and life: "These will go away into *eternal* punishment; but the righteous into *eternal* life." (See Matt. 25:46.) However we may try to qualify the word so that it means *age-long* rather than everlasting, we must apply the same qualification to the destinies of the righteous and the wicked. We cannot, consistently, deny eternal punishment without also denying eternal life. And "eternal life" is *everlasting* life. "Eternal" certainly means "everlasting" when it is applied to God. Why should it mean anything else when it modifies "punishment"?

There are, however, *degrees* of punishment in hell and of reward in heaven. Some, at the judgment seat of Christ in heaven, will suffer loss of reward because their works of "wood, hay, and stubble" will not stand the test of fire (1 Cor. 3:15). Their capacity for enjoyment, though unlimited in duration, will be less than that of others. Similarly, the wicked will be judged, "every man according to his works" (Rev. 20:13). "That servant who knew his Lord's will and prepared not himself, . . . shall be beaten with many stripes; but he that knew not, and did commit things worthy of stripes, shall be beaten with few stripes" (Luke 12:47-48).

God, in His love, has done everything necessary to deliver men from eternal punishment. His justice requires that He punish sin, but His love provides salvation freely for all who will accept it. Those in hell are there because they refused or ignored God's love; they are solely responsible for their condition. The realization of this truth will surely be one of the most painful experiences of perdition.

Heaven

The final destiny of the righteous is heaven. Heaven is most simply defined as where God is. It is a place of rest (Heb. 4:9), of glory (2 Cor. 4:17), of holiness (Rev. 21:27), of worship (Rev. 19:1), of fellowship with others (Heb. 12:23), and of being with God (Rev. 21:3). He "shall wipe away all tears from their eyes; and there shall be no more death, neither sorrow, nor crying, neither shall there be any more pain; for the former things are passed away" (Rev. 21:4).

Believers may receive one or more crowns—the crown of life (James 1:12), the crown of glory (1 Peter 5:4), and the crown of righteousness (2 Tim. 4:8). Those who have been won for Christ through our witness become our crown of rejoicing at His coming (1 Thes. 2:19).

Everything in heaven will be new: "The earth also, and the works that are therein, shall be burned up. . . . Nevertheless we, according to His promise, look for new heavens and a new earth, wherein dwelleth righteousness" (2 Peter 3:10, 13). John reports that he "saw a new heaven and a new earth; for the first heaven and the first earth were passed away, and there was no more sea. And I . . . saw the holy city, New Jerusalem, coming down from God out of heaven. . . . And they shall reign forever and ever" (Rev. 21:1-2; 22:5).

God's kingdom will be established when all things are put under His feet. Then, "at the name of Jesus, every knee shall bow and every tongue confess that Jesus Christ is Lord, to the glory of God the Father" (Phil. 2:10-11). The kingdoms of this world shall be the kingdoms of our Lord, and He shall reign forever and ever. His will will be done on earth as it is done in heaven.

Heaven will not be the boring experience of strumming a harp on a cloud, as some facetiously characterize it. It will be the most dynamic, expanding, exhilarating experience conceivable. Our problem now is that, with our finite minds, we cannot imagine it.

> When we've been there ten thousand years,
> Bright shining as the sun,
> We've no less days to sing His praise,
> Than when we first begun.

For Further Reading

Hamilton, Floyd. *The Basis of Millennial Faith*. Grand Rapids: Eerdmans, 1942.

Ladd, George E. *Crucial Questions About the Kingdom of God*. Grand Rapids: Eerdmans, 1952.

Pentecost, J. Dwight. *Things to Come*. Findlay, Ohio: Dunham Pub. Co., 1958.

Reese, Alexander. *The Approaching Advent of Christ*. London: Marshall, Morgan, & Scott, (n.d.).

Vos, Geerhardus, *The Pauline Eschatology*. Grand Rapids: Eerdmans, 1952.

KNOW WHY YOU BELIEVE

Dear Marie,

We have never met and perhaps never will. I had been intending to write Paul for many months. However, a few months ago, I heard him referred to as "the late Paul Little" on a radio broadcast, and I felt a portion of your sadness. I truly believe someday I will tell him directly some of the things I would like to share with you now.

God's timetable continually brings me to my knees. . . . I (an atheist and dead last on any list of people of the world who might have a conversion experience) wandered into a Christian bookstore with thoughts of picking up some *different* reading material to while away some upcoming quiet days at home. (As a busy physician, I was unable to accompany my family on their Wisconsin vacation.) After much indecision and with considerable doubt, I purchased *Know Why You Believe*.

That evening I became convinced in 30-45 minutes of reading that there was a man named Jesus. He died on the cross *and* He was resurrected by God. There was no particular emotional experience involved except considerable anger over why, after wandering for 40 years in the wilderness of my life, hadn't someone told me these things before?

Although I was not aware of it, in the next few months I experienced fluctuating stages in my belief in Jesus Christ akin to the stages of dying as described in Elizabeth Kübler-Ross' work on death: denial—"in the morning I'll wake up and come to my senses"—anger, depression, bargaining—("I'll take this and that, God, if I don't have to do this other thing")—and finally, acceptance.

My intellectual acceptance has received fantastic confirmation through seeing God's promises come true in my life. I can really relate to the old dying away, to a changed life, to power, love, peace, joy, and to the abundant life—these are not just words conveying nice thoughts; they are absolutely for real.

I set aside my will and accepted Christ into my heart at an Easter sunrise service. There is really no other rational choice if you *really* believe, is there? My faith is anchored to the Resurrection like a rock, and every time I tug on the anchor rope, I find it firmly attached.

In Christ's love,
Dave Wright, M.D.
Portland, Oregon

ONE

IS CHRISTIANITY RATIONAL?

"**W**hat is faith?" asked the Sunday School teacher. A young boy answered in a flash, "Believing something you know isn't true."

That many non-Christians feel this way is not surprising. That many believers overtly or secretly feel this way is tragic.

Frequently I have the opportunity to present the Gospel in a bull session format. After a presentation, we have questions from the floor. Following these discussions I am often gratified and often dismayed. Unbelievers say the session has been helpful because it's the *first time* they've heard something that makes sense. I'm also gratified, but more deeply dismayed, when Christians tell me the same thing! They're relieved to discover that the Gospel can be successfully defended in the open marketplace of ideas and to discover that they haven't kissed their brains good-bye in becoming Christians!

We live in an increasingly sophisticated and educated world. It is no longer enough to know *what* we believe. It is essential to know *why* we believe it. Believing something doesn't make it true. A thing is true or not regardless of whether anyone believes it. This is as true of Christianity as it is of everything else.

Erroneous Viewpoints

There are two equally erroneous viewpoints abroad among Christians today on the important question of whether Christianity is rational. The first is, in essence, an anti-intellectual approach to Christianity. Many misunderstand verses like Colossians 2:8: "Beware lest anyone spoil you through philosophy or vain deceit, after the traditions of men, after the rudiments of the world and not after Christ." Some use this verse in a way that gives the impression that Christianity is at least nonrational if not irrational. They fail to realize that a clearly reasoned presentation of the Gospel "is important—not as a rational substitute for faith, but as a *ground* for faith; not as a replacement for the Spirit's working but as a means by which the objective truth of God's Word can be made clear so that men will heed it as the vehicle of the Spirit, who convicts the world through its message." [1]

There are challengers to our faith on every hand. Modern communications have made the world a neighborhood. We are likely to be challenged by Muslims, Hindus, and Buddhists, all of them claiming valid religious experience that may approximate ours. From within Christendom we are now being told God is dead. Increasingly, in our scientific age, ethical humanism is having stronger appeal. Julian Huxley's *Religion Without Revelation* is a good example of this approach.

Montgomery further observes:

> The analytical philosopher, Antony Flew, in developing a parable from a tale told by John Wisdom, illustrates how meaningless to the non-Christian are religious assertions incapable of being tested objectively.
>
> "Once upon a time two explorers came upon a clearing in the jungle. In the clearing were growing many flowers and many weeds. One explorer says, 'Some gardener must tend this plot.' The other disagrees, 'There is no gardener.' So they pitch their tents and set a watch. No gardener is ever seen. 'But perhaps he is an invisible gardener.' So they set up a barbed wire fence. They electrify it. They patrol with bloodhounds. (For they remember how H. G. Wells' *The Invisible Man* could be both smelt and touched though he could not be seen.) But no shrieks ever suggest that some intruder has received a shock. No movements of the wire ever betray an invisible climber. The bloodhounds never give cry. Yet still the believer is not convinced. 'But there is a gardener, invisible, insensible to electric shocks, a gardener who comes secretly to look after the garden which he loves.' At last the skeptic despairs, 'But what remains of your original assertion? Just how does what you call an invisible, intangible, eternally elusive gardener differ from an imaginary gardener or even from no gardener at all?" [2]

"This parable is a damning judgment on all religious truth-claims save that of the Christian faith. For in Christianity we do not have merely an allegation that the garden of this world is tended by a loving Gardener; we have the actual, empirical entrance of the Gardener into the human scene in the person of

Christ (John 20:14-15), and this entrance is verifiable by way of His resurrection." [3]

On the other hand, there are those who naively trust a set of answers and try to argue people into the kingdom. This is an impossibility and is as doomed to failure as attempting to put a hole in a brick wall by shooting it with a water pistol! There is an intellectual factor in the Gospel, but there are also moral considerations. "The natural man receiveth not the things of the Spirit of God, for they are foolishness unto him; neither can he know them, because they are spiritually discerned" (1 Cor. 2:14). Apart from the work of the Holy Spirit, no man will believe. But one of the instruments the Holy Spirit uses to bring enlightenment is a reasonable explanation of the Gospel and of God's dealings with men.

Know the Gospel
Beyond these pragmatic considerations, however, are the biblical assertions of the reasonableness of the Gospel. Along with this there are clear biblical commands to Christians to be intelligent in their faith: "Be ready always to give an answer to every man that asketh you a reason of the hope that is in you with meekness and fear" (1 Peter 3:15). If we are unable to give reasons for our faith, and if we allow the same questions to defeat us in conversation time after time, we are being disobedient. By our own ignorance, we are confirming unbelievers in their unbelief.

There are sound practical reasons why this command has been given us. In the first place, it is necessary for the strengthening of our faith as Christians. If we know Jesus lives only because, as the hymn says, "He lives within my heart," we're going to be in trouble the first time we don't feel He's there. And when someone from a non-Christian position claims to have experienced the same thing from *his* god, our mouths will be stopped. We may choose to ignore doubts, but eventually they will "get to us." One cannot drive himself indefinitely to do by willpower something of which he is not intellectually convinced. Witnessing is an example. He eventually suffers emotional collapse. When someone tells us the only reason we believe is because of our parents and our religious background, we must be able to show ourselves and others that what we believe is *objectively true*, regardless of who told us.

A Rational Body of Truth
Many non-Christians fail to consider the Gospel seriously because no one has ever presented the facts to them cogently. They associate faith with superstition based primarily on emotional considerations, and therefore they reject it.

Further biblical indication of the rational basis of the Gospel appears in our Lord's command to "love the Lord thy God with all thy heart, . . . and with all thy mind" (Matt. 22:37). The whole man is involved in conversion—the mind, the emotions, and the will. Paul says that he is "set for the defense of the Gospel" (Phil. 1:17). All of this implies a clearly understandable Gospel which can be rationally understood and defended.

It is quite true that an unenlightened mind cannot come to the truth of God unaided, but enlightenment brings comprehension of a *rational body of truth.*

The Gospel is always equated with truth. Truth is always the opposite of error (2 Thes. 2:11-12). Non-Christians are defined by Paul as those who "do not obey the truth" (Rom. 2:8). These statements would be meaningless unless there were a way to establish objectively what the truth is. If there were no such possibility, truth and error would, for all practical purposes, be the same because we would have no way to tell one from the other.

In writing to the Romans, Paul makes it clear that men have enough knowledge from creation itself to know there is a God (Rom. 1:20). He goes on to show that the basic reason men do not know God is not because He cannot be known or understood but because men have rebelled against Him, their Creator. "When they knew God, they glorified Him not as God" (1:21), "changed the glory of the uncorruptible God into an image made like to corruptible man" (1:23), "changed the truth of God into a lie" (1:25), and, finally, "did not like to retain God in their knowledge" (1:28).

A Matter of the Will

The moral issue always overshadows the intellectual issue in Christianity. It is not that man *cannot* believe—it is that he "*will* not believe." Jesus pointed the Pharisees to this as the root of the problem. "You *will* not come to me," He told them, "that you might have life" (John 5:40). He makes it abundantly clear that moral commitment leads to a solution of the intellectual problem. "If any man *will* [wants to] do His will, he shall *know* of the doctrine, whether it be of God or whether I speak of Myself" (John 7:17). Alleged intellectual problems are often a smoke screen covering moral rebellion.

A student once told me I had satisfactorily answered all his questions. "Are you going to become a Christian?" I asked. "No," he replied. Puzzled, I asked, "Why not?" He admitted, "Frankly, because it would mess up the way I'm living." He realized that the real issue for him was not intellectual but moral.

The question is often asked, "If Christianity is rational and true, why is it that most educated people don't believe it?" The answer is simple. They don't believe it for the same reason that most *un*-educated people don't believe it. They don't *want* to believe it. It's not a matter of brain power, for there are outstanding Christians in every field of the arts and sciences. It is primarily a matter of the will.

John Stott struck a balance when he said, "We cannot pander to a man's intellectual arrogance, but we must cater to his intellectual integrity."

Is Doubt Healthy?

Many Christians become troubled when they think about their faith and sometimes even wonder if it's true. Doubt is a word that strikes terror to the soul and often it is suppressed in a way that is very unhealthy. This is a particularly acute problem for those who have been reared in Christian homes and in the Christian church. From their earliest years they have accepted the facts of Christianity solely on the basis of confidence and trust in parents, friends, and minister. As the educational process develops, a reexamination of their position takes place.

This is a healthy and necessary experience to bring virile faith into being. It's nothing to fear or to be shocked about. Occasionally I ask myself, as I walk down the street, "Little, how do you know you haven't been taken in by a colossal propaganda program? After all, you can't see God, touch Him, taste Him or feel Him." And then I go on to ask myself how I *know* the Gospel is true. I always come back to two basic factors: the objective, external, historical facts of the Resurrection, and the subjective, internal, personal experience of Christ that I have known.

When young people begin to think and seem to have doubts, they should be welcomed into a climate where they are free to "unload" and *express* their doubts. Many such young people have been driven underground and lost to the cause of Christ because the adults with whom they first talked had a high shock index. They implied that a good Christian would never doubt and that the questioner's spiritual life must be slipping because he was thinking. Young people aren't stupid. When they meet this response they quickly shift gears and mouth the party line, even though it doesn't come from the heart. They quietly wait until they are out from under pressure to conform, and then they shed a faith that had never become their very own.

Doubt and questioning are normal to any thinking person. Rather than express shock, it is better for us to hear the questioner out and, if possible, even sharpen the question a little more. Then an answer can be suggested. Because Christianity is about the One who is Truth, close examination can do it no harm.

Don't Hit the Panic Button

If we don't have the answer at the moment, we needn't hit the panic button. We can always suggest we'll be glad to *get* the answer. It is improbable that anyone thought up, last week, the question that will bring Christianity crashing down. Brilliant minds have thought through the profound questions of every age and have ably answered them.

We don't have full answers to every question because the Lord hasn't fully revealed His mind to us on everything. "The secret things belong unto the Lord our God; but those things which are revealed belong unto us and to our children forever" (Deut. 29:29). We possess enough information, however, to have a solid foundation under our faith. Faith in Christianity is based on evidence. It is reasonable faith. Faith in the Christian sense goes beyond reason, but not against it.

Despite these facts, many Christians are over-whelmed by a mountain of material which they erroneously think they must master if they are ever to answer the questions of thinking Christians and non-Christians. A little exposure to non-Christians, however, will help to dispel those fears. It will soon become apparent that the same few questions are being asked repeatedly. Further, these questions fall within a remarkably limited range. I frequently talk to audiences that are composed of 98 percent non-Christians. I can predict with a high degree of accuracy the questions that will be asked me in the course of a half-hour question period. The questions may vary in wording, but the underlying issues are the same. This consistency is a great help in knowing what to study to answer such questions.

A Doubter's Response

A doubter needs to see that he must come to a decision after having been given an answer. To make no decision is to decide against the Christian position. Continued doubt in the face of adequate information may be a cloak for unwillingness to believe, in which case the problem is the questioner's will has been set against God.

Recently a friend told of a time, after he had finished college, when he felt God was calling him to the mission field. He fought against the call by feigning intellectual problems concerning his faith, rather than by praying clearly about his unwillingness to go overseas.

This book is intended to spotlight commonly asked questions and to suggest at least preliminary answers.

For the strengthening of our own faith and for the help of others, we must be ready to give an answer to everyone who asks us a reason for the hope that is within us, for *Christianity is rational!*

TWO

IS THERE A GOD?

There is in human existence no more profound question demanding an answer. "Is there a God?" is the question that must be answered by every human being, and the answer is far-reaching in its implications.

Mortimer Adler in his essay on God, in the monumental *Great Ideas Syntopicon* says:

"With the exception of certain mathematicians and physicists, all the authors of the 'Great Books' are represented in this chapter. In sheer quantity of references, as well as in variety, it is the largest chapter. The reason is obvious. More consequences for thought and action follow the affirmation or denial of God than from answering any other basic question."

Adler spells out the practical implications: "The whole tenor of human life is affected by whether men regard themselves as supreme beings in the universe or acknowledge a superhuman being whom they conceive of as an object of fear or love, a force to be defied or a Lord to be obeyed. Among those who acknowledge a divinity, it matters greatly whether the divine is represented merely by the concept of God—the object of philosophical speculation—or by the living God whom men worship in all the acts of piety which comprise the rituals of religion." [1]

Scientific Proof?

We must be clear from the outset that it is not possible to *prove* God in the scientific method sense of the word. But it can be said with equal emphasis that you can't *prove* Napoleon by the scientific method. The reason lies in the nature of history itself, and in the limitations of the scientific method. In order for something to be *proved* by the scientific method, it must be repeatable. One cannot announce a new finding to the world on the basis of a single experiment. But history in its very nature is nonrepeatable. No one can *rerun* the beginning of the universe or bring Napoleon back or repeat the assassination of Lincoln or the crucifixion of Jesus Christ. But the fact that these events can't be *proved* by repetition does not disprove their reality as events.

There are many real things outside the scope of verification by the scientific method. The scientific method is useful only with measurable things. No one has ever seen three feet of love or two pounds of justice, but one would be foolish indeed to deny their reality. To insist that God be *proved* by the scientific method is like insisting that a telephone be used to measure radioactivity.

What evidence is there for God? It is very significant that recent anthropological research has indicated that among the farthest and most remote primitive peoples, today, there is a universal belief in God. And in the earliest histories and legends of peoples all around the world the original concept was of one God, who was the Creator. An original high God seems once to have been in their consciousness even in those societies which are today polytheistic. This research, in the last 50 years, has challenged the evolutionary concept of the development of religion, which had suggested that monotheism—the concept of one God—was the apex of a gradual development that began with polytheistic concepts. It is increasingly clear that the oldest traditions everywhere were of one supreme God.[2]

For our present purposes, however, it is enough to observe that the vast majority of humanity, at all times and in all places, has believed in some kind of god or gods. Though this fact is not conclusive proof, by any means, we should keep it in mind as we attempt to answer the big question.

Law of Cause and Effect

Then there is the law of cause and effect to consider. No effect can be produced without a cause. We as human beings, and the universe itself, are effects which must have had a cause. We come eventually to an uncaused cause, who is God.

Bertrand Russell makes an astounding statement in his *"Why I Am Not a Christian."* He says that when he was a child, "God" was given him as the answer to the many questions he raised about existence. In desperation, he asked, "Well, who created God?" When no answer was forthcoming, he says, "My entire faith collapsed"! But how foolish. God by definition is eternal and uncreated. Were God a created being, He would not and could not be God.

Universe's Order and Design

A further development of this line of thought has to do with the clearly observable order and design of the universe. No one would think a wrist watch could come into being without an intelligent designer. How much more incredible is it to believe that the universe, in its infinite complexity, could have happened by chance? The human body, for instance, is an admittedly astounding and complex organism—a continual marvel of organization, design, and efficiency. So impressed was he with this that Albert Einstein, generally considered to be one of the great scientists of all time, said, "My religion consists of a humble admiration of the illimitable superior Spirit who reveals Himself in the slight details we are able to perceive with our frail and feeble minds. That deeply emotional conviction of the presence of a superior reasoning power, which is revealed in the incomprehensible universe, forms my idea of God." [3]

Evidences of this design are abundant. It is unlikely that a monkey in a print shop could set Lincoln's *Gettysburg Address* in type. If we found a copy of it, we would conclude that an intelligent mind was the only possible explanation for the printing. It is likewise incredible that water, for instance, with all its qualities, could have just happened. Bernard Ramm, quoting L. J. Henderson, enumerates some of these properties:

> Water has a high specific heat. This means that chemical reactions within the (human) body will be kept rather stable. If water had a low specific heat we would 'boil over' with the least activity. If we raise the temperature of a solution by 10 degrees Celsius we speed up the reaction by two. Without this particular property of water, life would hardly be possible. The ocean is the world's thermostat. It takes a large loss of heat for water to pass from liquid to ice, and for water to become steam quite an intake of energy is required. Hence the ocean is a cushion against the heat of the sun and the freezing blast of the winter. Unless the temperatures of the earth's surface were modulated by the ocean and kept within certain limits, life would either be cooked to death or frozen to death.
>
> Water is the universal solvent. It dissolves acids, bases, and salts. Chemically, it is relatively inert, providing a medium for reactions without partaking in them. In the bloodstream it holds in solution the minimum of 64 substances. Perhaps if we knew the actual number it would be a staggering figure. Any other solvent would be a pure sludge! Without the pecu-

liar properties of water, life as we know it would be impossible.[4]

A. Rendle Short makes this observation about water:

It forms more than half the body weight of most animals and plants. It is not readily decomposed; it dissolves many substances; it makes dry substances cohere and become flexible; with salts in solution, it conducts electricity. This is a very important property in the animal body. Then alone, or almost alone, amongst fluids known to us, it reaches its greatest density when cooled, not at freezing point, but at 4 degrees Celsius. This has two important consequences. One is that lakes and ponds freeze at the top, and not from the bottom upwards. Fish life thus has a chance of surviving a very hard winter. Another consequence is that by its expansion freezing water disrupts the rocks (also, alas, our household water pipes), and thus breaks them down to form soil, carves out cliffs and valleys, and makes vegetation possible. Water has the highest heat of evaporation of any known substance. This, with other special properties, reduces the rise in temperature when a water surface is heated by the sun's rays.[5]

The earth itself is evidence of design.

If it were much smaller an atmosphere would be impossible (e.g., Mercury and the moon); if much larger the atmosphere would contain free hydrogen (e.g., Jupiter and Saturn). Its distance from the sun is correct—even a small change would make it too hot or too cold. Our moon, probably responsible for the continents and ocean basins, is unique in our solar system and seems to have originated in a way quite different from the other relatively much smaller moons. The tilt of the [earth's] axis insures the seasons, and so on.[6]

DuNoüy says that "the chance formulations of a typical protein molecule made up of 3,000 atoms is of the order of one of 2.02×10^{231}, or practically nil. Even if the elements are shaken up at the speed of the vibration of light, it would take 10^{234} billions of years to get the protein molecule [needed] for life, and life on the earth is limited to about two billion years." [7]

Law of Thermodynamics
In addition to design in the universe, there is the implication of the second law of thermodynamics, which is also called the law of entropy. Ramm explains it:

What the law asserts can be illustrated from a plastic oleo-margarine bag which contains white margarine and a small capsule filled with yellow coloring. When the capsule is broken, as the bag is massaged, the coloring is eventually spread throughout the mass of white margarine. If the bag is squeezed indefinitely the distribution of the coloring will proceed till the coloring is perfectly spread throughout the entire mass. No matter how much more we squeeze, we cannot reverse the process and get the coloring back into the capsule. There are some parts of the universe that are much hotter than other parts of the universe. The distribution of the heat is always 'down' from hotter regions to cooler regions. As the heat 'flows' from the hot regions to cooler regions, it becomes more and more evenly distributed throughout the universe. If the universe is infinitely old, the energy would have been evenly distributed by now. The fact that there are still hot bodies in the universe means that the furnace was stoked, so to speak, at some measurable time in the past. This would be the moment of creation, or of some creative activity.[8]

In the light of all these things we can conclude with Ramm's statement:

Genesis 1 now stands in higher repute than it could ever have stood in the history of science up to this point. We now have means whereby we can point to a moment of time, or to an event or cluster of events in time, which dates our present known universe. According to the best available data, that is of the order of four to five billion years ago. A series of calculations converge on about the same order of time. We cannot with our present information force a verdict for creation from the scientists, though that is not to be considered an impossibility. Perhaps the day will come when we have enough evidence from physics, astronomy, and astrophysics to get such a verdict from the scientists. In the meantime we can maintain that Genesis 1 is not out of harmony with the trend of scientific information.[9]

This is what the Apostle Paul had in mind when he wrote, "Because that which may be known of God is manifest in them; for God hath showed it unto them. For the invisible things of Him from the creation of the world are clearly seen, being understood by the things that are made, even His eternal power and Godhead; so that they are without excuse" (Rom. 1:19-20). The psalmist says the same thing: "The heavens declare the glory of God; and the firmament showeth His handiwork" (Ps. 19:1).

Prejudice Prevents Obvious Conclusions

A most remarkable admission of unscientific bias, which precludes an admission that God is the only plausible explanation of the origin of the universe, is made by J. W. N. Sullivan. At his death, *Time* magazine called him "one of the world's four or five most brilliant interpreters of physics to the world of common man." He said:

> The beginning of the evolutionary process raises a question which is as yet unanswerable. What was the origin of life on this planet? Until fairly recent times there was a pretty general belief in the occurrence of "spontaneous generation." It was supposed that lowly forms of life developed spontaneously from, for example, putrefying meat. But careful experiments, notably those of Pasteur, showed that this conclusion was due to improper observation, and it became an accepted doctrine that life never arises except from life. So far as actual evidence goes, this is still the only possible conclusion. But since it is a conclusion that seems to lead back to some supernatural creative act, it is a conclusion that scientific men find very difficult to accept. It carries with it what are felt to be, in the present mental climate, undesirable philosophic implications, and it is opposed to the scientific desire for continuity. It introduces an unaccountable break in the chain of causation, and therefore cannot be admitted as part of science unless it is quite impossible to reject it. For that reason most scientific men prefer to believe that life arose, in some way not yet understood, from inorganic matter in accordance with the laws of physics and chemistry.[10]

Here we have an example of how believing there is *no* God is also an act of faith. It is pure presupposition, as much as faith *in* God is a presupposition for belief. Unbelief is even more remarkable when it is admitted that the evidence, by which one is guided in science, points in the opposite direction! And science rejects the conclusion because it is an unpalatable one.

What Is God Like?

It is important to observe here that though there are many *indications* of God in nature, we could never know conclusively from nature that He *is* or what He is *like*. The question asked centuries ago, "Canst thou by searching find out God" (Job 11:7). The answer is NO! Unless God reveals Himself, we are doomed to confusion and conjecture.

It is obvious that among those who believe in God there are many ideas abroad today as to what God is like. Some, for instance, believe God to be a celestial killjoy. They view Him as peering over the balcony of heaven looking for anyone who seems to be enjoying life. On finding such a person, He shouts down, "Cut it out!"

Others think of God as a sentimental grandfather of the sky, rocking benignly and stroking His beard as He says, "Boys will be boys!" That everything will work out in the end, no matter what you have done, is conceded to be His general attitude toward man.

Others think of Him as a big ball of fire and of us as little sparks who will eventually come back to the big ball. Still others, like Einstein, think of God as an impersonal force or mind. Herbert Spencer, one of the popularizers of agnosticism of a century ago, observed accurately that a bird has never been known to fly out of space. Therefore he concluded by analogy that it is impossible for the finite to penetrate the infinite. His observation was correct, but his conclusion was wrong. He missed one other possibility: that the infinite could penetrate the finite. This, of course, is what God did.

God Has Visited Us
As the writer to the Hebrews puts it, "God, who at sundry times and in divers manners spake in time past unto the fathers by the prophets, hath in these last days spoken unto us by His Son" (Heb. 1:1-2).

God has taken the initiative, throughout history, to communicate to man. His fullest revelation has been His invasion into human history in the person of Jesus Christ. Here, in terms of human personality that we can understand, He has lived among us. If you wanted to communicate your love to a colony of ants, how could you most effectively do it? Clearly, it would be best to become an ant. Only in this way could your existence and what you were like be communicated fully and effectively. This is what God did with us. We are, as J. B. Phillips aptly put it, "the visited planet." The best and clearest answer to how we know there is a God is that He has visited us. The other indications are merely clues or hints. What confirms them conclusively is the birth, life, death, and resurrection of Jesus Christ.

Changed Lives
Other evidence for the reality of God's existence is His clear pres-

ence in the lives of men and women today. Where Jesus Christ is believed and trusted a profound change takes place in the individual, and ultimately, the community. One of the most moving illustrations of this is recorded by Ernest Gordon, now chaplain at Princeton University. In his *Valley of the Kwai* he tells how, during World War II, the prisoners of the Japanese on the Malay peninsula had been reduced almost to animals, stealing food from their buddies who were also starving. In their desperation the prisoners decided it would be good to read the New Testament.

Because Gordon was a university graduate, they asked him to lead. By his own admission he was a skeptic, and those who asked him to lead them were unbelievers too. He and others came to trust Christ on becoming acquainted with Him in all of His beauty and power through the uncluttered simplicity of the New Testament. How this group of scrounging, clawing humans was transformed into a community of love is a touching and powerful story that demonstrates clearly the reality of God in Jesus Christ. Many others today, in less dramatic terms, have experienced this same reality.

There is, then, evidence from creation, history, and contemporary life that there is a God and that this God can be known in personal experience.

THREE

IS CHRIST GOD?

It is impossible for us to know conclusively whether God exists and what He is like unless He takes the initiative and reveals Himself. We must know what He is like and His attitude toward us. Suppose we knew He existed, but that He was like Adolf Hitler—capricious, vicious, prejudiced, and cruel. What a horrible realization that would be!

We must scan the horizon of history to see if there is any clue to God's revelation. There is one clear clue. In an obscure village in Palestine, almost 2,000 years ago, a Child was born in a stable. His birth was feared by the reigning monarch, Herod. In an attempt to destroy this Baby, who was said to be the King of the Jews, Herod had many infants killed in what history knows as the "slaughter of the innocents."

The Baby and His parents settled in Nazareth, where Jesus learned His father's trade of carpentry. He was an unusual child. When He was 12 years old He confounded the scholars and rabbis in Jerusalem. When His parents remonstrated with Him because He had stayed behind after they departed, He made the strange reply, "Don't you realize I must be about My Father's business?" This answer implied a unique relationship between Him and God.

He lived in obscurity until He was 30, and then began a public ministry that lasted for three years. It was destined to change the course of history.

He was a kindly person and we're told that "the common people heard Him gladly." Unlike the religious teachers of His time, "He spoke with authority, and not as the scribes and Pharisees."

Jesus Said He Was the Son of God

It soon became apparent, however, that He was making shocking and startling statements about Himself. He began to identify Himself as far more than a remarkable teacher or a prophet. He began to say clearly that He was Deity. He made His identity the focal point of His teaching. The all-important question He put to those who followed Him was, "Whom do you say that I, the Son of man, am?" When Peter answered and said, "Thou art the Christ, the Son of the living God" (Matt. 16:15-16), He was not shocked, nor did He rebuke Peter. On the contrary, He commended him!

He made the claim explicitly, and His hearers got the full impact of His words. We are told, "Therefore the Jews sought the more to kill Him, because He not only had broken the Sabbath, but said also that God was His Father, making Himself equal with God" (John 5:18).

On another occasion He said, "I and My Father are one." Immediately the Jews wanted to stone Him. He asked them for which good work they wanted to kill Him. They replied, "For a good work we stone Thee not; but for blasphemy and because that Thou, being a man, makest Thyself God" (John 10:30-33).

Jesus clearly claimed attributes which only God has. When a paralytic was let down through a roof and placed at His feet, He said, "Son, thy sins be forgiven thee." This caused a great to-do among the scribes, who said in their hearts, "Why does this man thus speak blasphemies? Who can forgive sins but God only?" Jesus, knowing their thoughts, said to them, "Whether it is easier to say to the sick of the palsy, 'Thy sins be forgiven thee,' or to say, 'Arise, and take up thy bed and walk'?" (Then He said, in effect, "But that you may know that I, the Son of man, have power on earth to forgive sins [which you rightly say God alone can do, but which is invisible], I'll do something you can *see*.") Turning to the palsied man, He commanded him, "Arise, and take up thy bed, and go thy way unto thine house" (Mark 2:7-11).

That the title "Son of man" is an assertion of deity, rather than being a disclaimer of it as some have suggested, is seen in the attributes Jesus claims as Son of man. These obviously are true only of God.

At the critical moment when His life was at stake because of this claim, He asserted it to the high priest, who had put the question to Him directly: "Art Thou the Christ, the Son of the blessed?" He said, "I am." Then He continued, "And you shall see the Son of man sitting on the right hand of power and coming in the clouds of heaven." The high priest tore his clothes and said, "What need we of any further witnesses? You have heard the blasphemy" (Mark 14:61-64).

So close was His connection with God that He equated a man's attitude to Himself with the man's attitude to God. Thus, to know Him was to know God (John 8:19; 14:7). To see Him was to see God (12:45; 14:9). To believe in Him was to believe in God (12:44; 14:1). To receive Him was to receive God (Mark 9:37). To hate Him was to hate God (John 15:23). And to honor Him was to honor God (5:23).[1]

Viewing the Claims of Christ

As we face the claims of Christ, there are only four possibilities. He was either a liar, a lunatic, a legend, or the Truth. If we say He is not the Truth, we are automatically affirming one of the other three alternatives, whether we realize it or not. When friends of ours take this position, we should invite them to show us what evidence they have that would lead us to adopt it. Often they realize, for the first time, that there is no evidence to support their views. Rather, all the evidence points in the other direction.

• One possibility is that Jesus Christ lied when He said He was God—that He knew He was not God, but deliberately deceived His hearers to lend authority to His teaching. Few, if any, seriously hold this position. Even those who deny His deity affirm that they think Jesus was a great moral teacher. They fail to realize those two statements are a contradiction. Jesus could hardly be a great moral teacher if, on the most crucial point of His teaching—His identity —He was a deliberate liar.

• A kinder, though no less shocking possibility, is that He was sincere but self-deceived. We have a name for a person today who thinks he is God—or a poached egg! That name is *lunatic,* and it certainly would apply to Christ if He were deceived on this all-important issue.

But as we look at the life of Christ, we see no evidence of the abnormality and imbalance we find in a deranged person. Rather, we find the greatest composure under pressure. At His trial before Pilate, when His very life was at stake, He was calm and serene. As C. S. Lewis put it, "The discrepancy between the depth and sanity of His moral teaching and the rampant megalomania which must lie behind His theological teaching unless He is indeed God has never been satisfactorily got over."[2]

• The third alternative is that all of the talk about His claiming to be God is a legend—that what actually happened was that His enthusiastic followers, in the third and fourth centuries, put words into His mouth He would have been shocked to hear. Were He to return He would immediately repudiate them.

The problem with the legend theory is the discoveries of modern archeology. It has been conclusively shown that the four biographies of Christ were written within the lifetime of contemporaries of Christ. Some time ago Dr. William F. Albright, world-famous archeologist now retired from Johns Hopkins University, said that there was no reason to believe that any of the Gospels were written later than A.D. 70. For a mere legend about Christ, in the form of the Gospel, to have gained the circulation and to have had the impact it had, without one shred of basis in fact, is incredible.

For this to have happened would be as fantastic as for someone in our own time to write a biography of the late Franklin Delano Roosevelt and in it say he claimed to be God, to forgive people's sins, and to have risen from the dead. Such a story is so wild it would never get off the ground because there are still too many people around who knew Roosevelt! The legend theory does not hold water in the light of the early date of the Gospel manuscripts.

• The only other alternative is that Jesus spoke the truth.

From one point of view, however, claims don't mean much. Talk is cheap. Anyone can make claims. There have been others who have claimed deity. A recent one was Father Divine of Philadelphia, now deceased. I could claim to be God, and you could claim to be God, but the question all of us must answer is, "What credentials do we bring to substantiate our claim?" In my case it wouldn't take you five minutes to disprove my claim. It probably wouldn't take too much more to dispose of yours. It certainly wasn't difficult to show that Father Divine was not God. But when it comes to Jesus of Nazareth, it's not so simple. He had the credentials to back up His claim. He said, "Though you believe not Me, believe [My] works that you may know and believe that the Father is in Me and I in Him" (John 10:38).

What Were Jesus' Credentials?

• *First, His character coincided with His claims.* We saw earlier that many asylum inmates claim to be various people. But their claims are belied by their character. Not so with Christ. And we do not *compare* Christ with others—we *contrast* Him with all others. He is unique—as unique as God.

Jesus Christ was sinless. The caliber of His life was such that He was able to challenge His enemies with the question, "Which of you convinceth Me of sin?" (John 8:-6) He was met by silence, even though He addressed those who would have liked to point out a flaw in His character.

We read of the temptations of Jesus, but we never hear of a confession of sin on His part. He never asked for forgiveness, though He told His followers to do so.

This lack of any sense of moral failure on Jesus' part is astonishing in view of the fact that it is completely contrary to the experience of the saints and mystics in all ages. The closer men and women draw to God, the more overwhelmed they are with their own failure, corruption, and shortcoming. The closer one is to a shining light, the more he realizes his need of a bath. This is true also, in the moral realm, for ordinary mortals.

It is also striking that John, Paul, and Peter, all of whom were trained from earliest childhood to believe in the universality of sin, all spoke of the sinlessness of Christ: "Who did no sin, neither was guile found in His mouth" (1 Peter 2:22); "In Him is no sin" (1 John 3:5); Jesus "knew no sin" (2 Cor. 5:21).

Pilate, no friend of Jesus, said, "What evil has He done?" He implicitly recognized Christ's innocence. And the Roman centurion who witnessed the death of Christ said, "Truly this was the Son of God" (Matt. 27:54).

In Jesus we find the perfect personality. Ramm points out:

If God were a man, we would expect His personality to be true humanity. Only God could tell us what a true man should be like. Certainly there are anticipations of the perfect man in the piety of the Old Testament. Foremost must be a complete God-consciousness, coupled with a complete dedication and consecration of life to God. Then, ranked below this, are the other virtues, graces, and attributes that characterize perfect humanity. Intelligence must not stifle piety, and prayer must not be a substitute for work, and zeal must not be irrational fanaticism, and reserve must not become stolidity. In Christ we have the perfect blend of personality traits, because as God Incarnate He is perfect humanity. Schaff describes our Lord, with reference to this point of our discussion, as follows: "His zeal never degenerated into passion, nor His constancy into obstinacy, nor His benevolence into weakness, nor His tenderness into sentimentality. His unworldliness was free from indifference and unsociability or undue familiarity; His self-denial from moroseness; His temperance from austerity. He combined childlike innocency with manly strength, absorbing devotion to God with untiring interest in the welfare of man, tender love to the sinner with uncompromising severity against sin, commanding dignity with winning humility, fearless courage with wise caution, unyielding firmness with sweet gentleness!" [3]

• *Christ demonstrated a power over natural forces* which could belong only to God, the Author of these forces.

He stilled a raging storm of wind and waves on the Sea of Galilee. In doing this He provoked from those in the boat the awe-struck question, "What manner of man is this, that even the wind and the sea obey Him?" (Mark 4:41) He turned water into wine, fed 5,000 people from five loaves and two fish, gave a grieving widow back her only son by raising him from the dead, and brought to life the dead daughter of a shattered father. To an old friend He said, "Lazarus, come forth!" and dramatically raised him from the dead. It is most significant that His enemies did not deny this miracle. Rather, they tried to kill Him. "If we let Him thus alone," they said, "all men will believe on Him" (John 11:48).

• *Jesus demonstrated the Creator's power over sickness and disease.* He made the lame to walk, the dumb to speak, and the blind to see. Some of His healings were of congenital problems not susceptible to phychosomatic cure. The most outstanding was that of the blind man whose case is recorded in John 9. Though the man couldn't answer his speculative questioners, his experience was enough to convince *him*. "Whereas I was blind, now I see," he declared. He was astounded that his friends didn't recognize his Healer as the Son of God. "Since the world began was it not heard that any man opened the eyes of one that was born blind," he said. To him the evidence was obvious.

• *Jesus' supreme credential to authenticate His claim to deity was His resurrection from the dead.* Five times in the course of His life He predicted He would die. He also predicted how He would die and that three days later He would rise from the dead and appear to His disciples.

Surely this was the great test. It was a claim that was easy to verify. It either happened or it didn't.

The Resurrection is so crucial and foundational a subject we will devote a whole chapter to it. If the Resurrection happened, there is no difficulty with any other miracles. And if we establish the Resurrection, we have the answer to the big question of God, His character, and our relationship to Him. An answer to this question makes possible answers to all subsidiary questions.

Christ moved history as only God could do. Schaff very graphically says:

> This Jesus of Nazareth, without money and arms, conquered more millions than Alexander, Caesar, Muhammad, and Napoleon; without science and learning, He shed more light on matters human and divine than all philosophers and scholars combined; without the eloquence of schools, He spoke such words of life as were never spoken before or since and produced effects which lie beyond the reach of orator or

poet; without writing a single line, He set more pens in motion, and furnished themes for more sermons, orations, discussions, learned volumes, works of art, and songs of praise than the whole army of great men of ancient and modern times.

• *Finally, we know that Christ is God because we can experience Him in the 20th century.* Experience in itself is not conclusive, but combined with the historic objective fact of the Resurrection it gives us the basis for our solid conviction. There is no other hypothesis to explain all the data we have than the profound fact that Jesus Christ is God the Son.

FOUR

DID CHRIST RISE FROM THE DEAD?

Both friends and enemies of the Christian faith have recognized the resurrection of Christ to be the foundation stone of the faith. Paul, the great apostle, wrote to those in Corinth, who in general denied the resurrection of the dead: "If Christ be not risen, then is our preaching vain, and your faith is also vain." Paul rested his whole case on the bodily resurrection of Christ. Either He did or He didn't rise from the dead. If He *did,* it was the most sensational event in all of history and we have conclusive answers to the profound questions of our existence: Where have we come from? Why are we here? Where are we going? If Christ rose, we know with certainty that God exists, what He is like, and how we may know Him in personal experience; the universe takes on meaning and purpose, and it is possible to experience the living God in contemporary life. These and many other wonderful things are true if Jesus of Nazareth rose from the dead.

On the other hand, if Christ did *not* rise from the dead, Christianity is an interesting museum piece—nothing more. It has no objective validity or reality. Though it is a nice wishful thought, it certainly isn't worth getting steamed up about. The martyrs who went singing to the lions, and contemporary missionaries who have given their lives in Ecuador and Congo while taking this message to others, have been poor deluded fools.

Crux of the Matter

The attack on Christianity by its enemies has most often concentrated on the Resurrection because it has been correctly seen that this event is the crux of the matter. A remarkable attack was the one contemplated in the early 30s by a young British lawyer. He was convinced that the Resurrection was a mere tissue of fable and fantasy. Sensing that it was the foundation stone of the Christian faith, he decided to do the world a favor by once and for all exposing this fraud and superstition. As a lawyer, he felt he had the critical faculties to rigidly sift evidence and to admit nothing as evidence which did not meet the stiff criteria for admission into a law court today.

However, while Frank Morrison was doing his research, a remarkable thing happened. The case was not nearly as easy as he had supposed. As a result, the first chapter in his book *Who Moved the Stone?* is entitled, "The Book That Refused to Be Written." In it he described how, as he examined the evidence, he became persuaded against his will, of the fact of the bodily resurrection.

Data To Be Considered
What are some of the pieces of data to be considered in answering the question, "Did Christ rise from the dead"?

• *First, there is the fact of the Christian church.* It is worldwide in scope. Its history can be traced back to Palestine around A.D. 32. Did it just happen or was there a cause for it? These people who were first called Christians at Antioch turned the world of their time upside down. They constantly referred to the Resurrection as the basis for their teaching, preaching, living, and—significantly—dying.

• *Then, there is the fact of the Christian day.* Sunday is the day of worship for Christians. Its history can also be traced back to the year A.D. 32. Such a shift in the calendar was monumental, and something cataclysmic must have happened to change the day of worship from the Jewish Sabbath, the seventh day of the week, to Sunday, the first day. Christians said the shift came because of their desire to celebrate the resurrection of Jesus from the dead. This shift is all the more remarkable when we remember that the first Christians were Jews. If the Resurrection does not account for this monumental upheaval, what does?

• *Then there is the Christian book, the New Testament.* In its pages are contained six independent testimonies to the fact of the Resurrection. Three of them are by eyewitnesses: John, Peter, and Matthew. Paul, writing to the churches at an early date, referred to the Resurrection in such a way that it is obvious that to him and his readers the event was well known, and accepted without question. Are these men, who helped transform the moral structure of society, consummate liars or deluded madmen? These alternatives are harder to believe than the fact of the Resurrection, and there is no shred of evidence to support them.

Two facts must be explained by the believer and the unbeliever alike. They are the empty tomb and the alleged appearances of Jesus Christ.

How Can We Account for the Empty Tomb?

• *The earliest explanation circulated was that the disciples stole the body.* In Matthew 28:11-15, we have the record of the reaction of the chief priests and the elders when the guards gave them the infuriating and mysterious news that the body was gone. They gave the soldiers money and told them to explain that the disciples had come at night and stolen the body while they were asleep. That story was so obviously false that Matthew didn't even bother to refute it! What judge would listen to you if you said that while you were asleep your neighbor came into your house and stole your television set? Who knows what goes on while he's asleep? Testimony like this would be laughed out of any court.

Furthermore, we are faced with a psychological and ethical impossibility. Stealing the body of Christ is something totally foreign to the character of the disciples and all that we know of them. It would mean that they were perpetrators of a deliberate lie which was responsible for the deception and ultimate death of thousands of people. It is inconceivable that, even if a few of the disciples had conspired and pulled off this theft, they would never have told the others.

Each of the disciples faced the test of torture and martyrdom for his statements and beliefs. Men will die for what they *believe* to be true, though it may actually be false. They do not, however, die for what they *know* is a lie. If ever a man tells the truth, it is on his deathbed. And if the disciples *had* taken the body, and Christ was still dead, we would still have the problem of explaining His alleged appearances.

• *A second hypothesis is that the authorities, Jewish or Roman, moved the body.* But why? Having put guards at the tomb, what would be their reason for moving the body? But there is also a convincing answer for this thesis—the silence of the authorities in the face of the apostles' bold preaching about the Resurrection in Jerusalem. The ecclesiastical leaders were seething with rage, and did everything possible to prevent the spread of this message and to suppress it (Acts 4). They arrested Peter and John and beat and threatened them, in an attempt to close their mouths.

But there was a very simple solution to their problem. If they had Christ's body, they could have paraded it through the streets of Jerusalem. In one fell swoop they would have successfully smothered Christianity in its cradle. That they did not do this bears eloquent testimony to the fact that they did *not* have the body.

• *Another popular theory has been that the women, distraught and overcome by grief, missed their way in the dimness of the morning and went to the wrong tomb.* In their distress they *imag-*

ined Christ had risen because the tomb was empty. This theory, however, falls before the same fact that destroys the previous one. If the women went to the wrong tomb, why did the high priests and other enemies of the faith not go to the right tomb and produce the body? Further, it is inconceivable that Peter and John would succumb to the same mistake, and certainly Joseph of Arimathea, owner of the tomb, would have solved the problem. In addition, it must be remembered that this was a private burial ground, not a public cemetery. There was no other tomb nearby that would have allowed them to make this mistake.

• *The swoon theory has also been advanced to explain the empty tomb.* In this view, Christ did not actually die. He was mistakenly reported to be dead, but had swooned from exhaustion, pain, and loss of blood. When He was laid in the coolness of the tomb, He revived. He came out of the tomb and appeared to his disciples, who mistakenly thought He had risen from the dead.

This is a theory of modern construction. It first appeared at the end of the 18th century. It is significant that not a suggestion of this kind has come down from antiquity among all the violent attacks which have been made on Christianity. All of the earliest records are emphatic about Jesus' *death*.

But let us assume for a moment that Christ was buried alive and swooned. Is it possible to believe that He would have survived three days in a damp tomb without food or water or attention of any kind? Would He have survived being wound in spice-laden grave clothes? Would He have had the strength to extricate Himself from the grave clothes, push the heavy stone away from the mouth of the grave, overcome the Roman guards, and walk miles on feet that had been pierced with spikes? Such a belief is more fantastic than the simple fact of the Resurrection itself.

Even the German critic David Strauss, who by no means believes in the Resurrection, rejected this idea as incredible. He said:

It is impossible that One who had just come forth from the grave half dead, who crept about weak and ill, who stood in the need of medical treatment, of bandaging, strengthening, and tender care, and who at last succumbed to suffering, could ever have given the disciples the impression that He was a conqueror over death and the grave; that He was the Prince of Life. This lay at the bottom of their future ministry. Such a resuscitation could only have weakened the impression which He had made upon them in life and in death—or at the most, could have given in an elegiac voice—but could by no possibility have changed their sorrow into ethusiasm or elevated their reverence into worship.[1]

Finally, if this theory is correct, Christ Himself was involved in flagrant lies. His disciples believed and preached that He was dead but became alive again. Jesus did nothing to dispel this belief, but rather encouraged it.

The only theory that adequately explains the empty tomb is the resurrection of Jesus Christ from the dead.

The Appearances of Christ

The second piece of data that everyone, whether believer or unbeliever, must explain is the recorded appearances of Christ. These occurred from the morning of His resurrection to His ascension 40 days later. Ten distinct appearances are recorded. They show great variety as to time, place, and people. Two were to individuals, Peter and James. There were appearances to the disciples as a group, and one was to 500 assembled brethren. The appearances were at different places. Some were in the garden near His tomb, some were in the Upper Room. One was on the road from Jerusalem to Emmaus, and some were far away in Galilee. Each appearance was characterized by different acts and words by Jesus.

For the same reasons that the empty tomb cannot be explained on the basis of lies or legends, neither can we dismiss the statement of the appearances of Christ on this basis. This is testimony given by eyewitnesses fully and profoundly convinced of the truth of their statements.

The major theory advanced to explain away the accounts of the appearances of Christ is that they were hallucinations. At first, this sounds like a plausible explanation of an otherwise supernatural event. It is plausible until we begin to realize that modern medicine has observed that certain laws apply to such psychological phenomena. As we relate these principles to the evidence at hand, we see that what at first seemed most plausible is, in fact, impossible.

Hallucinations occur generally in people who tend to be vividly imaginative and of a nervous makeup. But the appearances of Christ were to all sorts of people. True, some were possibly emotional women, but there were also hardheaded men like the fisherman Peter, and others of various dispositions.

Hallucinations are extremely subjective and individual. For this reason, no two people have the same experience. But in the case of the Resurrection, Christ appeared not just to individuals but to *groups*, including one of more than 500 people. Paul said that more than half of them were still alive and could tell about these events (1 Cor. 15).

Hallucinations usually occur only at particular times and places, and are associated with the events fancied. But these appearances occurred both indoors and outdoors, in the morning, afternoon, and evening.

Generally these psychic experiences occur over a long period of time with some regularity. But these experiences happened during a period of 40 days, and then stopped abruptly. No one ever said they happened again.

But perhaps the most conclusive indication of the fallacy of the hallucination theory is a fact often overlooked. In order to have an experience like this, one must so intensely *want* to believe that he projects something that really isn't there and attaches reality to his imagination. For instance, a mother who has lost a son in the war remembers how he used to come home from work every evening at 5:30 o'clock. She sits in her rocking chair every afternoon musing and meditating. Finally, she thinks she sees him come through the door, and has a conversation with him. At this point she has lost contact with reality.

One might think that this is what happened to the disciples about the Resurrection. The fact is that the opposite took place—they were persuaded *against their wills* that Jesus had risen from the dead!

Mary came to the tomb on the first Easter Sunday morning with spices in her hands. Why? To anoint the dead body of the Lord she loved. She was obviously not expecting to find Him risen from the dead. In fact, when she first saw Him she mistook Him for the gardener! It was only after He spoke to her and identified Himself that she realized who He was.

When the other disciples heard, they didn't believe. The story seemed to them "as an idle tale."

When the Lord finally appeared to the disciples, they were frightened and thought they were seeing a ghost! They thought they were having a hallucination, and it jolted them. He finally had to tell them, "Handle Me and see, for a spirit hath not flesh and bones as you see Me have." He asked them if they had any food, and they gave Him a piece of broiled fish. Luke didn't add the obvious—ghosts don't eat fish! (Luke 24:36-43)

Finally, there is the classic case of which we still speak— Thomas the doubter. He was not present when the Lord appeared to the disciples the first time. They told him about it, but he scoffed and would not believe. In effect, he said, "I'm from Missouri. I won't believe unless I'm shown. I'm an empiricist. Unless I can put my finger into the nail wounds in His hands and my hand into His side, I will not believe." *He* wasn't about to have a hallucination!

John gives us the graphic story (John 20) of our Lord's appearance to the disciples eight days later. He graciously invited Thomas to examine the evidence of His hands and His side. Thomas looked at Him and fell down in worship: "My Lord and my God."

To hold the hallucination theory in explaining the appearances of Christ, one must completely ignore the evidence.

What was it that changed a band of frightened, cowardly disciples into men of courage and conviction? What was it that changed Peter from one who, the night before the Crucifixion, was so afraid for his own skin that he three times denied he even knew Jesus, into a roaring lion of the faith? Some 50 days later Peter risked his life by saying he had seen Jesus risen from the dead. It must be remembered that Peter preached his electric Pentecost sermon in Jerusalem, where the events took place and his life was in danger. He was not in Galilee, miles away, where no one could verify the facts and where his ringing statements might go unchallenged.

Only the bodily resurrection of Christ could have produced this change.

Contemporary Proof

Finally, there is the evidence for the Resurrection which is contemporary and personal. If Jesus Christ rose from the dead, He is alive today, ready to invade and change those who invite Him into their lives. Thousands now living bear uniform testimony that their lives *have* been revolutionized by Jesus Christ. He has done in them what He said He would do. The proof of the pudding is in the eating. The invitation still stands, "Taste and see that the Lord is good!" The avenue of experimentation is open to each person.

In summary, then, we can agree with Canon Westcott, a brilliant scholar at Cambridge, who said, "Indeed, taking all the evidence together, it is not too much to say that there is no historic incident better or more variously supported than the Resurrection of Christ. Nothing but the antecedent assumption that it must be false could have suggested the idea of deficiency in the proof of it." [2]

FIVE

IS THE BIBLE GOD'S WORD?

This is a crucial question and one which is very much in dispute today. It is, however, not the foremost question in evangelism. Many Christians think they must prove the Bible to be the Word of God before they begin to witness. This is not the case. The crucial issue in salvation is one's relationship to the Lord Jesus Christ —not his view of the Bible. The Bible *is* the Word of God, regardless of what a person may think about it, and he can be led to consider Scripture even before the question of its inspiration has been settled in his mind. After conversation with a believer, a person should realize that the issue is, "What think you of Christ?" rather than "What think you of the Bible?"

All we need do to confront a person with the claims of the Lord Jesus Christ is to show him that the Gospels are reliable historical documents. This is reasonably easy, as we shall see in a later chapter. After a person has trusted Christ, the logical question for him to ask is, "How did Christ view the Bible?" As we shall see, it is abundantly clear that the Lord Jesus Christ viewed Scripture as the authoritative Word of God. As a follower of Christ, the logical step of obedience is to accept His view of the Scripture.

But how can we answer this far-reaching question for ourselves as believers?

While the statements and claims of the Scriptures themselves are not proof, they are a significant body of data which cannot be ignored.

Biblical View of Inspiration

In 2 Timothy 3:16, we read, "All Scripture is given by inspiration of God, and is profitable for doctrine, for reproof, for correction, for instruction in righteousness." The word *inspired*, here, is not to be confused with the common usage of the word, as when we say Shakespeare was *inspired* to write great plays, or Beethoven was *inspired* to compose great symphonies. Inspiration, in the biblical sense, is unique. The word translated *inspired* (2 Tim. 3:16) actually means *God-breathed*. It refers, not to the writers, but to what is written. This is an important point to grasp.

Second Peter 1:20-21 is another important statement "No prophecy of the Scripture is of any private interpretation. For the prophecy came not in old time by the will of man; but holy men of God spake as they were moved by the Holy Ghost." Here again the divine origin of the Scripture is emphasized.

It is important to realize, too, that the writers of the Scripture were not mere writing machines. God did not punch them, like keys on a typewriter, to produce His message. He did not dictate the words, as the biblical view of inspiration has so often been caricatured. It is quite clear that each writer has a style of his own. Jeremiah does not write like Isaiah, and John does not write like Paul. God worked through the instrumentality of human personality, but so guided and controlled men that what they wrote is *what He wanted written.*

Other indications of the claim of supernatural origin of the Scripture are sprinkled throughout its contents. Prophets were consciously God's mouth-pieces, and spoke as such: "The word of the Lord came unto me" is a phrase that recurs frequently in the Old Testament. David says, "The spirit of the Lord spoke by me, and His word was in my tongue" (2 Sam. 23:2). Jeremiah said, "The Lord put forth His hand and touched my mouth. And the Lord said unto me, 'Behold, I have put My words in thy mouth' " (Jer. 1:9). And Amos cries out, "The Lord God hath spoken, who can but prophesy?" (3:8)

It is also very remarkable that when later writers of Scripture quote parts of the Scripture which had previously been recorded, they frequently quote it as words spoken by God rather than by a particular prophet. For instance, Paul writes, "And the Scripture, foreseeing that God would justify the heathen through faith, preached before the Gospel unto Abraham, saying, 'In thee shall all nations be blessed' " (Gal. 3:8).

There are other passages in which God is spoken of as if He were the Scriptures. For example, "Thou art God . . . who by the mouth of Thy servant David has said, 'Why do the heathen rage, and the people imagine a vain thing?' " (Acts 4:24-25 and Ps. 2:1) Benjamin Warfield points out that these instances of the Scriptures being spoken of as if they were God, and of God being spoken of as if He were the Scriptures, could only result from a habitual identification, in the mind of the writer, of the text of Scripture with God speaking. It became natural, then, to use the term "Scripture said," and to use the term, "God says," when what was really intended was, "Scripture, the Word of God, says. . . ." "The two sets of passages, together, thus show an absolute identification of "Scripture" with the "speaking God." [1]

It is equally clear that New Testament writers have the same prophetic claim to authority as Old Testament writers. Jesus said that John the Baptist was a prophet and more than a prophet (Matt. 11:9-15). As Gordon Clark has put it, "He was superior to all the Old Testament prophets. Yet the prophet who was least in New Testament times was a greater prophet than John. It follows, does it not, that the New Testament prophets were no less inspired than their forerunners?" [2]

Paul claims prophetic authority: "If any man think himself to be a prophet, or spiritual, let him acknowledge that the things that I write unto you are the commandments of the Lord" (1 Cor. 14:37).

Peter speaks of Paul's letters as what some "wrest, as they do also the *other* Scriptures, unto their own destruction" (2 Peter 3:16). His reference to them on the same level as "the other Scriptures" shows that he viewed them as having the prophetic authority of Scripture.

Jesus' View of Scripture

Most significant of all, however, is our Lord's view of the Scripture. What did *He* think of it? How did *He* use it? If we can answer these questions, we have the answer of the incarnate Word of God Himself. Surely He is the authority for anyone who claims Him as Lord!

What was our Lord's attitude toward the Old Testament? He states emphatically, "Verily I say unto you, Till Heaven and earth pass, one jot or one tittle shall in no wise pass from the Law, till all be fulfilled" (Matt. 5:18). He quoted Scripture as final authority, often introducing the statement with the phrase, "It is written," as in His encounter with Satan in the temptation in the wilderness (Matt. 4). He spoke of Himself and of events surrounding His life as being fulfillments of the Scripture (Matt. 26:54, 56).

Perhaps His most sweeping endorsement and acceptance of the Old Testament was when He declared with finality, "The Scripture cannot be broken" (John 10:35).

If, then, we accept Jesus as Saviour and Lord, it would be a contradiction in terms, and strangely inconsistent, if we rejected the Scripture as the Word of God. On this point we would be in disagreement with the One whom we acknowledge to be the eternal God, the Creator of the universe.

Some have suggested that in His view of the Old Testament, our Lord accommodated Himself to the prejudices of His contemporary hearers. They accepted it as authoritative, so He appealed to it to gain wider acceptance for His teaching, though He Himself did not subscribe to the popular view.

Grave difficulties beset this thesis, however. Our Lord's recognition and use of the authority of the Old Testament was not superficial and unessential. It was at the heart of His teaching concerning His person and work. He would be guilty of grave deception, and much of what He taught would be based on a fallacy. Then, too, why would He accommodate Himself at this one point, when on other seemingly less important points He abrasively failed to accommodate Himself to the prejudices of the time? This is most clearly illustrated in His attitude toward the Sabbath. And we could ask an even more basic question: How do we know, if accommodation is His principle of operation, when He is accommodating Himself to ignorance and prejudice and when He is not!

Helpful Definitions

Several definitions will be of great help in our understanding the Bible as the Word of God.

• *Those who accept the Bible as the Word of God are often accused of taking the Bible* literally. The question "Do you believe the Bible literally" is like the question, "Have you stopped beating your wife?" Either a Yes or a No convicts the one who responds. Whenever the question is asked, the term *literally* must be carefully defined. Taking a literal view of the Bible does not mean we can't recognize that figures of speech are used in the Scripture. When Isaiah spoke of "trees clapping their hands" (Isa. 55:12), and the psalmist of "mountains skipping like rams" (Ps. 114:4,6), it is not to be thought that one who takes the Bible literally views such statements as literal. No, there is poetry as well as prose and other literary forms, in the Bible. We believe that the Bible is to be interpreted in the sense in which the authors intended it to be received by readers. This is the same principle one employs when reading the newspaper. And it is remarkably easy to distinguish between figures of speech and those statements a writer intends his readers to take literally.

This view is in contrast with that of those who do not take the Bible *literally*. They frequently attempt to evade the clear intent of the authority, suggesting that the biblical records of certain events (for instance, the fall of man, and miracles) are merely nonfactual stories to illustrate and convey profound spiritual truth.

Those holding this view say that as the truth of "Don't kill the goose that lays the golden egg" does not hinge on the literal factuality of Aesop's fable, so we need not insist on the historicity of biblical events and records to enjoy and realize the truth they convey. Some modern writers have applied this principle even to the cross and the resurrection of Jesus Christ. The expression "Taking the Bible literally," therefore, is ambiguous and must be carefully defined to avoid great confusion.

• *Another very important term we must clearly define is* inerrancy. What does it mean and what does it not mean? Considerable confusion can be avoided by clear definition at this point.

A temptation we must avoid is that of imposing on the biblical writers our 20th century standards of scientific and historical precision and accuracy. For instance, the Scripture describes things phenomenologically—that is as they *appear* to be. It speaks of the sun rising and setting. Now, we know that the sun does not actually rise and set, but that the earth rotates. But we use *sunrise* and *sunset* ourselves, even in an age of scientific enlightenment, because this is a convenient way of describing what appears to be. So we cannot charge the Bible with error when it speaks phenomenologically. Because it speaks in this way, it has been clear to men of all ages and cultures.

In ancient times there were not the same standards of exactness in historical matters. Sometimes round numbers are used rather than precise figures. When the police estimate a crowd we know the figure is not accurate, but it is close enough for the purpose.

Some apparent errors are obviously errors in transcription, which means that careful work is necessary in establishing the true text. We will discuss this more fully in the chapter on whether or not we can trust the Bible documents.

There are some other problems which as yet do not yield a ready explanation. We must freely admit this, remembering that many times, in the past, problems resolved themselves when more data became available. The logical position, then, would seem to be that where there are areas of apparent conflict, we must hold the problem in abeyance, admitting our present inability to explain, but awaiting the possibility of new data. The presence of problems does not prevent our accepting the Bible as the supernatural Word of God.

Carnell puts it succinctly:

There is a close parallel between science and Christianity which surprisingly few seem to notice. As Christianity assumes that all in the Bible is supernatural, so the scientist assumes that all in nature is rational and orderly. Both are hypotheses—based, not on all of the evidence, but on the evidence "for the most part." Science devoutly holds to the hypothesis that all of nature is mechanical, though as a matter of fact the mysterious electron keeps jumping around as expressed by the Heisenberg principle of uncertainty. And how does science justify its hypothesis that all of nature is mechanical, when it admits on other grounds that many areas of nature do not seem to conform to this pattern? The answer is that since regularity is observed in nature "for the most part," the smoothest hypothesis is to assume that it is the same throughout the whole.[3]

A helpful guide to apparent contradictions in the Bible is *Some Alleged Discrepancies in the Bible*, by John W. Haley (Gospel Advocate).

• *A further indication that the Bible is the Word of God is in the remarkable number of fulfilled prophecies it contains.* These are not vague generalities like those given by modern fortunetellers—"A handsome man will soon come into your life." Such predictions are susceptible to easy misinterpretation. Many Bible prophecies are specific in their details, and the authentication and veracity of the prophet rests on them. The Scripture itself makes it clear that fulfilled prophecy is one of the evidences of the supernatural origin of the word of its prophets (Jer. 28:9). Failure of fulfillment would unmask a false prophet: "If thou say in thine heart, How shall we know the word which the Lord hath not spoken? When a prophet speaketh in the name of the Lord, if the thing follows not, nor comes to pass, that is the thing which the Lord hath not spoken, but the prophet hath spoken it presumptuously; thou shalt not be afraid of him" (Deut. 18:21-22).

Isaiah ties the unmasking of false prophets to the failure of their predictive prophecy. "Let them bring them forth and show us what shall happen; let them show the former things, what they be, that we may consider them and know the latter end of them, or declare us things for to come. Show the things that are to come hereafter, that we may know that you are gods" (Isa. 41:22-23).

There are various kinds of prophecies. One group has to do with predictions of a coming Messiah, the Lord Jesus Christ. Others have to do with specific historical events, and still others with the Jews. It is very significant that the early disciples quoted the Old Testament prophecies frequently to show that Jesus fulfilled in detail the prophecies made many years earlier.

We can mention only a small but representative number of these prophecies. Our Lord refers to the predictive prophecies about

Himself in what must have been one of the most exciting Bible studies in history. After conversation with two disciples on the road to Emmaus, He said, "O fools, and slow of heart to believe all that the prophets have spoken. . . . And beginning at Moses and all the prophets, He expounded unto them in all the Scriptures the things concerning Himself" (Luke 24:25, 27).

Isaiah 52:13—53:12 is the most outstanding example of predictive prophecy about Christ. It is full of contingencies which could not be rigged in advance in an attempt to produce fulfillment. They involve His life, His rejection in ministry, His death, His burial, and His reactions to the unjust judicial proceedings.

Micah 5:2 is a striking illustration of both a prediction about Christ and historic detail. "But thou, Bethlehem Ephratah, though thou be little among the thousands of Judah, yet out of thee shall He come forth unto Me that is to be Ruler in Israel, whose goings forth have been from of old, from everlasting." It took a decree from the mighty Caesar Augustus to bring this event to pass.

Predictions dealt not only with the coming Messiah, but with kings, nations, and cities. Perhaps the most remarkable (Ezek. 26) has to do with the city of Tyre. Here a whole series of little details are given as to how Tyre would be destroyed, the utter completeness of its destruction, and the fact that it would never be reconstructed (v. 4). How this prophecy was fulfilled by degrees, in Nebuchadnezzar's attack and through the savage onslaught of Alexander the Great, is a phenomenal illustration of the accurateness and reality of predictive prophecy in the Bible.

Finally, there are the remarkable prophecies about the Jewish people, the Israelites. Again, only a few of these startling prophecies may be cited.

Their dispersion was predicted by Moses and Hosea. "The Lord shall cause thee to be smitten before thine enemies: thou . . . shalt be removed into all the kingdoms of the earth" (Deut. 28:25). "My God will cast them away, because they did not harken unto Him: and they shall be wanderers among the nations" (Hosea 9:17). Persecution and contempt were predicted: "I will deliver them to be removed into all the kingdoms of the earth for their hurt, to be a reproach and a proverb, a taunt and a curse, in all places whither I shall drive them" (Jer. 24:9). Jeremiah 31 makes the astonishing prediction of the restoration of Israel as a nation. For centuries, this was considered to be unthinkable. Some events in our own time, however, may well be at least partial fulfillment of these prophecies. All observers agree that the reestablishment of Israel as a nation, in 1948, is one of the amazing political phenomena of our day.

One cannot gainsay the force of fulfilled prophecy. Many prophecies could not possibly have been written after the events predicted.

The Holy Spirit's Role

There are, then, a number of pieces of evidence on which one can reasonably base his belief that the Bible *is* the Word of God. As helpful as these evidences are, the testimony of the Holy Spirit is what finally makes one believe that the Bible is the Word of God. As he surveys the evidence and as he reads the Bible, "it dawns on him," to use Gordon Clark's phrase, that the Bible is the Word of God.[4] This realization is the work of the Holy Spirit. But the work of the Spirit is always toward some purpose. This involves the giving of *reasons* for belief, and the explanation of the Scripture message itself.

The two disciples on the road to Emmaus asked, "Did not our hearts burn within us?" This same experience becomes ours as, by the Holy Spirit, we come to the conviction that the Bible is the Word of God, we feed on it, and we share it with others.

SIX

ARE THE BIBLE DOCUMENTS RELIABLE?

Several years ago a leading magazine carried an article purporting to show there are thousands of errors in the Bible.

How do we know that the text of the Bible as we have it today, having come to us through many translations and versions over the centuries, is not just a pale reflection of the original? What guarantee do we have that deletions and embellishments have not totally obscured the original message of the Bible? What difference does the historical accuracy of the Bible make? Surely the only thing that counts is the message!

But Christianity is rooted in history. Jesus Christ was counted in a Roman census. If the Bible's historical references are not true, grave questions may be raised about the reliability of other parts of the message based on historical events. Likewise, it is crucial for us to know that we have substantially the same documents in our time as people had almost 2,000 years ago. And how do we know the books we now have are the ones that should be in the Bible? Or that others should not be included? These questions are worthy of answers.

If we believe the Bible to be the Word of God verbally inspired, the job of establishing the text accurately is an extremely important one. This task is called textual criticism. It has to do with the reliability of the text, i.e., how our current text compares with the originals and how accurately the ancient manuscripts were copied.

Examining the Data

Let us briefly examine the data for the Old and New Testaments.

It is evident that the work of a scribe was a highly professional and carefully executed task. It was also a task undertaken by a devout Jew with the highest devotion. Since he believed he was dealing with the Word of God, he was acutely aware of the need for extreme care and accuracy. There are no complete copies of the Hebrew Old Testament earlier than around A.D. 900, but it seems evident that the text was preserved very carefully and faithfully since at least A.D. 100 or 200.

A check is provided by comparing some translations from the Hebrew into Latin and Greek at about this time. This comparison reveals the careful copying of the Hebrew text during this period. The text dating from around A.D. 900 is called the "Massoretic Text" because it was the product of Jewish scribes known as the "Massoretes." All of the present copies of the Hebrew text which comes from this period are in remarkable agreement, attesting to the skill of the scribes in proofreading.

But how could we know about the accuracy and authenticity of the text in pre-Massoretic times? The history of the Jews was very turbulent, raising questions as to the carefulness of the scribes during this hectic period.

The Dead Sea Scrolls

In 1947 the world learned about what has been called the greatest archeologic discovery of the century. In caves, in the valley of the Dead Sea, ancient jars were discovered containing the now famous Dead Sea Scrolls. From these scrolls, it is evident that a group of Jews lived at a place called Qumran from about 150 B.C. to A.D. 70. Theirs was a communal society, operated very much like a monastery. In addition to tilling the fields, they spent their time studying and copying the Scriptures. It became apparent to them that the Romans were going to invade the land. They put their leather scrolls in jars and hid them in caves in the side of the cliffs west of the Dead Sea.

In the providence of God the scrolls survived undisturbed until discovered accidentally by a wandering Bedouin goat herdsman in February or March of 1947. The accidental discovery was followed by careful exploration, and several other caves containing scrolls have been located. The find included the earliest manuscript copy yet known of the complete book of Isaiah, and fragments of almost every book in the Old Testament. In addition, there is a fragmented copy containing much of Isaiah 38—66. The Books of Samuel, in a tattered copy, were also found at that time, along with two complete chapters of Habakkuk. A number of nonbiblical items, including the rules of the ancient community, were also discovered.

The significance of this find, for those who wonder about the accuracy of the Old Testament text, can easily be seen. In one dramatic stroke, almost 1,000 years were hurdled in terms of the age of the manuscripts we now possess. By comparing the Dead Sea

Scrolls with the Massoretic text, we would get a clear indication of the accuracy, or lack of it, of transmission over the period of nearly a millennium.

What was actually learned? In comparing the Qumran manuscript of Isaiah 38—66 with the one we had, scholars found that:

> The text is extremely close to our Massoretic text. A comparison of Isaiah 53 shows that only 17 letters differ from the Massoretic text. Ten of these are mere differences of spelling, like our 'honor' or 'honour' and produce no change in the meaning at all. Four more are very minor differences, such as the presence of the conjunction, which is often a matter of style. The other three letters are the Hebrew word for 'light' which is added after 'they shall see' in verse 11. Out of 166 words in this chapter, only this one word is really in question, and it does not at all change the sense of the passage. *This is typical of the whole manuscript.*[1]

The Septuagint

Other ancient witnesses attest the accuracy of the copyists who ultimately gave us the Massoretic text. One of these is the Greek translation of the Old Testament, called the Septuagint. It is often referred to as the LXX because it was reputedly done by 70 Jewish scholars in Alexandria. The best estimate of its date seems to be around 200 B.C.

Up till the discovery of the Dead Sea Scrolls there was a question, when the LXX was different from the Massoretic text, why the variations existed. It is now apparent that the Massoretic text has not changed significantly since around 200 B.C. Other scrolls among those discovered show a type of Hebrew that is very similar to that from which the LXX was translated. The Samuel scroll especially resembles the reading of the LXX. The LXX appears to be a rather literal translation, and our manuscripts are pretty good copies of the original translation.

Another ancient witness is the evidence for a third type of text similar to that which was preserved by the Samaritans. Copies of the old scrolls of the Pentateuch are extant today in Nablus, Palestine.

Three Families of Texts

Three main types of text existed in 200 B.C. The question for us is, "What is the *original* version of the Old Testament, in the light of these three 'families' of texts to choose from?"

We can conclude with R. Laird Harris:

We can now be sure that copyists worked with great care and accuracy on the Old Testament, even back to 225 B.C. At that time there were two or three types of text available for copying. These types differed among themselves so little, however, that we can infer that still earlier copyists had also faithfully and carefully transmitted the Old Testament text. Indeed, it would be rash skepticism that would now deny that we have our Old Testament in a form very close to that used by Ezra when he taught the Law to those who had returned from the Babylonian captivity.[2]

What of the New Testament?

Again, based on the evidence, the conviction comes that we have in our hands a text which does not differ in any substantial particular from the originals of the various books as they came from the hands of the human writers. The great scholar, F. J. A. Hort, said that apart from insignificant variations of grammar or spelling, not more than one thousandth part of the whole New Testament is affected by differences of reading.[3]

The New Testament was written in Greek. More than 4,000 manuscripts of the New Testament, or of parts of it, have survived to our time. These are on different materials. Papyrus was the common material used for writing purposes at the beginning of the Christian era. It was made from reeds and was highly durable. In the last 500 years many remains of documents written on papyrus have been discovered, including fragments of manuscripts of the New Testament.

The second material of which Greek manuscripts were made is parchment. This was the skin of sheep or goats, polished with pumice. It was used until the late Middle Ages, when paper began to replace it.

The dates of the New Testament documents indicate that they were written within the lifetime of contemporaries of Christ. People were still alive who could remember the things He said and did. Many of the Pauline letters are even earlier than some of the Gospels.[4]

The evidence for the early existence of the New Testament writings is clear. The wealth of materials for the New Testament becomes even more evident when we compare it with other ancient documents which have been accepted without question. Bruce observes that only nine or ten good manuscripts of Caesar's *Gallic War* exist. The oldest of these manuscripts was written some 900 years after Caesar's time. The *History of Thucydides* (ca. 460-400 B.C.) is known to us from eight manuscripts, the earliest belonging to around A.D. 900, and a few papyrus scraps that belong to about the beginning of the Christian era. The same is true of the *History of Herodotus* (ca. 480-425 B.C.). However, no classical scholar would listen to an argument that the authenticity of Herodotus or Thucydides is in doubt because of the earliest manuscripts of their work which are of any use to us are more than 1,300 years later than the originals.[5]

By contrast there are two excellent manuscripts of the New Testament from the fourth century. Fragments of papyrus copies of books of the New Testament date from 100 to 200 years earlier still. Perhaps the earliest piece of data we have is a fragment of a papyrus codex containing John 18:31-33, 37. It is dated around A.D. 130.

More Evidence

The authenticity of the New Testament comes from other sources. These are the references and quotations of the New Testament books by both friends and enemies of Christianity. The Apostolic Fathers, writing mostly between A.D. 90 and 160, give indication of familiarity with most of the books of the New Testament.

It seems apparent, from recent discoveries, that the Gnostic school of Valentinus was also familiar with most of the New Testament.[6]

There are two other sources of data for establishing the authenticity of the New Testament books. The first source is the versions. Versions are those manuscripts which were translated from the Greek into other languages. Three groups of these are of the most significance: the Syriac versions, the Egyptian or Coptic versions, and the Latin versions. By careful study of the versions, important clues have been uncovered as to the original Greek manuscripts from which they were translated.

Finally, there is the evidence of the lectionaries, the reading lessons used in public church services. By the middle of the twentieth century more than 1,800 of these reading lessons had been classified. There are lectionaries of the Gospels, The Acts, and the Epistles. Though they did not appear before the sixth century, the text from which they quote may itself be early and of high quality.[7]

Though there have been many changes in the many copyings of the New Testament writings, most of them are minor. The science of textual criticism, which is very exacting, has enabled us to be sure of the true text of the New Testament. Rather than share the *alarm* of *Look* magazine at all the *errors* which it chose to call those minor variations in the Bible, we can rest with the conclusion of the late Sir Frederic Kenyon, a world-renowned scholar of the ancient manuscripts. He said, "The interval, then, between the dates of original composition and the earliest extant evidence becomes so small as to be in fact negligible, and the last foundation for any doubt that the Scriptures have come down to us substantially as they were written has now been removed. Both the authenticity and the general integrity of the books of the New Testament may be regarded as finally established." [8]

The Question of the Canon

A question closely allied to that of the reliability of the texts we have is, "How do we know the books in our Bible, and no others, are the ones that should be there?" This is called the question of the canon. There are distinct questions involved for Old and New Testaments.

The Protestant Church accepts identically the same Old Testament books as the Jews had, and as Jesus and the apostles accepted. The Roman Catholic Church, since the Council of Trent in 1546, includes the books of the Apocrypha. The order in the English Bible follows that of the Septuagint. This is different from the Hebrew Bible, in which the books are divided into three groups: the Law (Genesis to Deuteronomy), known also as the Torah or the Pentateuch; the Prophets, including the Former Prophets (Joshua, Judges, Samuel, Kings) and the Latter Prophets (Isaiah, Jeremiah, Ezekiel, and the Book of the Twelve—Hosea to Malachi); and the Writings, the remaining books of our Old Testament canon.

The books were received as authoritative because they were recognized as utterances of men inspired by God to reveal His Word. As E. J. Young says, "When the Word of God was written, it became Scripture, and inasmuch as it had been spoken by God, it possessed absolute authority. Since it was the Word of God, it was canonical. That which determines the canonicity of a book, therefore, is the fact that the book is inspired of God. Hence, a distinction is properly made between the authority which the Old Testament books possess as divinely inspired and the recognition of that authority on the part of Israel." [9]

We can see this development in the work of Moses. The laws issued by him and by the later prophets were intended to be respected as the decrees of God Himself. They were so regarded then and also by later generations. The Law was neglected, to be sure, but its authority was recognized by Israel's spiritual leaders. It was the recognition of this authority that shook Josiah when he realized how long the Law had been neglected (2 Kings 22:11).

When we examine the writings of the prophets, it is obvious that they believed they spoke with authority. "Thus saith the Lord" and "The Word of the Lord came unto me saying" are common preambles to their messages.

It is not clear on what grounds the authority of the writings was accepted. That it *was* accepted, however, *is* clear. In New Testament times it was customary to describe at least some of these writings as the utterances of the Holy Spirit.

By the beginning of the Christian era the term *Scripture* had come to mean a fixed body of divinely inspired writings that were fully recognized as authoritative. Our Lord used the term in this sense and was fully understood by His hearers when He said, "The Scripture cannot be broken" (John 10:35). It is interesting that there was no controversy between our Lord and the Pharisees on the authority of the Old Testament. Contention arose because they gave *tradition* the same authority as Scripture.

At the Council of Jamnia, in A.D. 90, informal discussions were held about the canon. Whether any formal or binding decisions were made is problematic. The discussion seemed to center not on whether certain books should be included in the canon, but whether certain ones should be excluded. In any case, those present recognized what already was accepted. They did not bring into being what had not previously existed. In other words, they *recognized* but did not *establish* the canonicity of the Old Testament books as we have them.

The Apocryphal Books

The Apocryphal books, it is important to note, were never received into the Jewish canon and were not considered as part of the inspired Scriptures by Jews or Christians in the early centuries of the Christian era. This is evident from a study of the writings of Josephus, the Jewish historian, and of Augustine, the great North African Bishop of Hippo.

It is interesting that the New Testament writers do not once quote the Apocrypha.

The Apocryphal books do not claim to be the Word of God or the work of prophets. They vary greatly in content and value. Some, like 1 Maccabees, were probably written around 100 B.C. and are valuable as historical background. Others are more characterized by legend and are of little value. Though not included at first, these books were later added to the LXX. In this way they came to be included by Jerome in the Latin Vulgate. Even Jerome, however, accepted only the books in the Hebrew Canon. He viewed the others as having ecclesiastical value only. He was in conflict with the later action of the Council of Trent, in Reformation times, which elevated the Apocrypha to canonical status.

For the Old Testament we have, ultimately, the witness of our Lord to the canonicity of the 39 books we now have.

What about the Books of the New Testament?

Here, as for the Old Testament, the books possessed canonicity by virtue of their inspiration, not by virtue of their being *voted* into canonicity by any group. The history of the recognition of the New Testament's canonicity, however, is interesting. Much of the material of the New Testament claimed apostolic authority. Paul and Peter clearly wrote with this authority in mind. Peter specifically refers to Paul's letters as Scripture (2 Pet. 3:15-16).

Jude (v. 18) says 2 Peter 3:3 is a word from the apostles. Such early Church Fathers as Polycarp, Ignatius, and Clement mention a number of the New Testament books as authoritative.

The onslaught of heresy in the middle of the second century caused the concept of a canon to be revived in the thinking of Christians. What was authoritative and what was not came to be clearly delineated. Irenaeus and later Eusebius, in the third century, give us more light in their writings. The final fixation of the canon as we know it came in the fourth century. In the East, a letter of Athanasius in A.D. 367 clearly distinguishes between works in the canon which are described as the sole sources of religious instruction and others which believers were permitted to read. In the West, the canon was fixed by decision of a church council held at Carthage in A.D. 397.

Three criteria were generally utilized, throughout this period of time, to establish that particular written documents were the true record of the voice and message of apostolic witness. First, could authorship be attributed to an apostle? The Gospels of Mark and Luke do not meet this criterion specifically, but were accepted as the works of close associates of the apostles. Secondly, there was the matter of ecclesiastical usage—that is, recognition of a book by a leading church or majority of churches. Third, conformity to standards of sound doctrine.

These data are helpful and interesting, but in the final analysis, as with the question of the inspiration of the Scripture, canonicity is a question of the witness of the Spirit in the hearts of God's people.

In days of uncertainty, what a rock the Scripture is on which to stand! "Heaven and earth shall pass away," says our Lord, "but My Word shall never pass away!"

SEVEN

DOES ARCHEOLOGY HELP?

One of the strange paradoxes of our time is the extent to which more and more people are questioning the reliability of the Scripture, in spite of the fact that there is greater evidence than ever for its trustworthiness. More than a century ago critics questioned many historical statements in the Old Testament. They thought them fictional and highly imaginative. But our century is one of unprecedented discovery, and these discoveries have for the most part substantiated the biblical record. The statements of nonevangelical scholars are significant. Dr. W. F. Albright, professor emeritus of Johns Hopkins University says, "There can be no doubt that archeology has confirmed the substantial historicity of Old Testament tradition." [1]

Millar Burrows of Yale states:

On the whole, however, archeological work has unquestionably strengthened confidence in the reliability of the scriptural record. More than one archeologist has found his respect for the Bible increased by the experience of excavation in Palestine.[2] Archeology has in many cases refuted the views of modern critics. It has shown, in a number of instances, that these views rest on false assumptions and unreal, artificial schemes of historical development. This is a real contribution and not to be minimized.[3]

Sir Frederic Kenyon, a former director of the British Museum, writes:

It is therefore legitimate to say that, in respect of that part of the Old Testament against which the disintegrating criticism of the last half of the nineteenth century was chiefly directed, the evidence of archeology has been to reestablish its authority and likewise to augment its value by rendering it more intelligible through fuller knowledge of its background and setting. Archeology has not yet said its last word, but the results already achieved confirm what faith would suggest—that the Bible can do nothing but gain from an increase in knowledge.[4]

More recently, Nelson Glueck, renowned Jewish archeologist, made the remarkable statement, "No archeological discovery has ever controverted a biblical reference." [5]

Clearly then, archeology is of great value in giving us a clearer understanding of the biblical record and message by enabling us to understand the background into which it is set. It is also clear that certain points of apparent conflict between the biblical record and the information previously available have been cleared up as more information has been obtained. It would seem, then, that the logical attitude toward a still existing area of apparent conflict would be to hold the matter in abeyance. Rather than conclude that the Bible must be wrong, it would seem much more reasonable to admit the problem exists and to hold it open pending further discoveries. Since new discoveries, time after time in the past, have tended to confirm the Scripture, this would certainly be a more reasonable attitude than declaring the Bible wrong unequivocally.

Having said all this, however, it is important to point out that we cannot *prove* the Bible by archeology, nor do we *believe* the Bible on the basis of archeological *proof*. It is the Holy Spirit who ultimately confirms the truth of the Scripture to us. Spiritual truth can never be confirmed by archeology. But we can be thankful for the historical details which have been confirmed by archeology even though we recognize the apparent conflicts that still exist.

Specific Ways in Which Archeology Has Been of Help

More than 25,000 sites showing some connection with the Old Testament period have been located in Bible lands. Relatively few have been explored, so a wealth of material awaits discovery.

The largest body of evidence for comparison with Scriptures is found in the ancient Eastern inscriptions. Few contemporary documents from Old Testament times have been found in Palestine. Illustrations must be drawn from the writings of neighboring countries.

Another major source of information for comparison with biblical narratives has been the archeological excavation of biblical sites.

The field of information and correlation with biblical data is vast, so we can spotlight only a few of the major facets.

The life and times of Abraham are a good example of the help archeology can be to us. Critics of the latter part of the last century and the early years of this one were very dubious about the historicity of the biblical account of Abraham. They thought he was an ignorant nomad and quite primitive. They felt he would be unable to read and would have no more knowledge of law, history, commerce, and geography than a Bedouin sheik in the Arabian desert today. They believed that for him to move from Ur to Haran was merely a minor nomadic shift. But the discoveries of Sir C. Leonard Woolley in his excavations at Ur of the Chaldees have shown these ideas to have been serious mistakes.

We have discovered that the Ur of Abraham's time was a highly developed city. Archeologists have unearthed advanced housing and many clay tablets which were the equivalent of books. Some of these were receipts for business transactions; others were temple hymns; others were mathematical tables with formulae for calculating square and cube roots as well as simpler sums. In the temple storerooms, receipts were found for numberless objects—sheep, cheese, wool, cooper ore, oil for lubrication of hinges—and payrolls for female employees. It is all very practical and curiously modern.[6]

It "became clear that Abraham was a product of a brilliant and highly developed culture, and that it must have meant a good deal for him to leave by faith for unknown lands."[7]

How Can These Finds Be Dated?

These ancient cities were built and rebuilt on the same site, so that a whole succession of levels is usually found, the lowest naturally being the oldest. Fashions in pottery changed, and if at one excavated site a particular fashion can be dated, similar pottery found elsewhere will be of the same period. Kings usually inscribed their names on the hinge-sockets of temple doors, and the name of the god would be given. Inscribed stones were often laid under palace or temple walls in memory of the founder. Royal sepulchres can usually be identified in the same way. There exist copies, dating back before 2000 B.C., of lists drawn up by Sumerian scribes of the kings according to the successive dynasties with notes as to the lengths of their reigns. A few miles from Ur an inscribed foundation-stone was found, laid by a king of unknown name, of the First Dynasty of Ur, which the scribes speak of as the third dynasty after the Flood. This king seems to have reigned 3,100 years before Christ, more than a thousand years before Abraham.[8]

The Biblical Kings

Archeology provides considerable background information for the study of the biblical kings. Critics have questioned the historicity of these accounts. The accounts of Solomon's grandeur have met special skepticism. The Bible speaks of him as having a navy (1 Kings 9:26), though there is no suitable harbor on the coastline of Palestine. It describes his wealth as being staggering, the number of his horses and chariots as astounding (10:26). His building projects were numerous and extensive. He fortified the cities of Jerusalem, Hazor, Gezer, and Megiddo (9:15). Extensive excavation has been undertaken at Megiddo. Interesting details of this military installation have come to light. Of particular interest are Solomon's stables.

A wide paved street led from the city gate of Megiddo to the stables of Solomon. The southern stable compound measured about 70 by 92 yards. A row of five stable units faced north and opened onto a courtyard or parade ground approximately 60 yards on a side. A wall, more than a yard thick in some places, was then built around the grounds to prevent the sand from washing away. Near the center of the courtyard was a sunken cistern of mud-dried bricks which was probably used as a water tank for the horses; this was capable of holding some 2,775 gallons of water. Two rectangular rooms along one side of the enclosure probably served as chariot garages.

Each stable unit consisted of a central passage about ten feet wide, floored with lime plaster. On either side of this was an aisle of similar width, separated from the central passageway by a row of stone pillars alternating with stone mangers which had troughs measuring about five feet in width and paved with rubble. Each aisle was 26 yards in length and cared for 15 horses, making a total of 150 for the southern compound.[9]

Solomon's casting of metals is mentioned in 2 Kings. In the excavation of Ezion-Geber one of the most spectacular finds was the blast furnace. Nelson Glueck says, "The finest and largest smelting and refining plant ever discovered in the ancient Near East has been unearthed at the northwest corner of the site. It was provided with a complicated system of flues and air channels almost modern in aspect and function."[10] The fierce winds which blew through the Arabah to the north were harnessed to eliminate the necessity of artificial bellows. To this refinery in Solomon's seaport was brought ore which had been partially processed in ovens along the length of the southern Arabah (the valley extending from the south end of the Dead Sea to the Red Sea). Most of the present knowledge of these Arabah mining sites depends also upon the work of Nelson Glueck. For instance, he excavated Khirget Hahas (Arabic for "copper ruin") about 21 miles south of the Dead Sea. Ores were surface-mined near here and put through the initial roasting process.

> The site is oblong, pointed north and south. A semicircular range of high sandstone hills surrounds it. On the east is a small wadi (a stream that does not flow during the dry season). Between the hills on the south and west, with the wadi on the east and north sides, lies a large flat area packed with ruins of walls, large buildings, miners' huts, smelting furnaces, and huge heaps of black copper slag. Two furnaces, a square and a circular one, are almost intact. The square one is of roughly hewn blocks three yards square and contains two compartments, one above the other.[11]

A remarkable memorial, commemorating one of the few incidents in the history of Moab of which we have any record, has survived. After Ahab died, Mesha, the king of Moab, threw off the yoke of Jehoram, Ahab's son, and refused to pay tribute. He was put under siege by the kings of Israel, Judah, and Edom. So great was the pressure that Mesha finally offered his eldest son on the wall as a burnt offering to Chemosh, the god of the Moabites. What happened then is not clear, but the implication is that the three kings had to abandon their siege.

In 1868 a German named Klein found an inscribed stone at Dibon, in the land of Moab. While he was back in Europe to raise money for its purchase, the Arabs roasted the stone and threw cold water over it to break it into pieces and so get a larger price. Fortunately, an impression had been taken of the intact stone, so it was possible to restore the fragments and read the inscription. The stone is now at the Louvre in Paris. The inscription is an early form of the Phoenician alphabet and describes how the stone was set up by Mesha, king of Moab, to tell how he, with the help of Chemosh his god, had thrown off the yoke of the king of Israel. A number of biblical place-names are mentioned and the God of Israel is called Yahweh.[12]

New Testament Research

Archeological research and discovery for the New Testament has been of a different nature than for the Old. It is not so much a matter of digging for buried buildings or inscribed tablets; rather, New Testament archeology is primarily a matter of written documents.

These documents may be public or private inscriptions on stone or some equally durable material: they may be papyri recovered from the sand of Egypt recording literary texts or housewives' shopping lists; they may be private notes scratched on fragments of unglazed pottery; they may be legends on coins preserving information about some otherwise forgotten ruler or getting some point of official propaganda across to the people who used them. They may represent a Christian church's collection of sacred Scriptures, like the Chester Beatty Biblical Papyri; they may be all that is left of the library of an ancient religious community, like the scrolls from Qumran or the Gnostic texts from Nag Hammadi. But whatever their character, they can be as important and relevant for the study of the New Testament as any cuneiform tablets are for the study of the Old.[13]

Papyrus documents have yielded a wealth of information. The common people wrote letters on papyrus and kept the ordinary commercial accounts of life on it. An even cheaper writing material was broken pieces of pottery, called *ostraca*. These were used for odd notes. One of the great significances of these materials, discovered in ancient rubbish heaps, has been to show the connection between the everyday language of the common people and the Greek in which most of the New Testament is written. It has long been recognized that there are great differences between the Greek of classic literature and that of the New Testament. Some scholars went so far as to suggest that New Testament Greek was a heavenly language which came into being for the purpose of recording Christian revelation. But through the discoveries of the papyri it became evident that the New Testament Greek was very similar to the language of the common people.

In 1931 the discovery of a collection of papyrus texts of the Greek Scriptures was made public. They have come to be known as the "Chester Beatty Biblical Papyri." F. F. Bruce says that this collection evidently formed the Bible of some outlying church in Egypt; it comprises 11 fragmentary codices. Three of these, in their complete state, contained most of the New Testament. One contained the Gospels and Acts, another Paul's nine letters to churches and the Epistle to the Hebrews, and a third the Revelation. All three were written in the third century. The Pauline codex, oldest of the three, was written at the beginning of that century. Even in their present mutilated state, these papyri bear most important testimony to the early textual history of the New Testament. They have provided most valuable evidence for the identification of the "Caesarean" text-type.[14]

These examples show the importance of papyrus discoveries.

Stone Inscriptions

Inscriptions on stone have been another source of valuable information. An example of this is an edict of Claudius inscribed on limestone at Delphi in central Greece. "This edict is to be dated [as originating] during the first seven months of A.D. 52, and mentions Gallio as being proconsul of Achaia. We know from other sources that Gallio's proconsulship lasted only for a year, and since proconsuls entered on their term of office on July 1, the inference is that Gallio entered on his proconsulship on that date in A.D. 51. But Gallio's proconsulship of Achaia overlapped Paul's year and a half of ministry in Corinth (Acts 18:11-12) so that Claudius' inscription provides us with a fixed point for reconstructing the chronology of Paul's career." [15]

Luke makes so many specific references to people and places that his writings are more easily illustrated by this kind of material than other parts of the New Testament. His accuracy of detail has been thoroughly established. Where he has been questioned, new evidence has vindicated him a number of times. Bruce points out:

> For example, his reference in Luke 3:1 to "Lysanias, the tetrarch of Abilene," at the time when John the Baptist began his ministry A.D. 27 has been regarded as a mistake because the only ruler of that name in those parts known from ancient historians was King Lysanias, whom Antony executed at Cleopatra's instigation in 36 B.C. But a Greek inscription from Abila (18 miles west-northwest of Damascus), from which the territory of Abilene is named, records a dedication to one Nymphaeus, "freeman of Lysanias, the tetrarch" between A.D. 14-29, around the very time indicated by Luke.[16]

Early Relics

An unusual bit of data was discovered in 1945. Eleazar L. Sukenik found two ossuaries, or receptacles for bones, in the vicinity of the Jerusalem suburb of Talpioth. The burial chamber in which these were found was in use during the years preceding A.D. 50. It is possible, says Bruce, "that here we have relics from the Christian community in Jerusalem during the first 20 years of its existence." [17]

Coins have provided some background information for parts of

New Testament history. One of the crucial questions in establishing the chronology of Paul's career is the date of Felix's replacement by Festus as procurator of Judea (Acts 24:27). A new Judean coinage begins in Nero's fifth year, before October of A.D. 59. This may point to the beginning of the new procuratorship.

Some sacred sites have been definitely identified, and general locations have also been identified. General locations have been more easily established than exact spots where some of the great New Testament events transpired. Jerusalem was destroyed in A.D. 70 and a new pagan city was founded on the site in A.D. 135. This has complicated the identification of places in Jerusalem mentioned in the Gospels and Acts. Some, however, like the temple area and the pool of Siloam, to which our Lord sent the blind man to wash (John 9:11), have been clearly identified.

Archeology is a real help in understanding the Bible. It yields fascinating information which illuminates what might otherwise be obscured, and in some instances confirms what some might otherwise regard as doubtful.

We can agree with Sir Frederic Kenyon when he says:

> To my mind, the true and valuable thing to say about archeology is, not that it proves the Bible, but that it illustrates the Bible. . . . The contribution of archeology to Bible study has been to [illuminate] the Bible narrative, and especially of the Old Testament. . . . The trend of all this increased knowledge has been to confirm the authority of the books of the Old Testament while it illuminates their interpretation. Destructive criticism is thrown on the defensive; and the plain man may read his Bible confident that, for anything that modern research has to say, the Word of our God shall stand forever." [18]

EIGHT

ARE MIRACLES POSSIBLE?

"Do you really believe Jonah was swallowed by a whale? And do you seriously think that Christ *actually* fed 5,000 persons from five loaves of bread and two fish?" So goes the trend and tone of many modern questioners. Surely, they say, these "miracle" stories in the Bible must be quaint ways of conveying spiritual truth, and they are not meant to be taken literally.

With many questions, it is more important to discern the root problem than to become involved in discussing a twig on a branch. This is especially true of questions about miracles. The questioner's problem is generally not with a particular miracle, but with a whole principle. To establish the miracle in question would not answer his question. His controversy is with the whole principle of the possibility of miracles.

The Whole Concept of God
One who has problems with miracles often has difficulty with the validity of predictive prophecy. These problems stem from a weak view of God. The real problem is not with miracles or prophecy, but with the whole concept of God. Once we assume the existence of God, there is no problem with miracles, because God is by definition all-powerful. In the absence of such a God, however, the concept of miracles becomes difficult, if not impossible, to entertain.

This came to me very forcibly one day as I was talking about the deity of Christ with a Japanese professor friend. "I find it very difficult to believe," he said, "that a man could become God." Sensing his problem, I replied, "Yes, Kinichi, so do I, but I can believe that God became a man." He saw the difference in a flash, and not long afterward he became a Christian.

God Is Not Bound By Natural Law
The question, then, really is, "Does an all-powerful God, who

202

created the universe, exist?" If so, we shall have little difficulty with miracles in which He transcends the natural law of which He is the Author. It is important to keep this fundamental question in mind in discussing miracles.

Why we know God exists has already been discussed.

David Hume and others have defined a miracle as a violation of natural law. To take such a position, however, is practically to deify natural law, to capitalize it in such a way that whatever God there may be becomes the prisoner of natural law and, in effect, ceases to be God.

In this modern scientific age, men tend to personify science and natural law. They fail to realize that these are merely the impersonal results of observation. A Christian believes in natural law— i.e., that things behave in a certain cause-and-effect way almost all the time. But in maintaining this he does not restrict God's right and power to intervene when and how He chooses. God is over, above, and outside natural law, and is not bound by it.

Laws do not *cause* anything in the sense that God causes things. They are merely descriptions of what happens.

What, in Fact, Is a Miracle?

We use the term rather loosely today. If a scared student passes an exam he says, "It was a miracle!" Or if an old jalopy makes a successful trip from one city to another, we say, "It's a miracle the thing ran!" We use the term to mean anything that is unusual or unexpected. We do not necessarily mean that the hand of God has been at work.

In discussing miracles as they are thought of in the Bible, however, the word is used in an entirely different sense. Here we mean an act of God breaking into, changing, or interrupting the ordinary course of things.

To be sure, the Bible records various kinds of miracles, and some of them *could* have a *natural* explanation. For instance, the parting of the Red Sea was accomplished by the *natural* cause of the high winds which drove the waters back. Perhaps this *could* have happened apart from God's intervention. The miraculous part was the timing. That the waters should part just as the Israelites reached the shore, and should close on the Egyptians as they were in hot pursuit, and after every Israelite was safely on dry land, clearly proves the miraculous intervention of God.

Without Natural Explanations

On the other hand, there are many miracles for which there are no *natural* explanations. The resurrection of Lazarus from the dead and the resurrection of our Lord involved forces unknown to us and outside the realm of so-called natural law. The same is true with many of the miraculous healings. It has been fashionable to explain these in terms of psychosomatic response. We know today that many illnesses, rather than having an organic origin, originate in the mind. If the mental condition is corrected, the physical condition rights itself. Some medical authorities estimate that 80 percent of the illnesses in our pressurized society are psychosomatic.

Undoubtedly there was an element of this dimension in our Lord's healings, but some were clearly outside this category. Take, for instance, the healings of leprosy. Obviously these did not have a psychosomatic base. Lepers who were made well experienced the direct power of God. Then there are the clear cases of healing of congenital disease, such as the man born blind (John 9). Since this man was born with his blindness, it could obviously not be accounted for on a psychosomatic basis, and for the same reasons neither could his receiving his sight.

This case illustrates the fallacy of another notion common among modern thinkers. We must remember, it is said, that people in ancient times were exceedingly ignorant, gullible, and superstitious. They thought many things were miracles that we now know, with the benefit of modern science, were not miracles at all, but simply phenomena which people didn't understand. For instance, if we were to fly a modern jet over a primitive tribe today, they would probably fall to the ground in worship of this Silver Bird God of the sky. They would think that the sight they observed was a miraculous phenomenon. We, however, know that the plane is simply a result of the applied principles of aerodynamics, and we realize there is nothing miraculous about it at all.

The problem with this thesis, which sounds so plausible at first, is that many of the miracles are not of this order. In the case of the blind man, the people observed that since the beginning of time it had not been known for a man born blind to receive his sight. And we have no more *natural* explanation of this miracle now than was available then. And who, today, has any more explanation, in a natural sense, of our Lord's resurrection from the dead than was available when it happened? No one! We simply cannot get away from the supernatural aspects of the biblical record.

Not in Conflict with Natural Law

It is important to note, however, that miracles are not in conflict with natural law. Rather, "Miracles are *unusual* events caused by God. The laws of nature are generalizations about ordinary events caused by Him." [1]

There are two views among thinking Christians as to the relationship of miracles to natural law. Some suggest that miracles employ a "higher" natural law, which at present is unknown to us. It is quite obvious that despite all of the impressive discoveries of modern science, we are still standing on the seashore of an ocean of ignorance. When we have increased our knowledge sufficiently, this thesis says, we will realize that the things we today thought were miracles were merely the working out of higher laws of the universe, of which we were not aware at the time.

But a *law*, in the modern scientific sense, is that which is regular and acts uniformly. To say that a miracle is the result of a higher *law*, then, is to use the term in a way that is different from its customary usage and meaning.

An Act of Creation

On the other hand, there are those Christian thinkers who view miracles as an act of creation—a sovereign, transcendent act of God's supernatural power. It would seem that this is the more appropriate view.

Biblical miracles, in contrast to miracle stories in pagan literature and those of other religions, were never capricious or fantastic. They are not scattered helter-skelter through the record without rhyme or reason. There was always clear order and purpose to them. They cluster around three periods of biblical history; the Exodus, the prophets who led Israel, and the time of Christ and the early church. They always had as their purpose to confirm faith by authenticating the message and the messenger, or to demonstrate God's love by relieving suffering. They were never performed as entertainment, as a magician puts on a show for his patrons.

Miracles were never performed for personal prestige or to gain money or power. Our Lord was tempted by the devil in the wilderness to use His miracle power in just this way, but He steadfastly refused. As an evidence of the truth of the Christian message, however, our Lord referred to miracles frequently. In answer to the direct request of the Jews to tell them plainly if He was the Messiah, He said, "I told you, and you believed not; the works that I do in My Father's name, they bear witness of Me" (John 10:25). Again He says that if they had any hesitation in believing His claims they should believe Him "for the very works' sake" (14:11).

God confirmed the message of the apostles in the fledgling church with signs and wonders.

Why Not Now?

The question is often raised, "If God performed miracles *then*, why does He not do them *now?* If I *saw* a miracle I could believe!" This question was answered in our Lord's time. A rich man who was in the torment of hell lifted up his eyes and pleaded with Abraham that someone should warn his five brothers lest they too should come into the awful place. He was told that his brothers had the Scriptures. But the rich man protested that if one should rise from the dead, they would be shaken by the miracle and would take heed. The reply given applies as much today as then: "They have Moses and the prophets," Abraham said, "and if they hear not Moses and the prophets, neither will they be persuaded though one rose from the dead" (Luke 16:19-31). And so it is today. Many have made a rationalistic presupposition which rules out the very possibility of miracles. Since they *know* miracles are impossible, no amount of evidence would ever persuade them one had taken place. There would always be an alternate naturalistic explanation for them to advance.

We Have Reliable Records

Miracles are not necessary for us today because we already have reliable records of those miracles which have occurred. As Ramm observes, "If miracles are capable of sensory perception, they can be made matters of testimony. If they are adequately testified to, then the recorded testimony has the same validity for evidence as the experience of beholding the event." [2]

Every court in the world operates on the basis of reliable testimony by word of mouth or in writing. "If the raising of Lazarus was actually witnessed by John and recorded faithfully by him when still in soundness of faculties and memory, for purposes of evidence it is the same as if we were there and saw it." [3] Ramm then lists reasons we may know that the miracles have adequate and reliable testimony. We summarize:

• *First, many miracles were done in public.* They were not performed in secret before only one or two people, who announced them to the world. There was every opportunity to investigate the miracles on the spot. It is very impressive that the opponents of Jesus never denied the fact of the miracles He performed. They either attributed them to the power of Satan or else tried to suppress the evidence, as with the raising of Lazarus from the dead. They said, "Let's kill Him before the people realize what is happening and the whole world goes after Him!"

• *Second, some miracles were performed before unbelievers.* It is significant that the miracles claimed by cults and offbeat groups never seem to happen when the skeptic is present to observe. It was not so with Jesus.

• *Third, the miracles of Jesus were performed over a period of time and involved a great variety of powers.* He had power over nature, as when He turned the water to wine; He had power over disease, as when he healed the lepers and the blind; He had power over demons, as was shown by His casting them out; He had supernatural powers of knowledge, as in His knowing that Nathaniel was under a fig tree; He demonstrated His power of creation when He fed 5,000 people from a few loaves and fish; and He exhibited power over death itself in the raising of Lazarus and others.

• *Fourth, we have the testimony of the cured.* As noted earlier, we have it from those, like Lazarus, whose healings could not possibly have been psychosomatic or the result of inaccurate diagnosis.

• *Fifth, we cannot discount the Gospel miracles because of the extravagant claim of pagan miracles.*

Miracles are believed in non-Christian religions because the religion is already believed, but in the biblical religion, miracles are part of the means of establishing the true religion. This distinction is of immense importance. Israel was brought into existence by a series of miracles, the Law was given surrounded by supernatural wonders, and many of the prophets were identified as God's spokesmen by their power to perform miracles. Jesus came not only preaching but performing miracles, and the apostles from time to time worked wonders. It was the miracle authenticating the religion at every point.[4]

As C. S. Lewis writes, "All the essentials of Hinduism would, I think, remain unimpaired if you subtracted the miraculous, and the same is almost true of Muhammadanism, but you cannot do that with Christianity. It is precisely the story of a great Miracle. A naturalistic Christianity leaves out all that is specifically Christian."[5]

Pagan Miracles

Miracles recorded outside the Bible do not display the same order, dignity and motive as those in Scripture. But what is more important, they do not have the same solid authentication as the biblical miracles. We have discussed at some length the historical reliability of Bible records. Similar investigations into pagan records of miracles would soon show there is no basis for comparison.

The same could be said of many so-called miracles and alleged healings of our own time. They do not stand the full weight of investigation. But to take some ancient pagan miracle, or a contemporary claim, and to show their great improbability is not fair to biblical miracles. The fact that some miracles are counterfeits is no proof that *all* are spurious, any more than the discovery of some counterfeit currency would prove all currency spurious.

Exaggerated Reporting
Some attempts have been made to explain miracles on the basis of exaggerated reporting. It has been demonstrated that people are notoriously inaccurate in reporting events and impressions. Playing the simple parlor game of *rumor* is enough to confirm this fact. In the light of this tendency, we are told, it is obvious that the reliability of a human being as an observer may be severely questioned. Consequently, we can discount the Gospel accounts of miracles as the mistaken observations of inaccurate and imaginative observers.

It may be answered that despite this tendency, law courts have not ceased functioning, and eye-witnesses are still considered able to provide highly useful information. And though there may be some question about such details of an accident as the time, speed of the cars, etc., the accident cannot be said not to have happened because of discrepancies in witnesses' stories. As Ramm observes, the smashed cars and the injured people are irrefutable evidence on which all agreed.[6]

We must be careful to see the limitations of arguments such as the unreliability of witnesses. It will help us greatly to see that some of these arguments, pressed to their outer limits, refute the very assertions they set out to make. For instance, those conducting the experiments to establish the unreliability of human witnesses must assume their own reliability or they will have to throw out their own conclusions as being the result of human observation, which is unreliable!

Believers Can't Be Objective
Another erroneous idea, sometimes advanced, is that the miracle stories must be discarded because they are told by believing disciples and are therefore not *objective*. But the disciples were the ones on the scene who saw the miracles. The fact that they were disciples is neither here nor there. The question is, "Did they tell the truth?" As we have seen, eyewitness testimony is the best we can get, and most of the disciples faced the test of death as the test of their veracity.

We would not today, in a court of law, say that in order to guarantee objectivity on the part of witnesses, we will listen only to those who were not at the scene of an accident and had nothing to do with it. Nor would we say we would not take testimony from eyewitnesses, including the victims, because they would be *prejudiced*. The crucial question in each case is truthfulness, not proximity or relationship to the events.

The Question Is Philosophical

We have seen that the question of whether miracles are possible is not scientific, but philosophical. Science can only say miracles do not occur in the ordinary course of nature. Science cannot *forbid* miracles because natural laws do not cause, and therefore cannot forbid, anything. They are merely descriptions of what happens. The Christian embraces the concept of natural law. "It is essential to the theistic doctrine of miracles that nature be uniform in her daily routine. If nature were utterly spontaneous, miracles would be as impossible of detection as it would be to establish a natural law." [7]

It is "scientism," rather than science, which says miracles cannot happen. The scientist, like anyone else, can only ask, "Are the records of miracles historically reliable?"

Further, we have seen the miracles in the Bible are an inherent part of God's communication to us—not a mere appendage of little significance. We have seen that the whole question ultimately depends on the existence of God. Settle that question and miracles cease to be a problem. The very uniformity against which a miracle stands in stark contrast depends on an omnipotent Author of natural law, Who is also capable of transcending it to accomplish His sovereign ends.

NINE

DO SCIENCE AND SCRIPTURE CONFLICT?

If ever there was a question the attemped answer to which has generated more heat than light, this is it. Most of the apparent conflict stems from making the Bible say things it really does not say and from *scientism,* a philosophic interpretation of facts. These interpretations are distinct from the facts themselves.

To the question, "Have some scientists and some Christians conflicted?" the answer would have to be a resounding "Yes!" We need only recall the church's persecution of Galileo, the Scopes trial of 1925, or the unfortunate confrontation a century ago between Bishop Wilberforce and T. H. Huxley, to know this is the case.

Dating Creation

Part of the problem, as we have indicated, stems from some well-meaning but misguided Christians who make the Bible say what it does not say. One classic and harmful example is the Bible chronology which was calculated by Bishop James Ussher (1581-1656), a contemporary of Shakespeare. He worked out a series of dates from the genealogies in the Bible and concluded that the world was created in 4004 B.C.

It is thought by many non-Christians, including the famous Lord Bertrand Russell, that Fundamentalists actually believe creation occurred in 4004 B.C. Some time ago I was visiting a non-Christian student on a Midwestern state university campus. He picked up a true-false exam in a course on Western Civilization. One question read, "According to the Bible, the world was created in 4004 B.C."

"I suppose your instructor wants you to mark this question true," I said.

"That's right," the student replied.

"Interesting," I mused. Pulling an Oxford edition of the Bible from my pocket, I said, "I wonder if you could show me where the Bible says that."

The student was puzzled that he couldn't immediately find the date on the first page of Genesis. Trying to be helpful, the Christian student who was with me volunteered, "It's on page 3."

It was news to both of them that Bishop Ussher's dates, which appear in many (but not *all*) English Bibles, are not part of the original text.

On the other hand, some scientists are given to making statements that go beyond the facts. These statements are, in fact, philosophic interpretations of data which do not carry the same weight of authority as the data themselves. Unfortunately, the facts and the interpretations are seldom distinguished in the minds of listeners.

When a Scientist Speaks

When a scientist speaks on *any* subject, he is likely to be believed. He may be speaking outside his field, but the same respect that should rightfully be given to his statements from *within* his field are almost unconsciously transferred to *everything* he says. For instance, Anthony Standen quotes R. S. Lull, professor of paleontology at Yale, as saying, "Since Darwin's day, evolution has been more and more generally accepted, until now, in the minds of informed thinking men, there is no doubt that it is the only logical way whereby creation can be interpreted and understood. We are not so sure as to the *modus operandi,* but we may rest assured that the process has been in accordance with great natural laws, some of which are as yet unknown and are perhaps unknowable." [1]

But one may be tempted to ask, "If some of the great natural laws are as yet unknown, how do we know they are there? And if some of them are perhaps unknowable, how do we know they are *logical?*"

Honest Differences

If we limit ourselves to what the Bible actually says and to what the scientific facts actually are, we shrink the area of controversy enormously. It should be noted here that there may be honest differences of opinion among equally orthodox and committed Christians as to what the Bible means in some instances—for instance, the meaning of *day* in Genesis 1. We must be slow to condemn as a heretic someone whose interpretation of a particular passage may differ from ours. As long as one agrees that what the Bible teaches is authoritative, he is within the bounds of orthodoxy. It is when one admits the Bible is teaching something clearly, like a historic Adam (Rom. 5) but does *not accept* it, that he has crossed the line of biblical orthodoxy.

Faith Is Suspect

Another area in which conflict has arisen is on the question of whether those things which cannot be verified by the scientific method are valid and real. Some people consciously, and others unconsciously, assume that if a statement cannot be proved in a laboratory by the methods of natural science, it is untrustworthy and cannot be accepted as reliable. The findings of science are considered to be objective and therefore real; statements that must be accepted by faith are looked upon as suspect.

But there are ways and means other than the laboratory to acquire real and genuine knowledge. Consider the process of falling in love. This surely is not done in a laboratory, with a battery of instruments, but anyone who has ever experienced it would be the last to admit that his knowledge of love is uncertain or unreal. We have seen earlier that the scientific method is valid only for those realities which are measurable in physical terms. God is a different kind of reality from the world of nature which science examines. God does not await man's empirical investigation; He is a personal Being who has revealed Himself in love and can be known in personal presence.

Scientific Methods

Faith is no detriment to the apprehension of reality. In fact, science itself rests on presuppositions which must be accepted by faith before research is possible. One such assumption is that the universe is orderly, that it operates according to a pattern, and that therefore one can predict its behavior.

It should be observed here that the scientific method, as we know it today, began in the 16th century among men who were Christians. Breaking with the Greek polytheistic concepts which viewed the universe as capricious and irregular, and therefore not capable of systematic study, they reasoned that the universe must be orderly and worthy of investigation because it was the work of an intelligent Creator. In pursuing scientific research, they were convinced they were thinking God's thoughts after Him.

Another unprovable presupposition that must be accepted by faith is the reliability of our sense perceptions. One must believe that our senses are trustworthy enough to get a true picture of the universe and enable us to understand the orderliness we observe.

Science Is Only One Way to Truth

Christians, then, believe that science is one avenue to the discovery of truth about physical things, but that there are other nonmaterial realities and other means of attaining truth. A Christian exercises faith and has presuppositions, as does a scientist, and in this he sees nothing incompatible with reason or intelligence. It is apparent that there are many Christians who are scientists. They do not consider themselves intellectual schizophrenics, but rather view themselves as following in the footsteps of the Christian founders of modern science.

It should further be recognized that science is incapable of making value judgments about the things it measures. Many men on the frontiers of science are realizing that there is nothing inherent in science to guide them in the application of the discoveries they make. There is nothing in science itself which will determine whether nuclear energy will be used to destroy cities or destroy cancer. This is a judgment outside the scientific method to determine.

Further, science can tell us how something works but not *why* it works that way. Whether there is any purpose in the universe can never be answered for us by science. As one writer put it, "Science can give us the 'know-how,' but it cannot give us the 'know-why.' " [2]

We are dependent on revelation for many kinds of information, the absence of which leaves us with a quite incomplete picture. The Bible does not purport to tell us the *how* of many things, but it clearly gives us the *whys*.

This is not to say that when the Scriptures refer to matters of science and history they are inaccurate, but rather to point out the focus of their attention.

A Valuable Virtue

Humility, then is a valuable virtue for a non-Christian scientist and for a Christian, be he scientist or not. Incalculable harm has been done by the use of argument by ridicule. A sarcastic remark is always good for a long loud laugh from some of the faithful, but invariably it loses the thoughtful person, wavering in his conviction, and the timid unbeliever making his first tentative investigation.

Some have erroneously thought that God was necessary to explain areas of life and existence for which at the moment there was no other explanation. Unbelieving scientists seize on this concept to point out that these gaps are narrowing. "Give us enough time," they say, "and man will be able to explain how everything in the universe works."

Those who adopt this point of view forget that God is not only Creator, but also Sustainer. "He is before all things, and by Him all things consist" (Col. 1:17). The universe would fall apart without His sustaining power. Even if man understands and explains everything, he will still need God. Knowing how the universe is sustained is not the same thing as sustaining it.

For instance, there is much talk today about the possibility of scientists creating life in a test tube. (It should be noted that one's definition of life has much to do with how close he thinks he is to the threshold of creating it.) Some earnest Christians fear that should this event take place, God will somehow have been torn from His throne. But what in fact would have happened? What will it prove? Only that life did not come by blind chance, but by an intelligent mind. It will be apparent to even the most simpleminded that this new *life* has not come into being by the random coincidence and interaction of matter, but as a result of prodigious thought and work under the most rigidly controlled conditions. It would clearly argue for theism. And we still must account for the elements used to produce life. Where did *they* come from? The most logical explanation is that God made them. If man can, in fact, think God's thoughts after Him, it should not be so inconceivable that man may be able to bring life out of a test tube—but he has not thereby become God.

Evolution

Perhaps no greater contemporary battleground is being faced daily by evangelical Christians in educational institutions than the question of evolution. The very word starts the adrenal glands working overtime. Part of the tension arises from casting the problem into black-and-white terms. Many think that either a person believes in total fiat creation or he is an agnostic or atheistic evolutionist.

Whenever the term *evolution* is used, however, we should be careful to define what we mean and to ask others, when they use it, to define what they mean. There are many theories on evolution. Ramm has a helpful list.[3]

Different Brands

• *First there is an anti-Christian, naturalistic theory of evolution.* Evolution as a theory has been expanded to fields far outside biology and, in fact, has become for many a philosophy of life which explains history, society, and religion. With this expansion of the theory of evolution into a philosophy of life there is no common ground with evangelical Christianity. We repudiate it completely.

Not all who hold a form of evolution fit into this category, however. There are those who hold it in a spiritual context. The modern Thomistic interpretation of evolution says that evolution is merely the way God chose to work, and that there would be no evolution if there were no God.

• *Then there is the theory of emergent evolution.* Those holding this view believe life and mind appeared miraculously. From original life to mind, life kept emerging on higher and higher levels. The new levels were not reached by chance evolution, but were sudden and novel appearances.

• *Then there are a few people in the evangelical camps who hold to theistic evolution.* They see no conflict between this view and their Christian faith. Among them were such stalwarts as James Orr and A. G. Strong. Most orthodox Catholic theologians also believe in theistic evolution.

The above is merely to show that the alternatives are not fiat creation and atheistic evolution. And in evangelism, it is useless to get into a discussion of evolution. I first ask an evolutionist whether he is concluding from his position that there is no God and that everything happened by chance, or whether he concedes God is the Author of life. If he accepts the latter, I confront him directly with Jesus Christ. *He* is the real issue in salvation, not one's view of evolution. When the issue of Christ is settled, other less important ones settle themselves in due course.

Two extremes must be avoided. First is the assumption that evolution has been proved without doubt and that anyone with a brain in his head must accept it. The second is the notion that evolution is "only a theory," with little evidence for it.

A Constantly Moving Train

Scientific theory is a matter of the highest degree of probability based on the data available. There are no absolutes in it. Furthermore, science is a train that is constantly moving. Yesterday's generalization is today's discarded hypothesis. This is one reason for being somewhat tentative about accepting any form of evolutionary theory as the final explanation of biology. It is also why it is dangerous to try to *prove* the Bible by science. If the Bible becomes wedded to today's scientific theories, what will happen to it when science, ten years from now, has shifted?

Thoughtful evolutionists are ready to concede that the matter is not an open-and-shut case, but they feel the theory must be accepted despite some seeming contradictions and unexplained factors.

The following is of such interest that I quote it at length to illustrate this point. After discussing how pathetically theology students at Cambridge, in a former century, accepted dogma and teachings they did not fully understand or personally investigate, G. A. Kerkut, an evolutionist, points out that many present-day undergraduates have succumbed to the same unthinking tendencies in their studies in general, and in accepting evolution in biology in particular.

For some years now (he writes), I have tutored undergraduates on various aspects of biology. It is quite common, during the course of conversation, to ask the student if he knows the evidence for evolution. This usually evokes a faintly superior smile. . . . "Well, sir, there is the evidence from paleontology, comparative anatomy, embryology, systematics, and geographical distributions," the student would say in a nursery rhyme jargon, sometimes even ticking off the words on his fingers. He would then sit and look fairly complacent and wait for a more difficult question, such as the nature of the evidence for natural selection. Instead I would continue on evolution.

"Do you think that the evolutionary theory is the best explanation yet advanced to explain animal interrelationships?" I would ask.

"Why, of course, sir," would be the reply. "There *is* nothing else, except for the religious explanation held by some fundamentalist Christians, and I gather, sir, that these views are no longer held by the more up-to-date churchmen."

"So you believe in evolution because there is no other theory?"

"Oh, no, sir, I believe in it because of the evidence I just mentioned."

"Have you read any book on the evidence for evolution?" I would ask.

"Yes, sir." And here he would mention the names of authors of a popular school textbook. "And of course, sir, there is that book by Darwin, *The Origin of Species*."

"Have you read this book?" I would ask.

"Well, not all through, sir."

"The first 50 pages?"

"Yes, sir, about that much; maybe a bit less."

"I see. And that has given you your firm understanding of evolution?"

"Yes, sir."

"Well, now, if you really understand an argument you will be able to indicate to me not only the points in favor of the argument, but also the most telling points against it."

"I suppose so, sir."

"Good. Please tell me, then, some of the evidence against the theory of evolution."

"But there isn't any, sir."

Here the conversation would take on a more strained atmosphere. The student would look at me as if I were playing a very unfair game. He would take it rather badly when I suggested that he was not being very scientific in his outlook if he swallowed the latest scientific dogma and, when questioned, just repeated parrot-fashion the views of the current Archbishop of Evolution. In fact he would be behaving like certain of those religious students he affected to despise. He would be taking on faith what he could not intellectually understand and, when questioned, would appeal to authority of a "good book," which in this case was *The Origin of Species.* (It is interesting to note that many of these widely quoted books are read by title only. Three of such that come to mind are the Bible, *The Origin of Species,* and *Das Kapital.*)

I would suggest that the student should go away and read the evidence for and against evolution and present it as an essay. A week would pass and the same student would appear armed with an essay on the evidence for evolution. The essay would usually be well done, since the student might have realized that I should be rough to convince. When the essay had been read and the question concerning the evidence against evolution came up, the student would give a rather pained smile. "Well, sir, I looked up various books but could not find anything in the scientific books against evolution. I did not think you would want a religious argument."

"No, you were quite correct. I want a scientific argument against evolution."

"Well, sir, there does not seem to be one, and that in itself is a piece of evidence in favor of the evolutionary theory."

I would then indicate to him that the theory of evolution was of considerable antiquity, and would mention that he might have looked at the book by Radi, *The History of Biological Theories.* Having made sure the student had noted the book down for future reference I would proceed as follows:

Before one can decide that the theory of evolution is the best explanation of the present-day range of forms of living material, one should examine all the implications that such a theory may hold. Too often the theory is applied to, say, the development of the horse, and then, because it is held to be applicable there, it is extended to the rest of the animal kingdom with little or no further evidence.

There are, however, seven basic assumptions that are often not mentioned during discussions of evolution. Many evolutionists ignore the first six assumptions and consider only the seventh.

The first assumption is that nonliving things gave rise to living material, i.e., that spontaneous generation occurred.

The second assumption is that spontaneous generation occurred only once.

The third . . . is that viruses, bacteria, plants, and animals are all interrelated.

The fourth . . . is that the protozoa gave rise to the metazoa.

The fifth . . . is that the various invertebrate phyla are interrelated.

The sixth . . . is that the invertebrates gave rise to the vertebrates.

The seventh . . . is that the vertebrates and fish gave rise to the amphibia, the amphibia to the reptiles, and the reptiles to the birds and mammals. Sometimes this is expressed in other words, i.e., that the modern amphibia and reptiles had a common ancestral stock, and so on.

For the initial purposes of this discussion on evolution I shall consider that the supporters of the theory of evolution hold that all these seven assumptions are valid, and that these assumptions form the general theory of evolution.

The first point that I should like to make is that *the seven assumptions by their nature are not capable of experimental verification.* [Italics mine.] They assume that a certain series of events has occurred in the past. Thus, though it may be possible to mimic some of these events under present-day conditions, this does not mean that these events *must* therefore have taken place in the past. All that it shows is that it is *possible* for such a change to take place. Thus, to change a present-day reptile into a mammal, though of great interest, would not show the way in which the mammals *did* arise. Unfortunately, we cannot bring about even this change; instead we have to depend upon limited circumstantial evidence for our assumptions, and it is now my intention to discuss the nature of this evidence.[4]

As Ramm observes, "There as yet remains the proof of the inorganic origin of life. It may be assumed, but it is not yet verified. There is the problem of the rugged species which have endured without change for millions of years. There is the problem of the sudden appearance of new forms in the geologic record."[5] It is erroneous to speak of the missing link. In fact there are thousands of missing links.

There is the further problem of the apparent conflict of the evolutionary theory with the second law of thermodynamics. This is also called the law of entropy. It says, in essence, that "in any energy transfer or change, though the total amount of energy remains unchanged, the amount of usefulness and availability that the energy possesses is always decreased." [6] Evolution and entropy are seemingly incompatible. The universe is running down, not building up. As Ramm says, "We are faced clearly with the two theories of (1) the recoverability of energy and (2) the irrecoverability of energy. If energy is irrecoverable we are faced with the doctrine of creation. To this hour no known process of recoverability is proven." [7]

The Definition of Species
Much of the problem and controversy over evolution hinges on the definition of species. It seems to me that once this is understood a good bit of hassling among evangelicals becomes unnecessary. If we identify species as we know them scientifically today with the term *kind* in Genesis 1, then we have enormous problems when we speak of the fixity of species. But this is an incorrect identification. Even so staunch an antievolutionist as Henry M. Morris says in the following:

> It is well to observe . . . that the Bible does not teach the fixity of species, and for this simple reason no one knows just what a species is. There are few issues more alive among biologists today than this matter of what constitutes a species. *Certainly, according to many definitions of the term, many new species have been evolved since the original creation* [italics mine]. Genetic research has proved conclusively that chromosome changes, gene mutation, and hybridization can produce, and in fact, have produced, many distinctly new varieties in both plants and animals. These varieties are often considered new species, or even genera, by most modern methods of classification.
>
> However, all evidence thus far in the genetic field seems to prove conclusively that these agencies of change cannot go beyond certain comparatively narrow limits, and can very definitely not produce new kinds. The Genesis account merely says that each created group was to produce *after its kind,* with no clear indication as to what constitutes a *kind,* except the implication that different kinds would not be interfertile (if they were, they would not be reproducing after their respective kinds). Thus, the biblical account leaves ample room for just such conditions of change within the smaller groups, and stability within the larger groups, as is indicated by modern discovery. [8]

In the same vein, Russell Mixter says:

"As a creationist I am willing to accept the origin of species from other species, called micro-evolution." [9] He rejects macro-evolution, which would be evolution of everything from one original. Carnell likewise thinks there is a wide possibility of change within the kinds originally created by God. These variations, however, cannot cross certain prescribed boundaries. He says, "Observe therefore that the conservative may scrap the doctrine of the 'fixity of species' also without jeopardizing his major premise in the least." [10]

We reiterate that the so-called conflicts of science and the Bible are often conflicts between interpretations of the facts.

The presupposition one brings to the facts, rather than the facts themselves, determines one's conclusion. For instance, one might be told that his wife was seen riding around town with another man. Knowing his wife, he draws a different conclusion from this fact than does the town gossip. The different conclusions result, not from different facts, but from different presuppositions brought to the fact.

In everything we read and in everything we hear we must ask, "What is this person's presupposition?" so that we may interpret conclusions in this light. There is no such thing as total objectivity, in science or in anything else.

While there are problems for which there is as yet no explanation, there is no fundamental conflict between science and Scripture.

TEN

WHY DOES GOD ALLOW SUFFERING AND EVIL?

This is one of the most pressing questions of our time. More pressing than the question of miracles or science and the Bible is the poignant problem of why innocent people suffer, why babies are born blind, or why a promising life is snuffed out as it is on the rise. Why are there wars in which thousands of innocent people are killed, children burned beyond recognition, and many maimed for life?

In the classic statement of the problem, either God is all-powerful but not all-good, and therefore doesn't stop evil; or He is all-good but unable to stop evil, in which case He is not all-powerful.

The general tendency is to blame God for evil and suffering and to pass on all responsibility for it to Him.

No Easy Answers
This profound question is not one to be treated lightly or in a doctrinaire fashion. We must never forget that when God created man, He created him perfect. Man was not created evil. He did, however, as a human being, have ability to obey or disobey God. Had man obeyed God there would never have been a problem. He would have lived an unending life of fellowship with God and enjoyment of Him and His creation. This is what God intended for man when He created him. In fact, however, the first man rebelled against God—and every one of us has ratified that rebellion. "Wherefore, as by one man sin entered into the world, and death by sin; and so death passed upon all men, for that all have sinned" (Rom. 5:12). The point we must keep in mind is that *man* is responsible for sin—not God.

But many ask, "Why didn't God make us so we couldn't sin?" To be sure, He *could* have, but let's remember that if He had done so we would no longer be human beings, we would be machines.

How would you like to be married to a chatty doll? Every morning and every night you could pull the string and get the beautiful words, "I love you." There would never be any hot words, never any conflict, never anything said or done that would make you sad! But who would want that? There would never be any love, either. Love is voluntary. God could have made us like robots, but we would have ceased to be men. God apparently thought it worth the risk of creating us as we are. In any case He did it and we must face the realities.

God Could Stamp Out Evil!

Jeremiah reminds us, "It is of the Lord's mercies that we are not consumed, because His compassions fail not" (Lam. 3:22). A time is coming when He will stamp out evil in the world. The devil and all his works will come under eternal judgment. In the meantime, God's love and grace prevail and His offer of mercy and pardon is still open.

If God were to stamp out evil today, He would do a *complete* job. We want Him to stop war but stay remote from us. If God were to remove evil from the universe, His action would be complete and would have to include our lies and personal impurities, our lack of love, and our failure to do good. Suppose God were to decree that at midnight tonight *all* evil would be removed from the universe—who of us would still be here after midnight?

God Has Done Something About the Problem of Evil

He has done the most dramatic, costly, and effective thing possible by giving His Son to die for evil men. It is possible for man to escape God's inevitable judgment on sin and evil. It is also possible to have its power broken by entering into a personal relationship with the Lord Jesus Christ. The ultimate answer to the problem of evil, at the personal level is found in the sacrificial death of Jesus Christ.

To speculate about the origin of evil is endless. No one has the full answer. It belongs in the category of "the secret things [that] belong unto the Lord our God" (Deut. 29:29).

Part of our problem arises from our limited definition of the word *good* and our applying this term to God. Hugh Evan Hopkins observes:

In his famous essay on Nature, John Stuart Mill clearly sets out the problem with which thinkers all through history have wrestled: If the law of all creation were justice and the Creator omnipotent, then in whatever amount suffering and happiness might be dispensed to the world, each person's share would be exactly proportioned to that person's good or evil deeds. No human being would have a worse lot than another without worse deserts; accident or favoritism would have no part in such a world, but every human life would be playing out a drama constructed like a perfect moral tale. Not even on the most distorted and contracted theory of good which ever was framed by religious or philosophical fanaticism can the government of nature be made to resemble the work of a being at once both good and omnipotent.[1]

The problem arises largely from the belief that a *good* God would reward each man according to his deserts and that an *almighty* God would have no difficulty in carrying this out. The fact that rewards and punishments, in the way of happiness and discomfort, appear to be haphazardly distributed in this life drives many to question either the goodness of God or His power.[2]

Exact Reward Concept

But would God be good if He were to deal with each person exactly according to his behavior? Consider what this would mean in your own life! The whole of the Gospel as previewed in the Old Testament and broadcast in stereo-television in the New Testament is that God's goodness consists not *only* in His justice but also in His love, mercy, and kindness. How thankful we and all men should be that "He hath not dealt with us after our sins; nor rewarded us according to our iniquities. For as the heaven is high above the earth, so great is His mercy toward them that fear Him" (Ps. 103: 10-11).

Such a concept of the goodness of God is also based on the faulty assumption that happiness is the greatest good in life. Happiness is usually thought of in terms of comfort. True, genuine, deep-seated happiness, however, is something much more profound than the ephemeral fleeting enjoyment of the moment. And true happiness is not precluded by suffering. Sometimes, in His infinite wisdom, God knows that there are things to be accomplished in our character that can be brought only through suffering. To shield us from this suffering would be to rob us of a greater good. Peter refers to this when he says, "But the God of all grace, who hath called us unto His eternal glory by Christ Jesus, after that you have suffered awhile, make you perfect, stablish, strengthen, settle you" (1 Pet. 5:10).

To see the logical consequence of Mill's *exact reward* concept of God in His dealings with us, we need only turn to Hinduism. The law of Karma says that all of the actions of life today are the result of the actions of a previous life. Blindness, poverty, hunger, physical deformity, outcastness, and other social agonies are all the out-working of punishment for evil deeds in a previous existence.

It would follow that any attempt to alleviate such pain and mis-ery would be an interference with the just ways of God. This con-cept is one reason why the Hindus did so little for so long for their unfortunates. Some enlightened Hindus today are talking about and working toward social progress and change, but they have not yet reconciled this new concept with the clear, ancient doctrine of Karma, which is basic to Hindu thought and life.

This Karma concept, however, *does* serve as a neat, simple, clearly understood explanation of suffering: suffering is all the result of previous evil-doing.

But is there not a sense in which it is true that Christianity also holds that suffering is punishment from God?

Certainly, in the minds of many, it is. "What did I do to deserve this?" is often the first question on the lips of a sufferer. And the conviction of friends, expressed or unexpressed, frequently operates on this same assumption. The classic treatment of the problem of suffering and evil in the Book of Job shows how this cruel assump-tion was accepted by Job's friends. It compounded his already stag-gering pain.

It is clear from the teaching of both the Old and the New Testa-ment that suffering *may* be the judgment of God, but that there are many instances when it is totally unrelated to personal wrongdoing. An automatic assumption of guilt and consequent punishment is totally unwarranted.

To be sure, God is not a sentimental, beard-stroking, grand-father of the sky with a "boys-will-be-boys" attitude. "Whatsoever a man soweth, that shall he also reap" (Gal. 6:7) is a solemn warn-ing to any who would tweak God's nose in arrogant presumption. God afflicted Miriam with leprosy for challenging the authority of Moses, her brother, whom God had appointed leader. He took the life of David's child, born of his adulterous relationship with Bath-sheba.

Other examples could be cited. In the New Testament we have the startling example of Ananias and Sapphira, who were struck dead for lying, cheating, and hypocrisy. That there may be a con-nection between suffering and sin is evident, but that it is not al-ways so is abundantly clear. We have the unambiguous word of our Lord Himself on the subject. The disciples apparently adhered to the direct retribution theory of suffering. One day when they saw a man who had been blind from birth, they wanted to know who had sinned to cause this blindness—the man or his parents. Jesus made it clear that neither was responsible for his condition, "but that the works of God should be made manifest in him" (John 9:1-3).

On receiving word of some Galileans whom Pilate had slaughtered, Jesus went out of his way to point out that they were not greater sinners than other Galileans. He said that the 18 people who had been killed when the tower of Siloam fell on them were not greater sinners than others in Jerusalem. From both incidents He made the point, "Except you repent, you shall all likewise perish" (Luke 13:1-3).

Clearly, then, we are jumping the gun if we assume automatically, either in our own case or in that of another, that the explanation of any given tragedy or suffering is the judgment of God. Further, as Hopkins observes, it seems clear from biblical examples that if one's troubles are the just rewards of misdeeds, the sufferer is never left in any doubt when his trouble is a punishment.

Judgment Preceded by Warning

Indeed, one of the profound truths of the whole of Scripture is that the judgment of God is preceded by warning. Throughout the Old Testament we have the repeated pleadings of God and warning of judgment. Only after warning is persistently ignored and rejected does judgment come. God's poignant words are an example. "I have no pleasure in the death of the wicked; . . . turn you, turn you from your evil ways, for why will you die, O house of Israel?" (Ezek. 33:11)

The same theme continues in the New Testament. What more moving picture of God's love and long-suffering is there than our Lord as He weeps over Jerusalem, "O Jerusalem, Jerusalem . . . how often would I have gathered thy children together, even as a hen gathereth her chickens under her wings, and you would not!" (Matt. 23:37) And we have the clear word of Peter that "the Lord is . . . not willing that any should perish, but that all should come to repentance" (2 Pet. 3:9).

When the question, "How could a good God send people to hell?" comes up, we should point out that, in a sense, God sends no one to hell. Each person sends himself. God has done all that is necessary for us to be forgiven, redeemed, cleansed, and made fit for heaven. All that remains is for us to receive this gift. If we refuse it, God has no option but to give us our choice. Heaven, for the person who does not want to be there, would be hell.

Though the judgment of God sometimes explains suffering, there are several other possibilities to consider. Man, as we saw earlier, was responsible for the coming of sin and death into the universe.

We must not forget that his wrongdoing is also responsible for a great deal of misery and suffering in the world today. Negligence in the construction of a building has sometimes resulted in its collapse in a storm, with consequent death and injury. How many lives have been snuffed out by the murder of drunken driving? The cheating, lying, stealing, and selfishness which are so characteristic of our society today all reap a bitter harvest of suffering. But we can hardly blame God for it! Think of all the misery that has its origin in the wrongdoing of man—it is remarkable how much suffering is accounted for in this way.

The Presence of an Enemy

But man is not alone on this planet. By divine revelation we know of the presence of an enemy. He appears in various forms, we are told, appropriate to the occasion. He may appear as an angel of light or as a roaring lion, depending on the circumstances and his purposes. His name is Satan. It was he whom God allowed to cause Job to suffer. Jesus, in the parable of the good seed and the tares, explains the ruining of the farmer's harvest by saying, "An enemy hath done this" (Matt. 13:28). Satan finds great pleasure in ruining God's creation and causing misery and suffering. God allows him limited power, but he cannot touch the one in close fellowship with God. "Resist the devil and he will flee from you" (James 4:7), we are assured. Nevertheless Satan accounts for some of the disease and suffering in the world today.

In answer to the question of why God allows Satan power to bring suffering, we can learn from Robinson Crusoe's answer to his Man Friday.

"Well," says Friday, "you say God is so strong, so great; has He not as much strong, as much might as the devil?"

"Yes, yes," says I; "Friday, God is much stronger than the devil."

"But if God much strong, much might as the devil, why God no kill the devil so make him no more do wicked?"

"You may as well ask," answers Crusoe reflectively, "Why does God not kill you and me when we do wicked things that offend Him?"

God Feels Our Suffering

In considering pain and suffering, whether it be physical or mental, another important consideration must be kept in mind. God is not a distant, aloof, impervious potentate, far removed from His people and their sufferings. He not only is aware of suffering—He *feels* it. No pain or suffering has ever come to us that has not first passed through the heart and hand of God. However greatly we may suffer, it is well to remember that God is the great Sufferer. Comforting are the words of Isaiah the prophet, foretelling the agony of Christ: "He is despised and rejected of men, a Man of sorrows and acquainted with grief" (Isa. 53:3). The writer of Hebrews reminds us, "For in that He himself hath suffered being tempted, He is able to succor them that are tempted" (Heb. 2:18). And "We have not a High Priest which cannot be touched with the feeling of our infirmities, but was in all points tempted like as we are, yet without sin" (Heb. 4:15).

The problem of evil and suffering is one of the profound problems of the ages. It is becoming increasingly acute in our time, with the advent of the Bomb. There are no easy answers, and we do not have the last word. There are, however, clues.

Risky Gift of Free Will
First, as J. B. Phillips has put it:

> Evil is inherent in the risky gift of free will.[3] God could have made us machines, but to do so would have robbed us of our precious freedom of choice, and we would have ceased to be human. Exercise of free choice in the direction of evil, in what we call the "fall" of man, is the basic reason for evil and suffering in the world. It is man's responsibility, not God's. He could stop it, but in so doing would destroy us all. It is worth noting "that the whole point of real Christianity lies not in interference with the human power to choose, but in producing a willing consent to choose good rather than evil." [4]

Unless the universe is without significance, the actions of every individual affect others. No man is an island. To have it otherwise would be like playing a game of chess and changing the rules after every move. Life would be meaningless.

Second, much of the suffering in the world can be traced directly to the evil choices men and women make. This is quite apparent when a holdup man kills someone. Sometimes it is less apparent and more indirect, as when crooked decisions are made in government or business that may bring deprivation and suffering to many people unknown to those who make the decisions. Even the results of natural disasters are sometimes compounded by man's culpability in refusing to heed warnings of tidal waves, volcanic eruptions, floods, etc.

Third, some—but not all—suffering is allowed by God as judgment and punishment. This is a possibility which must always be considered. God usually allows such suffering with a view to restoration and character formation, and those suffering as a result of their deeds usually know it.

Fourth, God has an implacable enemy in Satan. He has been defeated at the Cross, but is free to work his evil deeds until the final judgment. That there is in the world a force of evil stronger than man himself is clear from revelation and from experience.

Fifth, God Himself is the great Sufferer and has fully met the problem of evil in the gift of His own Son, at infinite cost to Himself. The consequence of evil for eternity is forever removed as we embrace the Lord Jesus Christ. Our sin is forgiven and we receive new life and power to *choose* what is right as the Holy Spirit forms the image of Christ in us.

Greatest Test of Faith

Perhaps the greatest test of faith for the Christian today is to believe that God is good. There is so much which, taken in isolation, suggests the contrary. Helmut Thielecke of Hamburg points out that a fabric viewed through a magnifying glass is clear in the middle and blurred at the edges. But we know the edges are clear because of what we see in the middle. Life, he says, is like a fabric. There are many edges which are blurred, many events and circumstances we do not understand. But they are to be interpreted by the clarity we see in the center—the cross of Christ. We are not left to guess about the goodness of God from isolated bits of data. He has clearly revealed His character and dramatically demonstrated it to us in the Cross. "He that spared not His own Son, but delivered Him up for us all, how shall He not with Him also freely give us all things?" (Rom. 8:32)

God never asks us to understand; we need only trust Him in the same way we ask that our child only trust *our* love, though he may not understand or appreciate our taking him to the doctor.

Peace comes when we realize we are able to see only a few threads in the grand tapestry of life and God's will, and that we do not have the full picture.

Then we can affirm, with calm relief and joy, that "all things work together for good to them that love God, to them who are the called according to His purpose" (Rom. 8:28).

At times it is our reaction to suffering, rather than the suffering itself, that determines whether the experience is one of blessing or of blight. The same sun melts the butter and hardens the clay.

When by God's grace we can view all of life through the lens of faith in God's love, we can affirm with Habakkuk, "Although the fig tree shall not blossom, neither shall fruit be in the vine; the labor of the olive shall fail, and the fields shall yield no meat; the flock shall be cut off from the fold, and there shall be no herd in the stalls. Yet I will rejoice in the Lord, I will joy in the God of my salvation" (Hab. 3:17-18).

ELEVEN

DOES CHRISTIANITY DIFFER FROM OTHER WORLD RELIGIONS?

This question is asked frequently in our shrinking modern world. There is, currently, a meeting of cultures, nations, races, and religions on a scale unprecedented in history. In this jet age we are no more than 24 hours away from any spot on the earth. Television brings the coronation of a pope, the burning of a Buddhist monk, and a Muslim ceremony conducted by a political leader into our living rooms.

Almost 250,000 students from more than 150 countries of the world come to the United States every year to study in more than 2,000 colleges and universities in every one of the 50 states. Brightly colored saris on graceful Indian women and striking turbans on erect Sikhs are not unfamiliar sights in our metropolitan areas or small college towns. In addition, there are multiplied thousands of diplomatic, business, and tourist visitors every year.

Many of these visitors find their way into Parent-Teacher Association meetings, service clubs, and churches to speak on their cultural and religious backgrounds. They are sincere, educated, and intelligent. They are often interested in learning about Christianity, and we may learn from them.

As one has contact with these friends from overseas and becomes aware of their religious beliefs, the question naturally arises as to whether or not Christianity is unique among world religions. Or is it only a variation on a basic theme running through all religions? To put it another way, "Does not the sincere Muslim, Buddhist, Hindu, or Jew worship the same God as we do, but under a different name?" Or, quite bluntly, "Is Jesus Christ the *only* way to God?"

In answering this question, it is extremely important that we first empty it of its potentially explosive emotional content. When a Christian asserts that Jesus Christ is the only way to God, and that apart from Him there is no salvation, he is not suggesting that he thinks he is—or that Christians in general think they are—better than anyone else. Some people erroneously view Christians as having formed a bigoted club, like a fraternity with a racial segregation clause. If only the fraternity and the Christians were less bigoted, such people think, they would vote to change their membership rules and, in the case of the Christians, let in anyone who believes in God. "Why bring Jesus Christ into it?" we are often asked. "Why can't we just agree on God?" And this brings us to the fundamental issue.

Christians assert that Jesus Christ is the only way to God because Scripture says, "There is none other name under heaven given among men whereby we must be saved" (Acts 4:12). Christians believe this, not because they have made it *their* rule, but because Jesus Christ our Lord taught it (John 14:6). A Christian cannot be faithful to his Lord and affirm anything else. He is faced with the problem of truth. If Jesus Christ is who He claims to be, then we have the authoritative word of God Himself on the subject. If He is God and there is no other Saviour, then obviously He is the *only* way to God. Christians could not change this fact by a vote or by anything else.

It is helpful to point out, to those who ask this question, that there are some laws the penalty for which is socially determined. There are other laws of which this is not true. For instance, the penalty for driving through a stop light is determined by society. It is not inherent in the act itself. The penalty could be set at $25 or at $5, or it could be abolished completely.

With the law of gravity, however, the penalty for violation is not socially determined. People could vote unanimously to suspend the law of gravity for an hour, but no one in his right mind would jump off the roof to test it! No, the penalty for violating that law is inherent in the act itself, and the person who violated it would be picked up with a blotter despite the unanimous resolution!

As there are inherent physical laws, so there are inherent spiritual laws. One of them is God's revelation of Himself in Christ. Another is Christ's death as the only atonement for sin.

In proclaiming the exclusiveness of Christ, a Christian does not assume a superior posture. He speaks as a sinner saved by grace. As D. T. Niles, of Ceylon, so beautifully put it, "Evangelism is just one beggar telling another beggar where to find food."

The Question of Truth

After defusing the emotional bomb, it is then important to move on to the important question of truth. Sincerely believing something does not make it true, as anyone will testify who has ever picked a wrong bottle out of a medicine cabinet in the dark. Faith is no more valid than the object in which it is placed, no matter how sincere or how intense the faith is. A nurse very sincerely put carbolic acid instead of silver nitrate in the eyes of a newborn baby. Her sincerity did not save the baby from blindness.

These same principles apply to things spiritual. Believing something doesn't make it true any more than failing to believe truth makes it false. Facts are facts, regardless of people's attitudes toward them. In religious matters, the basic question is always, "Is it true?"

Take, for instance, the fact of the deity, death, and resurrection of the Lord Jesus Christ. Christianity affirms these facts as the heart of its message. Islam, on the other hand, denies the deity, death, and resurrection of Christ. On this very crucial point, one of these mutually contradictory views is wrong. They can't simultaneously be true, no matter how sincerely both are believed by how many people.

A great deal is said about the similarity of world religions. Many Christians naively assume that other religions are basically the same, making the same claims and essentially doing what Christianity does, but in slightly different terms. Such an attitude reveals complete ignorance of other religions.

Though there are some similarities, the differences far outweigh, and are much greater than, the similarities.

Is the Golden Rule Enough?

One of the similarities is the essence of the Golden Rule, which is contained in almost every religion. From Confucius' time we have the statement, in various forms, that one should do unto others as he would have others do unto him. Many wrongly assume that this is the essence of Christianity. But if all Jesus Christ did was to give us the Sermon on the Mount and the Golden Rule, He actually increased our frustration. As we have already seen, man has had the Golden Rule since Confucius' time. Man's problem has never been not knowing what he should do. His problem, rather, has been that he lacks power to do what he knows he should.

Christ raised the ethical level and thereby made the requirements higher. This by itself raises our frustration level. But that is not *all* Christ did, and this is a major difference between Christianity and other religions. Christ offers us His power to live as we should. He gives us forgiveness, cleansing, and His own righteousness, all as a free gift. He reconciles us to God. He does something for us we cannot do for ourselves.

Every other religious system, however, is essentially a do-it-yourself proposition. Follow this way of life, they say, and you will gain favor with God and eventually achieve salvation. In a sense, other religious systems are sets of swimming instructions for a drowning man. Christianity is a life-preserver.

A Free Gift

D. T. Niles has also observed that in other religions good works are an "in order to." In Christianity, they are a "therefore." In other religions, good works are the means by which one hopes to earn salvation. In Christianity salvation is received as a free gift, through the finished work of Christ, the "therefore" of good works becomes an imperative love of God. Or, as another has put it, other religions are *do;* Christianity is *done.*

Christianity is what God has done for man in seeking him and reaching down to help him. Other religions are a matter of man seeking and struggling toward God.

Because of this profound difference, Christianity alone offers *assurance* of salvation. Because our salvation depends on what God has done for and given us, we can say with the same wonderful certainty of the Apostle Paul, "To be absent from the body is to be present with the Lord" (2 Cor. 5:8).

You Never Know in a Works Religion

In every *works* religion, however, it is impossible ever to have assurance. When do you know that you have done enough good works? You *never* know, and never *can* know. Fear persists because there is no assurance of salvation.

What salvation is, and what we are pointing toward, is quite different in the world's religions from what it is in Christianity.

In Buddhism, for instance, the ultimate goal is nirvana, or the extinction of desire. According to Buddha's teaching, all pain and suffering come from *desire.* If this desire can be overcome by following the Eightfold Path to Enlightenment, one can achieve nirvana, which is total nothingness. It is likened to the snuffing out of a candle. This is what is supposed to happen to life and consciousness when nirvana has been achieved.

In Hinduism the ultimate goal is also nirvana, but the term here has a different meaning. Nirvana is ultimate reunion with Brahma, the all-pervading force of the universe which is the Hindu's God. This experience is likened to the return of a drop of water to the ocean. Individuality is lost in the reunion with God, but without the total self-annihilation of Buddhism. Nirvana, in Hinduism, is achieved through a continuous cycle of birth, life, death, and rebirth. As soon as any animal, insect, or human being dies, it or he is immediately reborn in another form. Whether one moves up or down the scale of life depends on the quality of moral life one has lived. If it has been a good life, one moves up the scale with more comfort and less suffering. If one has lived a bad life, he moves down the scale into suffering and poverty. If he has been bad enough he is not reborn as a human being at all, but as an animal or insect. This law of reaping in the next life the harvest of one's present life is called the law of Karma. It explains why Hindus will not kill even an insect, not to mention a sacred cow, though these inhibitions pose grave sanitation and public health problems. What seems strange, curious, and even ludicrous to us of the western world has a very clear rationale to the Hindu, and to us once we understand his thinking.

In Islam, heaven is a paradise of wine, women, and song. It is achieved by living a life in which, ironically, one abstains from the things with which he will be rewarded in paradise. In addition to this abstention, one must follow the Five Pillars of Islam: repeating the creed, making a pilgrimage to Mecca, giving alms to the poor, praying five times daily, and keeping the fast of the month of Ramadan.

Again, there is no possibility of assurance. I have often asked Hindus, Muslims, and Buddhists whether they would achieve nirvana or go to paradise when they died. I have not yet had one reply in the affirmative. Rather, they referred to the imperfection of their lives as being a barrier to this realization. There is no assurance in their religious systems because there is no atonement and because salvation depends on the individual's gaining enough merit.

Concept of God

Even the fundamental concept of God, on which there is a plea that we should agree, reveals wide divergences. To say that we can unite with all who believe in God, regardless of what this God is called, fails to recognize that the term God means nothing apart from the definition given it.

Buddha, contrary to popular belief, never claimed to be deity. In fact, he was agnostic about the whole question of whether God even existed. If God existed, the Buddha taught emphatically, He could not help an individual achieve enlightenment. Each person must work this out for himself.

Hindus are pantheistic. *Pan* means *all* and *theistic* means *God*. Hindus believe that God and the universe are identical. The concept of *maya* is central to their thinking. Maya means that the material world is an illusion and that reality is spiritual and invisible. Brahma is the impersonal, all-pervading force of the universe, and the ultimate goal is for man to be reunited with this *God* in nirvana. Buddhism also teaches that the material world is an illusion. It is readily apparent why modern science came to birth through Christians, who believed in a personal God and an orderly universe, rather than in the context of Oriental philosophy. It is clear why most scientific progress has come from the West rather than the East. Why would one investigate what he believes is an illusion?

In Islam and Judaism we have a God much closer to the Christian concept. Here God is personal and transcendent, or separate from His creation. Surely, we are urged, we may get together with those who believe in God in personal terms.

But as we examine the Muslim concept of God—*Allah* as He is called in the *Koran*—we find he is not the God and Father of our Lord Jesus Christ, but rather, as in all other instances, a God of man's own imagination. Our knowledge of Allah comes from the Koran, which came through Muhammad. Muhammad, like Buddha and unlike Jesus Christ, did not claim deity. He taught that he was only the prophet of Allah. The picture of God which comes through to us in the pages of the Koran is of one who is totally removed from men, one who is capricious in all of His acts, responsible for evil as well as for good, and certainly not the God who "so loved the world that He gave His only begotten Son, that whosoever believeth in Him should not perish but have everlasting life." It is this totally distant concept of God that makes the idea of the Incarnation utterly inconceivable to the Muslim. How could their god, so majestic and beyond, have contact with mortal man in sin and misery? The death of God the Son on the cross is likewise inconceivable to a Muslim, since this would mean God was defeated by His creatures, an impossibility to them.

The Jewish God Is Close

The Jewish concept of God is closest of all to the Christian. Isn't the God whom they worship the God of the Old Testament, which we accept? Surely we can get together on this!

Again, however, closer examination shows that the Jews would not admit their God was the Father of Jesus Christ. In fact, it was this very issue that precipitated such bitter controversy in our Lord's time. God we accept, they said to Christ, but we do not accept You because as a man You make Yourself God, which is blasphemy.

In a conversation with the Jews, our Lord discussed this question. "God is our Father," they said. Jesus said to them, "If God were your Father, you would love Me, for I proceeded forth and came from God. . . . He that is of God heareth God's words; you therefore hear them not because you are not of God" (John

8:42, 47). In even stronger words He says, "You are of your father the devil" (v. 44).

Here, in our Lord's own words, we have the clue as to what our attitude should be toward those who are sincerely seeking *God*. If they are seeking the true God, their sincerity will be evidenced by the fact that they will receive Christ when they hear about Him. Missionary history has numerous examples of those who have been following other gods or an unknown god but who have responded when presented with the truth about the Lord Jesus Christ. They have immediately realized that He is the true God, whom they have been seeking.

Scripture is clear throughout the Old Testament and in the New that worship of gods other than the true God originates with the devil. "And they shall no more offer their sacrifices unto devils" (Lev. 17:7), and "But I say, that the things which the Gentiles sacrifice, they sacrifice to demons (Greek), and not to God" (1 Cor. 10:20).

Christ Alone Claims Deity

Of the great religious leaders of the world, Christ alone claims deity. It really doesn't matter what one thinks of Muhammad, Buddha, or Confucius as individuals. Their followers emphasize their *teachings*. Not so with Christ. He made *Himself* the focal point of His teaching. The central question He put to His listeners was, "Whom do you say that *I* am?" When asked what doing the works of God involved, Jesus replied, "This is the work of God, that you believe on Him whom He hath sent" (John 6:29).

On the question of who and what God is, the nature of salvation and how it is obtained, it is clear that Christianity differs radically from other world religions. We live in an age in which tolerance is a key word. Tolerance, however, must be clearly understood. (Truth, by its very nature, is intolerant of error.) If two plus two is four, the total cannot at the same time be 23. But one is not regarded as intolerant because he disagrees with *this* answer and maintains that the only correct answer is *four*.

The same principle applies in religious matters. One must be tolerant of other points of view and respect their right to be held and heard. He cannot, however, be forced in the name of tolerance to agree that all points of view, including those that are mutually contradictory, are equally valid. Such a position is nonsense.

The Only Way to God

It is not true that "it doesn't matter what you believe as long as you believe it." Hitler's slaughter of six million Jews was based on a sincere view of race supremacy, but he was desperately wrong. What we believe must be true in order to be real. Jesus said, "I am the Way, the Truth, and the Life. No man cometh unto the Father, but by Me" (John 14:6). There are many ways to Christ, but if we are to know the true and living God in personal experience, it must be through Christ, the only Way to God.

TWELVE

IS CHRISTIAN EXPERIENCE VALID?

"You could get the same response from that table lamp if you believed it possessed the same attributes as your God," said the young law student. This articulate skeptic was telling me what thousands feel—that Christian experience is completely personal and subjective, and has no objective, eternal, and universal validity.

The premise behind this notion is that the mind is capable of infinite rationalization. Belief in God is seen as mere wish-fulfillment. In adults, it is a throw-back to our need for a father-image.

The assumption, whether expressed or not, is that Christianity is for emotional cripples who can't make it through life without a crutch.

It is claimed that Christian conversion is a psychologically induced experience brought about by *brainwashing* as used by both Fascists and Communists. An evangelist is just a master of psychological manipulation. After pounding away at an audience, people become putty in his hands. He can get them to do anything if he asks for a *decision* at the right time and in the right way.

Some go further. Christian experience, they claim, is sometimes positively harmful. More than one student has been packed off to a psychiatrist by unbelieving parents after he has come to personal faith in Christ. "Look at all the religious nuts in mental asylums. It's their religion that put them there." Those who feel this way have succumbed to the "common-factor fallacy" pointed out by Anthony Standen. He tells of a man who got drunk each Monday on whiskey and soda water; on Tuesday he got drunk on brandy and soda water; and on Wednesday on gin and soda water. What caused the drunkenness? Obviously the common factor, soda water! [1]

"The Last Stop on the Train"
For many, the church is thought of as the last stop on the train

before being institutionalized. A careful scrutiny of a truly disoriented person, however, would reveal imbalance and unreality in other areas as well as in his religious life. It is actually a credit to the church that she is willing to offer help to these people. On the other hand, some mental disturbances have spiritual roots. As *these* people come into a right relationship with God through Jesus Christ they find immediate release and healing.

So strong is the prejudice in some quarters against the validity of Christian experience that academic degrees have been denied. A friend, studying in one of our best known universities, was denied a Ph.D. degree in social science. He was told, "Believing what you do about God, you are by definition crazy."

It is suggested by some skeptics that all Christian experience can be explained on the basis of conditioned reflexes. This thinking has its roots in experiments by Pavlov, the famous Russian scientist. He placed measuring devices in a dog's mouth and stomach to determine the production of digestive juices. Then he would bring food to the dog and at the same time ring a bell. After doing this repeatedly over a period of time, Pavlov rang the bell without producing the food and the dog salivated as usual. The inference drawn is that by such repeated conditioning, the mind can be made to produce desired physical reactions. It is on this basis that we can explain all political, social, and religious conversions, say the proponents of this view.

These are serious, far-reaching charges. Some of them have an air of plausibility.

Is Christian Experience Valid?

At the outset, we must concede the possibility of manipulating human emotions in some circumstances. And we would have to admit that some evangelists consciously or unconsciously play on the emotions of their audiences with deathbed stories, histrionic performances, and other devices. Our Lord, in the parable of the sower, implicitly warns against merely stirring the emotions in evangelism. He describes those who have received the seed of the Word into stony places as those that have heard the Word and received it with joy but who have no roots in themselves. They endure until tribulation and persecution come, and then they are *soon offended*. All of us have known people who have made what appears to be a tremendous response to the Gospel, only to fall by the wayside. Often this happens when they learn that it *costs* something to be a Christian and are not prepared to pay the price. Their emotions are stirred but their wills had not been bent to obey the Lord in total commitment.

A Matter of the Will

Dr. Orville S. Walters, a Christian psychiatrist, has pointed out that the will is like a cart pulled by two horses, the emotions and the intellect. With some people the will is reached more quickly through the emotions. With others it is reached through the mind. But in every case there is no genuine conversion unless the will has been involved.[2]

Realizing these potentialities for manipulating emotions, even unconsciously, all who are involved in evangelistic work, whether with children or with adults, must eliminate, so far as is humanly possible, factors and techniques which could produce these abortive results. But to attempt to explain *all* Christian experience on a psychological basis does not fit the facts. In passing, it is well to observe a principle that applies here as well as in other areas, i.e., to describe something is not the same thing as explaining it. To be sure, Christian experience can be described psychologically, but this does not explain *why* it happens nor negate its reality.

One evidence that Christianity is true is the reality of the experience of those who embrace Jesus Christ. One of the challenges a Christian throws out to skeptics is, "Taste and see that the Lord is good" (Ps. 34:8). Verify for yourself, in the laboratory of life, the hypothesis that Jesus Christ is the living Son of God. The reality of Christian experience is evidence of the validity of Christianity.

A Conditioned Reflex?

What of the objections that Christian experience is merely a conditioned reflex? First we must ask, as Dr. D. Martyn Lloyd-Jones does in answering the influential book, *Battle for the Mind,* by William Sargant, whether the comparison between men and animals is a strictly legitimate one. Man has reason and a critical faculty, and has powers of self-analysis, self-contemplation, and self-criticism which make him quite different from animals. "In other words, the comparison is only valid at times (like war) when what differentiates man has been knocked out of action and a man, because of terrible stress, has been reduced for the time being to the level of an animal."[3]

Second, if we are only creatures of conditioned reflexes, then this must also explain acts of great heroism and self-sacrifice in which man has taken pride. Such acts must be nothing but responses to a given stimulus at a given point. Taken to its logical conclusion, a deterministic view of human behavior eliminates moral responsibility. The little girl who said, "It ain't my fault, it's my glands," was right. It is significant, however, that those holding a deterministic point of view philosophically tend to operate on a different basis in daily life: like anyone else, they want a wallet stealer arrested promptly!

We cannot explain Christian experience on a conditioned reflex basis, however. Since thousands reared in Christian homes unfortunately never become Christians, the fact that many others really trust Christ cannot be explained exclusively on the basis of background. Though personal faith in Christ is the only door to becoming a Christian, the roads that lead to that door are almost as many as the number who enter it. I have known persons who became Christians *the first time* they heard the Gospel. It is significant, by contrast, that in political brainwashing, as with Pavlov's experiments, the stimulus must be applied repeatedly for some time in order to get the desired result.

Those who have become Christians, out of every conceivable religious background and out of no background at all, testify uniformly to an experience through personal commitment to Jesus Christ. The evidence of their changed lives testifies to the reality of the experience. This result cannot be gained from a bridge lamp by positive thinking. If positive thinking were the answer to everything, we would have no problems. As a matter of fact, the law student previously referred to committed his life to Christ in the course of the week's lectures that followed.

Victims of Autohypnosis?

But how do we Christians know that we are not victims of autohypnosis? How do we know we are not just whistling in the dark? Subjective experience as such does not prove anything. Many have claimed experiences—the reality of which—we may legitimately question. There must be more than experience on which to base our conviction, or we could be in difficulty.

For instance, suppose a man with a fried egg over his left ear came through the door of your church. "Oh," he glows, "this egg really gives me joy, peace, purpose in life, forgiveness of sins, and strength for living!" What would you say to him? You can't tell him he hasn't experienced these things. One of the powers of personal testimony is that it can't be argued. The blind man mentioned in John 9 couldn't answer many of the questions put to him, but he was sure of the fact that now he could see. His testimony was eloquent in its power.

But we could ask several questions of our friend with the fried egg. These are questions we Christians must also be prepared to *answer*.

First, who else has had the same experience with the fried egg? Presumably our friend would be hard put to produce others. The late Harry Ironside was preaching, some years ago, when a heckler shouted, "Atheism has done more for the world than Christianity!"

"Very well," said Ironside, "tomorrow night you bring a hundred men whose lives have been changed for the better by atheism, and I'll bring a hundred who have been transformed by Christ."

Needless to say, his heckler friend did not appear the next night. With Christianity, there are hundreds from every race, every country, and every walk of life who bear testimony to an experience through Jesus Christ.

Secondly, we should ask our friend with the fried egg: What objective reality outside of himself is his internal subjective experience tied to? How does he *know* he is not a victim of autohypnosis? Of course he will have nothing to say. In Christianity our personal subjective experience is tied into the objective historical fact of the Resurrection of Christ. If Christ had not risen from the dead we would not experience Him. It's because He rose from the dead and is living today that we can actually know Him.

Objective Historical Fact

Christian experience is not induced by belief in unrealities. It is not like the fraternity boy who died of fright when tied to a railroad track one night during hazing. He was told that a train would be coming in five minutes. He was not told that the train would pass on a parallel track. He thought there was only one track. When he heard the train approaching he suffered heart failure. With Christianity, nothing happens if there is "no one out there."

Because Christ is really *there,* all the possibilities of His life within us are realizable. It is only half the story when we sing, "He lives within my heart." The other crucial half is that we know He lives because He rose from the dead *in history.* Our personal subjective experience is based on objective historical *fact.*

In commenting on the truth that people, in suffering, speak of drawing upon power outside themselves, J. B. Phillips says:

> I know perfectly well that I am merely describing subjective phenomena. But the whole point is that when I have observed results in *objective* phenomena—courage, faith, hope, joy, and patience, for instance—and these qualities are very readily observed. The man who wants everything proved by scientific means is quite right in his insistence on "laboratory conditions" if he is investigating, shall we say, water-divining, clairvoyance, or telekinesis. But there can be no such thing as "laboratory conditions" for investigating the realm of the human spirit unless it can be seen that the "laboratory condi-

tions" are in fact human life itself. A man can only exhibit objectively a change in his own disposition, a faith which directs his life—*in the actual business of living.*[4]

It is in these objective results in personal life that we see some of the dynamic relevance of Christ. He meets man in his deepest needs.

Purpose and Direction

Christ gives purpose and direction to life. "I am the Light of the world," He says. "He that followeth Me shall not walk in darkness, but shall have the Light of life" (John 8.12). Many are in the dark about the purpose of life in general and about their own lives in particular. They are groping around the room of life looking for the light switch. Anyone who has ever been in a dark, unfamiliar room knows this feeling of insecurity. When the light goes on, however, a feeling of security results. And so it is when one steps from darkness to the light of life in Christ.

God in Christ gives our lives cosmic purpose, tying them in with His purpose for history and eternity. A Christian lives not only for time, but for eternity. Even routine is transformed as we live the whole of our lives in God's purpose and obey the admonition, "Whether, therefore, you eat or drink, or whatsoever you do, do all to the glory of God" (1 Cor. 10:31). This purpose embraces every aspect of life. It is also an unending, eternal purpose. Undoubtedly a non-Christian has such temporary purposes as family, career, and money that give limited satisfaction. But these, at best, are transient and may fail with a change in circumstances.

To an age in which life has been described as meaningless and absurd by existentialist philosophers, nothing could have more power and meaning than this verifiable claim of Christ.

We Have Been Made for God

The late Carl Gustav Jung said, "The central neurosis of our time is emptiness." When we do not have money, fame, success, power, and other externals, we think we'll achieve final happiness after we attain them. Many testify to the disillusionment experienced when these have been achieved and the realization sets in that one is still the same miserable person. The human spirit can never be satisfied "by bread alone"—by material things. We have been made for God and can never find rest until we rest in Him.

An automobile, however shiny, high-powered, and full of equipment, will not run on water. It was made to run *only* on gasoline. So man can find fulfillment only in God. He was made this way by

God Himself. Christian experience offers this fulfillment in a personal relationship to Christ. He said, "I am the Bread of life; he that cometh to Me shall never hunger, and he that believeth on Me shall never thirst" (John 6:35). When one experiences Christ, he comes to an inner contentment, joy, and spiritual refreshment which enables him to transcend circumstances. It was this reality that enabled Paul to say, "I have learned, in whatsoever state I am, therewith to be content" (Phil. 4:11). This supernatural reality enables a Christian to rejoice in the middle of difficult circumstances.

Our Quest Is for Peace

"Peace in our time" expresses the longing of all men as they view the international scene. We hope against hope that the current brush-fire wars will not erupt into a large-scale conflict.

Peace is the quest of every human heart. If it could be bought, people would pay millions for it. The skyrocketing sales of books dealing with peace of mind and soul testify that they have touched a resonant chord in the lives of millions. Psychiatrists' offices are jammed.

Jesus says, "Come unto Me, all you that labor and are heavy laden, and I will give you rest" (Matt. 11:28). Christ alone gives peace that passes understanding, a peace the world cannot give or take away. It is very moving to hear the testimony of those who have restlessly searched for years and have finally found peace in Christ. The current rise in narcotic addiction, alcoholism, and sex obsession are vain hopes of gaining the peace which is in Christ alone. "He is our peace" (Eph. 2:14).

A Radical Power Needed

Today's society is experiencing a profound power failure—a moral power failure. Parents know what is right for themselves and their children, but for lack of backbone they find it easier to go along with the crowd. Children readily pick up this attitude. The result is rapid deterioration of the moral fabric of society. Merely to give good advice to either the old or young is like putting iodine on cancer. What is needed is radical *power*. Christianity is not the putting of a new suit on a man, but the putting of a new man into the suit. Jesus Christ said, "I am come that they might have life, and that they might have it more abundantly" (John 10:10). He offers us His power. Not only is there power and freedom from things like alcohol and narcotics, but power to forgive those who have wronged us, to resist temptation, and to love the unlovely. Twice-born men have new appetites, new desires, new loves. They are, in fact, "new creatures" (2 Cor. 5:17). Salvation is a literal coming from death to spiritual life.

Guilt Problem Solved

Christian experience solves the guilt problem. Every normal person feels guilt. A guilt complex is an *irrational* feeling that has no basis in fact. But guilt felt over something done wrongly, in violation of an inherent moral law, is *normal*. The absence of any guilt feeling is abnormal. A person who feels nothing after deliberately killing or hurting an innocent person is abnormal. Guilt must not be rationalized away. In Christ, there is an objective basis for forgiveness. Christ died for our sins; the sentence of death that belonged to us has been taken by Him. "There is therefore now no condemnation to them which are in Christ Jesus" (Rom. 8:1). Forgiveness at the personal level is a reality.

Christianity speaks to man's loneliness, which is so characteristic of modern society. It is ironic that in a period of population explosion man is more lonely than ever. Christ is the Good Shepherd (John 10:14) who will never leave us nor forsake us. And He introduces us into a worldwide family and a fellowship closer than a blood-relationship with an unbeliever.[5]

Conversion Affects the Entire Personality

Finally, in recognizing the validity of Christian experience we should realize that a psychological description of it is valid as far as it goes. But it is only a *description,* not a *cause.* A man who is converted has a new spiritual life within him. This new life will thoroughly affect his entire personality. One part of man's nature cannot be altered without affecting the rest of him.

Man's brain and nervous system may be analyzed in the same way as his heart and kidneys. The body and spirit are inextricably intertwined. Man is this totality. He is not merely a spirit encased in a body. On the other hand, his mind is a reality. The mechanical and spiritual aspects of life are complementary. Dr. Donald M. MacKay puts it very helpfully:

> One familiar illustration is that of the use of lamps to signal from ships at sea. When a man sends a message from ship to shore, in one sense all that is coming from the ship is a series of flashes of light, but the trained sailor who sits on the shore watching this light says, "I see a message ordering so-and-so to proceed somewhere," or "Look, they're in trouble!" Why does he say this? All he has seen is "nothing but" flashes of light. The whole pattern of activity can be correctly labeled

thus by a physicist, and described so completely that he is able to reproduce at any time exactly what the man on shore saw. He does not add "the message" as a kind of "extra" at the end of his description, and it would clearly be silly to say he is "leaving out the message" as if it were very wrong of him to do so. What he has done is to choose one way of approaching a complex unity, namely the sending-of-a-message-from-ship-to-shore, one aspect of which is a purely physical allowing of complete description in such terms as the wave lengths of the light and the time-pattern. On the other hand, if he reads it also as a message, it is not as if he had found something mysterious, as well as the flashing, going on. Instead he has discovered that the whole thing, when he allows it to strike him in a different way, can be *read* and can also make sense in nonphysical terms. The message here is related to the flashing of light, not as an effect is to a cause, but rather as one aspect of a complex unity is related to another aspect.

Take another illustration. Two mathematicians start arguing about a problem in geometry. With a piece of chalk, they make a pattern of dots and lines on the board, and the fun waxes fast and furious. Can we imagine some nonmathematician coming in and saying, in amazement, "I can't see what you're arguing about—there's nothing there but chalk"? Once again this would illustrate what I like to call the fallacy of "nothing-buttery"—the idea that because, in one sense, at one level, or viewed from one angle, there is nothing there but chalk, therefore it is unnecessary . . . to talk about what is there in any other terms. Again, if the mathematicians protest, "But there is a geometrical figure there; we are talking about these angles," they are not suggesting that the other man's eyes are failing to detect something that they are seeing on the board. Both of them are responding to exactly the same light waves. It is not that the mathematicians have a sixth sense or anything queer that enables them to receive from the board some invisible emanations that the other fellow is not receiving. The point is that, as a result of a different attitude to what is there, they have power to see in it, or, if you like, to abstract from it, an aspect of significance which the other misses. Of course, in this case he can be trained to discover it. There is no great difficulty in their eventually coming to agreement, and he then realizes that the geometrical pattern is related to the chalk on the board, not indeed as effect is to a cause, but in a still more intimate way.

I want to clarify this alternative to "a cause and effect,"

because it bears on questions that are often raised about the "causation" of bodily action by mental activity. If an argument were to come up as to whether the light causes the message or the message causes the light, whether the chalk-distribution causes the geometrical figure or the geometrical figure causes the chalk-distribution, we would see at once that the word "cause," in the scientific sense, is the wrong one here. Causality in science is a relationship between two events or sets of events, the cause and the effect. Here we have not two events or situations, but one. You cannot have the flashing of the light without the message: they are one set of events. You cannot have the chalk-distribution without there being, at the same time, the figure on the board. On the other hand, the two do have a certain kind of independence. It would be possible to reproduce the same message or figure in a quite different embodiment—in ink or pencil, for example. It is for this reason that I prefer to say that the one "embodies" the other.[6]

As Christians, we need not fear psychological descriptions of Christian experience. They are not explanations. The fact that some Christian experiences can be produced by other means is a warning against the temptation to manipulate human personality. The fact that solid Christian experience is also sound mental health is an asset rather than a detriment, and is an evidence of the Gospel's validity.

Notes: Know What You Believe

Chapter 1

[1] B.B. Warfield, *The Inspiration and Authority of the Bible* (New York: Oxford University Press, 1927), p. 299.
[2] T.C. Hammond, *In Understanding Be Men* (Downers Grove, Ill.: Inter-Varsity Press, 1968), p. 13.
[3] J.N. Birdsell, "Canon of the New Testament," in *New Bible Dictionary* (Grand Rapids: Eerdmans, 1962), p. 194 (hereafter cited as *NBD*).
[4] W.F. Albright, *Archaeology and the Religion of Israel* (Baltimore: Johns Hopkins Press, 1942), p. 176.
[5] Nelson Glueck, *Rivers in the Desert* (New York: Farrar, Straus, & Giroux, 1959), p. 31.

Chapter 2

[1] A.H. Strong, *Systematic Theology* (Philadelphia: Judson Press, 1907), p. 255.
[2] T.C. Hammond, *In Understanding Be Men* (Downers Grove, Ill.: Inter-Varsity Press, 1968), p. 44.
[3] R.A. Finlayson, "Holiness," in *NBD* (Grand Rapids: Eerdmans, 1962), p. 530.
[4] Ibid.
[5] R.A. Finlayson, "Trinity," *NBD*, p. 1298.
[6] Ibid.
[7] Ibid., p. 1300.
[8] Hammond, *In Understanding*, p. 54.
[9] Finlayson, "Trinity," *NBD*, p. 1300.
[10] Hammond, *In Understanding*, p. 66.
[11] Ibid., p. 56.
[12] J.I. Packer, *Evangelism and the Sovereignty of God* (Downers Grove, Ill.: InterVarsity Press, 1961), pp. 18-19.

Chapter 3

[1] A.H. Strong, *Systematic Theology* (Philadelphia: Judson Press, 1907), p. 676.
[2] Ibid., p. 673.
[3] T.C. Hammond, *In Understanding Be Men* (Downers Grove, Ill.: Inter-Varsity Press, 1968), p. 101.
[4] R.A. Finlayson, *The Story of Theology* (Downers Grove, Ill.: Inter-Varsity Press, 1963), pp. 24-25.
[5] Hammond, *In Understanding*, p. 105.

Chapter 4

[1] Leon Morris, "Atonement," in *NBD* (Grand Rapids: Eerdmans, 1962), p. 108.

[2] Leon Morris, "Propitiation," *NBD*, p. 1046.

[3] A.H. Strong, *Systematic Theology* (Philadelphia: Judson Press, 1907), p. 740.

[4] R.A. Finlayson, *The Story of Theology* (Downers Grove, Ill.: InterVarsity Press, 1963), p. 38.

[5] Strong, *Theology*, p. 766.

[6] James Denney, *The Death of Christ* (Downers Grove, Ill.: InterVarsity Press, 1964), p. 3.

[7] T.C. Hammond, *In Understanding Be Men* (Downers Grove, Ill.: Inter-Varsity Press, 1968), p. 122.

[8] Robert J. Little, *Here's Your Answer* (Chicago: Moody Press, Chicago, 1967), p. 206.

Chapter 5

[1] T.C. Hammond, *In Understanding Be Men* (Downers Grove, Ill.: Inter-Varsity Press, 1968), p. 71.

[2] D.M. Edwards, "Image," in *International Standard Bible Encyclopedia* (Grand Rapids: Eerdmans, 1939), p. 1450 (hereafter cited as *ISBE*).

[3] R.J. Wallace, "Man," in *NBD* (Grand Rapids: Eerdmans, 1962), p. 777.

[4] Hammond, *In Understanding*, p. 77.

[5] John Murray, "Sin," *NBD*, p. 1190.

Chapter 6

[1] G.W. Walters, "Holy Spirit," in *NBD* (Grand Rapids: Eerdmans, 1962), p. 531f.

[2] E.Y. Mullins, "Holy Spirit," in *ISBE* (Grand Rapids: Eerdmans, 1939), p. 1450.

[3] A.H. Strong, *Systematic Theology* (Philadelphia: Judson Press, 1907), p. 342.

[4] T.C. Hammond, *In Understanding Be Men* (Downers Grove, Ill.: Inter-Varsity Press, 1968), p. 131.

Chapter 7

[1] D.W.B. Robinson, "Church," in *NBD* (Grand Rapids: Eerdmans, 1962), pp. 228-29.

[2] A.H. Strong, *Systematic Theology* (Philadelphia: Judson Press, 1907), p. 887.

[3] Ibid., p. 890.

[4] Leon Morris, *Ministers of God* (Chicago: InterVarsity Press, 1969), p. 91.

[5] T.C. Hammond, *In Understanding Be Men* (Downers Grove, Ill.: Inter-Varsity Press, 1968), p. 162f.

[6] Morris, *Ministers of God,* pp. 92ff.
[7] John Dall, *Encyclopedia of Religion and Ethics* (Edinburgh: T. & T. Clark, 1918), p. 264.

Chapter 8

[1] Robert J. Little, *Here's Your Answer* (Chicago: Moody Press, 1946), p. 191.
[2] Ibid., p. 186.

Chapter 9

[1] Leon Morris, "Faith," in *NBD* (Grand Rapids: Eerdmans, 1962), p. 413.
[2] A.H. Strong, *Systematic Theology* (Philadelphia: Judson Press, 1907), p. 809.
[3] J.I. Packer, "Election," *NBD,* p. 360.
[4] Charles Simeon, *Expository Outlines on the Whole Bible* (Grand Rapids: Zondervan, reprint 1956), vol. 1, xvii-xviii.

Chapter 10

[1] Helmut Thielecke, *The Waiting Father* (New York: Harper, 1959).
[2] George E. Ladd, "Eschatology," in *NBD* (Grand Rapids: Eerdmans, 1962), p. 390.
[3] William Evans, *The Great Doctrines of the Bible* (Chicago: Moody Press, 1949), p. 254.
[4] A.H. Strong, *Systematic Theology* (Philadelphia: Judson Press, 1907), p. 1034.
[5] Geerhardus Vos, "Eschatology of the New Testament," in *ISBE* (Grand Rapids: Eerdmans, 1939), p. 991.

Notes: Know Why You Believe

Chapter 1

[1] John W. Montgomery, "The Place of Reason," *His,* March 1966, p. 16.
[2] Antony Flew, "Theology and Falsification," *New Essays in Philosophical Theology,* eds. Antony Flew and Alasdair Macintyre (London: SCM Press, 1955), n. p.
[3] On the issue of theological verification, cf. John W. Montgomery, "Inspiration and Inerrancy: a New Departure," *Evangelical Theological Society Bulletin* 8 (Spring 1956): pp. 45-75.

Chapter 2

[1] Mortimer Adler, *Great Books of the Western World,* ed. Robert Maynard Hutchins, vol. 2 (Chicago: Encyclopaedia Britannica, n.d.), p. 561.
[2] Samuel Zwemer, *The Origin of Religion,* (Neptune, N.J., Loizeaux Bros., 1945).
[3] Lincoln Barnett, *The Universe and Dr. Einstein* (New York: Bantam, 1974), p. 95.
[4] Bernard Ramm, *The Christian View of Science and Scripture* (Grand Rapids: Eerdmans, 1955), p. 148.
[5] A. Rendle Short, *Modern Discovery and the Bible* (London: Inter-Varsity Christian Fellowship, 1949), p. 39.
[6] R.E.D. Clark, *Creation* (London: Tyndale Press, 1946), p. 20.
[7] Ramm, *Science and Scripture,* p. 148.
[8] Ibid., p. 154.
[9] Ibid.
[10] J.W.N. Sullivan, *The Limitations of Science* (New York: New American Library, 1956), p. 94.

Chapter 3

[1] John R.W. Stott, *Basic Christianity* (Downers Grove, Ill.: InterVarsity Press, 1964), p. 26.
[2] C.S. Lewis, *Miracles,* in Stott, *Basic Christianity,* p. 32.
[3] Bernard Ramm, *Protestant Christian Evidences* (Chicago: Moody Press, 1953), p. 177.

Chapter 4

[1] David Strauss, *The Life Of Jesus for the People,* 2d ed. (London, 1879), 1:412.
[2] B.F. Westcott, *The Gospel of the Resurrection,* 4th ed. (London, 1879), pp. 4-6.

Chapter 5

[1] B.B. Warfield, *The Inspiration and Authority of the Bible* (New York: Oxford University Press, 1927), pp. 299ff.

[2] Gordon Clark, *Can I Trust My Bible?* (Chicago: Moody Press, 1963), pp. 15-16.

[3] E.J. Carnell, *An Introduction to Christian Apologetics* (Grand Rapids: Eerdmans, 1950), p. 208.

[4] Clark, *My Bible*, p. 27.

Chapter 6

[1] R. Laird Harris, "How Reliable Is the Old Testament Text?" in Gordon Clark, *Can I Trust My Bible?* (Chicago: Moody Press, 1963), p. 124.

[2] Ibid., pp. 129-130.

[3] B.F. Westcott and F.J.A. Hort, eds., vol. 2 *New Testament in Original Greek* (London, 1881), p. 2.

[4] F.F. Bruce, *The New Testament Documents; Are They Reliable?* (Grand Rapids: Eerdmans, 1959). Contains a full discussion of the dating of documents.

[5] Ibid., pp. 16-17.

[6] Ibid., p. 19.

[7] A. Berkley Mickelsen, "Is the Text of the New Testament Reliable?" in Clark, *My Bible*, p. 160.

[8] Sir Frederic Kenyon, *The Bible and Archaeology*, in Bruce, *New Testament Documents*, p. 20.

[9] E.J. Young, "The Canon of the Old Testament," in *Revelation and the Bible*, ed. C.F. Henry (Grand Rapids: Baker Book House, 1956), p. 156.

Chapter 7

[1] W.F. Albright, *Archaeology and the Religion of Israel*, in Howard F. Vos, *An Introduction to Bible Archaeology* (Chicago: Moody Press, n.d.), p. 121.

[2] Millar Burrows, *What Mean These Stones?* in Vos, *Bible Archaeology*.

[3] Ibid., pp. 291-292.

[4] Sir Frederic Kenyon, *The Bible and Archaeology*, in F.F. Bruce, *The New Testament Documents: Are They Reliable?* (Grand Rapids: Eerdmans, 1959), p. 279.

[5] Nelson Glueck, *Rivers in the Desert* (New York: Farrar, Straus, & Giroux, 1959), p. 31.

[6] A. Rendle Short, *Modern Discovery and the Bible* (London: Inter-Varsity Christian Fellowship, 1949), p. 137.

[7] Howard F. Vos, *Genesis and Archaeology* (Chicago: Moody Press, 1963), p. 52.

[8] Short, *Modern Discovery*, p. 138.

[9] Vos, *Bible Archaeology*, p. 75.

[10] Nelson Glueck, "Ezion-Geber," *Bulletin of the American Schools of Oriental Research,* in Vos, *Bible Archaeology,* p. 75.

[11] Vos, *Bible Archaeology,* pp. 79-80.

[12] Short, *Modern Discovery,* p. 184.

[13] F.F. Bruce, "Archaeological Confirmation of the New Testament," in *Revelation and the Bible,* ed. C.F. Henry (Grand Rapids: Baker Book House, 1958), p. 320.

[14] Ibid., p. 323.

[15] Ibid., p. 324.

[16] Ibid., p. 327.

[17] Ibid., p. 328.

[18] Short, *Modern Discovery.*

Chapter 8

[1] J.N. Hawthorne, *Questions of Science and Faith* (London: Tyndale Press, 1960), p. 55.

[2] Bernard Ramm, *Protestant Christian Evidences* (Chicago: Moody Press, 1953), p. 140.

[3] Ibid., pp. 140-141.

[4] Ibid., pp. 142-143.

[5] C.S. Lewis, *Miracles,* in Ramm, *Christian Evidences,* p. 143.

[6] Ramm, *Christian Evidences,* p. 160.

[7] Ibid., p. 40.

Chapter 9

[1] R.S. Lull, *Organic Evolution,* in Anthony Standen, *Science Is a Sacred Cow* (New York: E.P. Dutton, 1962), p. 106.

[2] J.N. Hawthorne, *Questions of Science and Faith* (London: Tyndale Press, 1960), p. 4.

[3] Bernard Ramm, *The Christian View of Science and Scripture* (Grand Rapids: Eerdmans, 1954), pp. 261ff.

[4] G.A. Kerkut, "Implications of Evolution," *International Series of Monographs of Pure and Applied Biology,* vol. 4 (Pergamon Press, 1960), p. 3.

[5] Ramm, *The Christian View,* p. 273.

[6] Henry Morris, *The Bible and Modern Science* (Chicago: Moody Press, 1953), p. 14.

[7] Ramm, *The Christian View,* p. 276.

[8] Morris, *The Bible,* p. 45.

[9] Russell Mixter, "The Science of Heredity and the Source of the Species," *Creation and Evolution,* in Ramm, *The Christian View,* p. 288.

[10] E.J. Carnell, *An Introduction to Christian Apologetics,* in Ramm, *The Christian View,* p. 289.

Chapter 10

[1] Hugh Evan Hopkins, *Mystery of Suffering,* (Downers Grove, Ill.: Inter-

Varsity Press, 1959) in J.S. Mill, *Nature and Utility of Religion: Two Essays,* ed. George Nakhnikian (Indianapolis: Bobbs, 1958), p. 38.

[2] Ibid., p. 13.

[3] J.B. Phillips, *God Our Contemporary* (New York: Macmillan, 1960), p. 88.

[4] Ibid., p. 89.

Chapter 12

[1] Anthony Standen, *Science Is a Sacred Cow* (New York: E.P. Dutton, 1962), p. 25.

[2] Orville S. Walters, *You Can Win Others* (Winona Lake, Ind.: Light and Life Press, 1950), n.p.

[3] D. Martyn Lloyd-Jones, *Conversions: Psychological or Spiritual* (Downers Grove, Ill.: InterVarsity Press, 1959), p. 13.

[4] J.B. Phillips, *God Our Contemporary* (New York: Macmillan, 1960), pp. 22-23.

[5] For an expansion of these experiences and their relevancy to life, see the author's *How to Give Away Your Faith* (Chicago: InterVarsity Press, 1966), p. 83f.

[6] Donald M. MacKay, *Christianity in a Mechanistic Universe* (London: Inter-Varsity Fellowship, 1965), pp. 57-59.